CAMILLE SAINT-SAËNS and the FRENCH SOLO CONCERTO

Saint-Saëns is a capital musician! His fourth piano concerto could cure anyone of an aversion to music . . . such Sardou-like technique and elegance! How well conceived, how pleasing the balance of common sense and subtle ingenuity, of logic and grace.

Hans von Bülow, 1890

MICHAEL STEGEMANN

CAMILLE SAINT-SAËNS and the FRENCH SOLO CONCERTO from 1850 to 1920

Translated by Ann C. Sherwin
Reinhard G. Pauly, General Editor

AMADEUS PRESS
Portland, Oregon

To my parents

Jacket illustrations: (Front) Camille Saint-Saëns, drawing by H. Meyer, 1890. Collection Roger-Viollet, Paris. (Back) Autograph sketch for Saint-Saëns's 5th Piano Concerto, Op. 103.

Frontispiece: Camille Saint-Saëns, drawing by P. Renouard. Collection Roger-Viollet, Paris.

ISBN 0-931340-35-7

Printed in Singapore

AMADEUS PRESS
9999 S.W. Wilshire
Portland, Oregon 97225

Library of Congress Cataloging-in-Publication Data

Stegemann, Michael.
[Camille Saint-Saëns und das französische Solokonzert von 1850 bis 1920. English]
Camille Saint-Saëns and the French solo concerto from 1850 to 1920 / Michael Stegemann ; translated by Ann C. Sherwin ; Reinhard G. Pauly, general editor.
p. cm.
Translation of: Camille Saint-Saëns und das französische Solokonzert von 1850 bis 1920.
Includes bibliographical references and index.
ISBN 0-931340-35-7
1. Saint-Saëns, Camille, 1835-1921. Concertos. 2. Concerto--France--19th century. 3. Concerto--France--20th century.
I. Pauly, Reinhard G. II. Title.
ML410.S15S713 1991
784.2'3'092--dc20

90-40053
CIP
MN

Contents

We are grateful to Editions Durand, Paris, for permission to reprint numerous musical examples.

List of Music Examples

List of Figures

List of Tables

Preface

My study of the life and work of the French composer Charles-Camille Saint-Saëns (1835–1921) began in 1971. Four years later, at the prompting of Yves Gérard of Paris, I decided to write an academic treatise using my extensive research findings. Mr. Gérard briefed me on the current status of Saint-Saëns research. Two excellent dissertations had recently been submitted—one by Sabina Ratner on Saint-Saëns's piano works, and one by Daniel Fallon on the composer's orchestral works through the Third Symphony. A study of Saint-Saëns's chamber music by Elizabeth Harkins was in progress at that time and since then has been completed. Therefore, I decided to concentrate my further studies on the concertante works of the composer. I later learned that Curtis Stotlar was planning a dissertation on the piano concertos, but it was never completed.

First of all, I must express my thanks to Yves Gérard. Without his help my work could not have been completed. From the outset he was at my side to advise me. In innumerable consultative sessions he helped me organize the vast quantity of material chronologically and analyze it. In addition, he placed his private collection of important documents and manuscripts at my disposal.

I also owe a debt of thanks to François Lesure and Jean-Michel Nectoux, curators of the Bibliothèque Nationale in Paris, and to Mr. Laisné, curator of the Bibliothèque Municipale in Dieppe. They assisted me in countless ways and granted me access to the material in their archives, much of which is not yet cataloged.

I also wish to thank Guy Kaufmann of Paris, general director of Editions Durand, who graciously allowed me to look at his publisher's archives and microfilm or photocopy the manuscripts and scores by Saint-Saëns that are still under copyright.

Hans Schneider of Tutzing provided information about the composer's *Fantaisie pour Orgue-Eolian* preserved in his archives.

Sabina Ratner of Quebec entrusted me with important notes and was a valuable advisor in our many conversations.

I am also indebted to pianists Gabriel Tacchino of Paris and Roberto Szidon of Abersdorf, and to violinist Ulf Hoelscher of Heidelberg, for insights into the particularities of instrumental technique in the compositions I studied.

Nicole Geeraert of Steinfurt was an invaluable help in solving linguistic problems that arose in transcribing handwritten documents and in translating French texts into German.

Finally, I would like to acknowledge an interview I was privileged to hold in 1971 with Jean Guibon of Dieppe, who was then 97 years old. He had met with Saint-Saëns on numerous occasions as chairman of the city's cultural committee in the early decades of this century.

My deepest gratitude goes to my parents, who lovingly promoted my musical development, and to Professor Maria Elisabeth Brockhoff, who has supervised my work since 1975 and helped me in every way possible.

Introduction

Sources Consulted

A major portion of this study was done during my stay in Paris in 1976–77. At that time I was primarily interested in the autographs of Saint-Saëns's concertante works, most of which had been collected and preserved at the Bibliothèque Nationale. In addition, I was interested in the composer's handwritten sketches and the first editions of his published concertos and concertinos, which were also housed at the Bibliothèque Nationale.

Upon examining 29 works, I thought I had completely covered the composer's concertante work. Thus, I was greatly surprised in August 1980, after my research was completed, when Hans Schneider informed me that the complete autograph of Saint-Saëns's *Fantaisie pour Orgue-Eolian* was among the antiquarian holdings of his music shop. The existence of this work was unknown; only in the composer's correspondence was there any reference to it. Though Mr. Schneider could not let me look at the score itself, he graciously provided photocopies of the first three pages and the last one. References to this composition, based upon these copies, have been incorporated into Appendices A and B. A detailed study must be left to further research.

The thematic catalogue of Camille Saint-Saëns's concertos and concertante works in Appendix A gives information about the sources on which I based my studies.

Saint-Saëns's eminent role in the development of the solo concerto in France can only be demonstrated through a comparison of his concertante works with those of his French contemporaries. Therefore, I examined the form and style of more than 100 concertante works performed in Paris between 1850 and 1920. A chronological survey of these, along with Saint-Saëns's concertante compositions and the most notable concertos that originated outside France during that period, is also given in Appendix B. Of course, this table cannot claim to be complete, but though I limited myself to the works preserved in the Bibliothèque Nationale in Paris, I believe I have offered a representative sample.

Because the impact of Saint-Saëns's solo concertos in France is inseparable from the history of their reception, I located as many contemporary performance reviews as possible. These are cited chronologically in Chapter 1.

The extensive list of secondary literature in the bibliography comes mainly from my private library and the Bibliothèque Nationale, but a number of the supplemental listings are courtesy of the private archives of Yves Gérard. Most of the publications on the life and work of Saint-Saëns appeared while he was still living. Among them is the only previous comprehensive study of the composer in the German language.[1] However, it was published as early as 1899 and is thus far from complete.

A biography of Saint-Saëns by Englishman James Harding has had a disastrous effect on current perceptions of the composer.[2] Except for musicological treatises, this biography is the only publication on the composer in recent times, and as such, it appeared to be one of the most important sources. But I soon discovered a myriad of inaccuracies and factual errors that totally invalidated its worth. To the extent that the errors touched on my field of study, I have corrected them. Possibly more serious than the factual shortcomings of the book—which, regrettably, is considered a reliable source and is quoted repeatedly—is the fact that Harding parrots his documentary material with absolutely no reflection. In some instances he even distorts it, thereby adding more fuel to the fire of unjust and prejudicial criticism of Saint-Saëns that raged at the beginning of this century, fanned mainly by Debussy and his associates. I tried to persuade the author, with whom I corresponded for years, to correct the errors prior to reprinting the book, but my efforts were in vain. Therefore, in light of these circumstances, I thought it advisable to offer a brief biography of the composer before presenting the analytical part of my research.

In conclusion, I must also mention Saint-Saëns's letters and writings, which afforded me valuable insights into his personality, his sense of aesthetics, and his manner of composing. This correspondence is housed at the Bibliothèque Municipale of Dieppe—more or less unordered and certainly not systematically catalogued. Except for a few original editions, I have based the bibliography on reprint editions.

Purpose and Arrangement of the Work

Over the many years that I have devoted to the study of Saint-Saëns, I have repeatedly felt that the current estimation of the composer is in dire need of revision. Although he gained recognition and acclaim during his lifetime that went far beyond the reaches of his native land, a countercurrent began to emerge as early as the 1870s. The Société Nationale de Musique, which Saint-Saëns had established in 1871 to encourage young French composers, dissociated itself from its founder shortly thereafter, at the instigation of Vincent d'Indy, a pupil of César Franck and an admirer of Richard Wagner. Saint-Saëns's commitment to a national French style of music was soon forgotten, and when Claude Debussy called for a revival of the music of the old masters of the harpsichord around the turn of the century, no one remembered that 50 years earlier Saint-Saëns had spoken up not only for Gluck but also for Rameau and Couperin, and that he had edited their works.

The beginnings of Saint-Saëns's career as a composer, pianist, and organist came at a time when the Paris music world was influenced by the successes of Italian bel canto opera and by the instrumental virtuosos who appeared primarily in the salons. The fact that Saint-Saëns favored Bach, Mozart, Beethoven, and Schumann, and that he composed chamber music not at all in keeping with the popular taste, soon earned him the reputation of an unwelcome innovator.[3] Ironically, on the basis of these same issues, he was labeled decades later as a stuffy academic.

On the other hand, Saint-Saëns consistently enjoyed a positive reception in Germany. As a pianist, he was a frequent and celebrated guest at orchestra concerts in Berlin, Leipzig, and Dresden, and his works were performed in Germany more often than those of other

French composers. It was the premiere performance of *Tannhäuser* in Paris that cast the first shadow on his success east of the Rhine. Saint-Saëns took a very objective position in the Wagner controversy, which neither the German nor the French side appreciated. During the wars of 1870–71 and 1914–18, the press became a battlefield for the cultural struggle, and the resulting strong Francophobe sentiment utterly destroyed Saint-Saëns's standing abroad.[4]

With the rise of Debussy and the new generation of French composers, Saint-Saëns's star finally waned in his own country as well. Attesting to this is a comment by Romain Rolland: "Oddly enough, you can talk with musicians for hours about the music of France, yet it would never occur to anyone to mention the name Saint-Saëns."[5]

Nevertheless, into the 1920s Saint-Saëns was still among the most performed French composers, and contemporary opinions of him were at least based on firsthand knowledge of the works praised or criticized.

The limited portion of his work that managed to hold its ground in the concerto repertoire in the ensuing years is certainly not a sufficient basis for an overall assessment. The *Carnival of the Animals* is still regarded as representative of his style, which was the very thing the composer feared when he adamantly refused to allow the work to be published during his lifetime. The grandiose *Organ Symphony* is often played, but its significance is far too seldom recognized. Widespread ignorance of a substantial fraction of his work has led to the assertion that Saint-Saëns is an intellectual eclectic whose musical language is at best noncommittal.

One of my main objectives in this treatise is to reverse this judgment. The inaccurate assessment is disproved principally by Saint-Saëns's concertante works, from which French music both before and after Debussy gained decisive momentum. The 30 works I have examined are doubtless among the most significant instrumental compositions produced in France between 1850 and 1920. But ironically, it was the less interesting concertos and concertante pieces that, due to their virtuoso character, repeatedly attracted the attention of artists and thus were performed. The public accepted these works as the norm, so that for years the far more substantial portion of Saint-Saëns's concertante works was denied the recognition it deserved. An example of this unbalanced assessment is the January 1972 edition of the authoritative

Schwann record catalog, which lists eight recordings of Saint-Saëns's First Cello Concerto but not one recording of his considerably more significant Second Cello Concerto. [The Fall 1987 edition only lists *one* recording. Ed.] Only in the last few years, fostered by the media's growing interest, has a positive change occurred.

In my study, I have not presented an exhaustive musicological analysis of the works selected. While such analysis was necessary preparation for this study, I have incorporated into "The Concertante Works of Camille Saint-Saëns" (Chapters 2–6) only as much as I deemed necessary to characterize the composer's concerto style. After outlining a structure, I have not noted its repeated occurrences in other concertante works. More importantly, I have sought to substantiate Saint-Saëns's outstanding significance to the Romantic era by comparison.

I have passed over several of the composer's works whose structures are concertante in part, because I did not consider them directly relevant to my purpose. These include *Carnival of the Animals,* which, though it calls for two solo pianos, is classified as chamber music; the Third Symphony, whose organ part is fully integrated with the orchestra and is not concertante in character; concertante segments of larger works that are not concertante as a whole, such as the prelude to the oratorio *Le Déluge* (solo violin) or the ballet music for the opera *Ascanio* (flute solo), since they offer no real analysis of the genre under study; and finally, all the rearrangements of chamber music compositions for solo and orchestra, done by others, such as the Suite Op. 16 for Violoncello and Piano or the Cavatina Op. 144 for Trombone and Piano.

1

A Biographical Sketch

Charles-Camille Saint-Saëns was born in Paris on 9 October 1835, the only child of attorney Vincent Saint-Saëns and his wife, Clémence Françoise, née Collin.[1] Three months later Camille lost his father who succumbed to a tubercular illness at the age of 37. Thereafter the child was raised by his mother, together with her aunt Charlotte Masson.[2]

The great musical talent of Saint-Saëns was evident from his earliest childhood. At the age of 2½ he tried his hand at the piano; his first composition, a little piano piece whose autograph is preserved in the Bibliothèque Nationale, was given an exact date by his great aunt: 22 March 1839. At the age of five he was introduced to Mozart's *Don Giovanni,* and he held its composer up as a model throughout his life.

Saint-Saëns made a successful public debut in July 1840, but the triumphant prelude to his career as a pianist was his concert performance in the Salle Pleyel on 6 May 1846. The program included Mozart's Concerto in B-flat Major, K. 450, in which Saint-Saëns performed a cadenza of his own, and then, as solo works, Thema con variationi and a fugue by Handel, a toccata by Kalkbrenner, a sonata by Hummel, and a prelude with fugue by Bach. The concluding number was Beethoven's Concerto in C Minor, Op. 37.[3]

Both audience and press celebrated Saint-Saëns as a new Mozart. It was also pointed out that his talent was not limited to the field of music. For example, a review of the concert in *L'Illustration* reported, "It is not only by virtue of his brilliant musical formation that the child stands out. He shows equal facility in the study of languages, the exact sciences, natural history, and mechanics."[4] This universality, already evident in the 10-year-old, is typical of Saint-Saëns's open-minded attitude. He always strove to be as objective as possible, as exemplified by the stands he took in the Wagner controversy and the political events of 1870–71 and 1914–18.

Soon after his first concert, Saint-Saëns entered the Paris Conservatory, initially as a pupil in François Benoist's organ class, and then in 1850 as a composition pupil of Halévy. He competed for the coveted Prix de Rome in 1852 but was unsuccessful. His friendship with singer Pauline Viardot also dates from his school years at the Conservatory.

It was also in 1852 that Saint-Saëns won a composition contest with his *Ode à Sainte-Cécile.* The contest was sponsored by the Société Sainte-Cécile, which had been founded by Belgian violinist François Seghers. Through Seghers, Saint-Saëns made the acquaintance of Franz Liszt, and the two became lifelong friends. In December of that year Saint-Saëns began as organist at the Church of Saint-Merry, where he remained for five years.[5]

Saint-Saëns's most important composition of this period was the Symphony in E-flat Major, Op. 2, his first symphony according to the official count. Its first performance by the Société Sainte-Cécile under Seghers's direction took place 18 December 1853, in Paris. An 1860 article reflects what it meant in those days for a composer to devote himself to symphonic composition:

> At this time it is necessary for a composer of instrumental music to make a double sacrifice, the sacrifice of his popularity and the sacrifice of his fortune; it is not only that a composer does not become popular by writing quartets and symphonies, but it costs a great deal to mount these kinds of productions and have them heard. There is little encouragement as you see.[6]

On the printed program, three stars appeared in place of the composer's name.[7] The performance was an enormous success, and when the name was revealed, no one could believe that such a mature score had been composed by an 18-year-old. The technical mastery of this symphony earned Saint-Saëns the friendship of Berlioz and Gounod, both of whom rejected the Italian bel canto style that was so in vogue at the Paris Opéra and had led to a general disdain for instrumental music.

During these years, Saint-Saëns was a frequent guest at the soirées in Rossini's home, a meeting ground for artists and art patrons. On one of these evenings Saint-Saëns's Tarantella, Op. 6, was premiered, obviously influenced by Rossini.[8] In 1858 Saint-Saëns was called to succeed Louis Lefébure-Wély as organist at Madeleine Church, a position as lucrative as it was prestigious, and one which Saint-Saëns held until 1877.

The Concerto in C Major for Violin and Orchestra was also written in 1858, though it was not published until 1879, as Op. 58, no. 2. None of Saint-Saëns's biographers have adduced the occasion for its composition nor the immediate circumstances surrounding it. The only detailed comment is that of Emile Baumann:

> The Concerto in C Major of 1858 reflects the Italian taste prevalent at the time; indeed the flexibility of the violin as it runs up and down the scales, its adroitness, makes it ideal for leaps, octave arpeggios, and lengthy cadenzas. And yet the Allegro maestoso exudes youthful bravura with its brilliant emphases, its overflowing animation; the Andante begins with an ingeniously simple cantilena, and the finale is a playful bit of deviltry, which recurs even more stunningly in the Rondo capriccioso.[9]

It is generally agreed that his meeting with Pablo de Sarasate (1844–1908) finally led Saint-Saëns to develop an original style in his violin compositions. The C-Major Concerto still adheres strongly to the tradition represented by the Ecole Liégoise.[10] The typical mixture of virtuosity and cantabile is also acknowledged by Dandelot: "Suffice it to say that it [the C-Major Concerto] is particularly well suited to giving the virtuoso a chance to shine, yet the true artist can also be heard to good advantage in the poetic cantilena."[11]

Far greater brilliance is displayed in the Concerto No. 1 in D Major for Piano and Orchestra, Op. 17, which was also composed in 1858, and according to the composer, was "inspiré par la forêt de Fontainebleau [inspired by the forest at Fontainebleau]."[12] Here again, Baumann's assessment seems well worth citing:

> The Concerto in D Major exhibits youthful hyperbole: runs and arpeggios of exorbitant proportions, an ambitious sortie into grandiose prolixity. In places, the piano is no more than a

> whimsical companion to the orchestra. But aside from these exaggerations, the stature and élan of the piece are still of heroic measure. Furthermore, the interplay of voluptuous and playful phrases softens the emotional tension. The virtuoso passages—where it is often hard to escape the "tyranny of the fingers," the formulas—are themselves original, as is the concluding twist of the Andante movement, which, after bursting forth with a trill, ends with chromatic ornamentation in a low *pianissimo.*
>
> This work in which virtuosity played an excessive role was not really a very personal one. In the finale, Allegro con fuoco, the composer carries his rhythms playfully from one measure to the next, but the Andante is quite drab.[13]

It is striking that Baumann singles out the middle movement as drab in this description, even though it far surpasses the first and last movements in originality and anticipates Maurice Ravel's *Jeux d'eau* in its almost-impressionistic tone language. Again, this goes to show that even biographers with the best of intentions are not infallible.

In October 1859, Saint-Saëns was invited to visit Richard Wagner at his Paris residence. Many false allegations circulated about the relationship between the two composers. Particularly in times of political conflict between France and Germany, agitators tried to blow up artistic differences into nationalistic hostilities. But actually, at least in the early period of their relationship, Wagner was very much taken with Saint-Saëns, as his journal testifies.[14] He even regarded him as "the best musician of his country."[15]

Likewise Saint-Saëns, with his cosmopolitan mind-set, was careful never to fall prey either to fanatical hatred of Wagner or to blind adoration of the master from Bayreuth. Rising above all political considerations in his review of the *Ring* performance in Bayreuth, Saint-Saëns wrote of Wagner:

> To label him as an enemy of our nation is simply absurd. He was an enemy only to those who were hostile toward his music. They may well be justified in the latter; but they are certainly unjust in labeling the composer of the works they ridicule a monster by birth and lineage.
>
> Wagnermania is an excusable error, but Wagnerphobia is a children's disease.[16]

Although Saint-Saëns was able to judge Wagner's musical side with objective detachment, the latter's work *Eine Kapitulation* caused Saint-Saëns to regard Wagner as his bitterest personal enemy. In this parody, occasioned by the war of 1870–71, Wagner had "humiliated the French race in a most cruel manner and exposed its cultural representatives to ridicule."[17] Saint-Saëns could not be appeased, even by Wagner's comment that this sorry effort had merely been a bad joke. As late as 1915, again against a backdrop of political dissension, Saint-Saëns wrote, "I am combating him [Wagner], and it is not my fault if he undermines his own cause by including *Eine Kapitulation* in his complete works, rather than letting it be forgotten."[18] Saint-Saëns deserves all the more credit for standing by his artistic judgment of Wagner despite their personal differences: "Wagner invented everything; before him there was no music at all, and there can no longer be any afterwards."[19]

A major stimulus for Saint-Saëns's violin works was his acquaintance with the Spanish violinist Pablo de Sarasate, who called on him in 1859, when he was only 15 years old but already a widely acclaimed virtuoso.

> He had been good enough to ask me, in the most casual way imaginable, to write a concerto for him. Greatly flattered and delighted at the request, I made him a promise and kept my word with the Concerto in A Major to which—I do not know why—the German title of *Concertstück* has been given.[20]

Op. 20 (1859), published in 1868 as Saint-Saëns's first violin concerto, before the C-Major work (Op. 58), was an important step toward mastery of the classic solo concerto tradition. The concentrated single-movement form, totally misunderstood by many biographers even in recent times as a "Concertstück" or concertino, summarizes the essence of the solo concerto in just under 10 minutes.

> This concerto will stand as the prototype of its genre; our finest virtuosos often perform it frequently under the foreign-language title *Concertstück,* since it really is a single piece in which each section merges into the next.[21]

Nevertheless, Saint-Saëns's Concerto in A Major is a full-fledged three-part concerto.

Emile Baumann, a personal friend of Saint-Saëns and a dependable source of biographical details, maintains that the composer preferred his Op. 20 to the other two concertos and "qu'il eut le plus de joie à écrire [that he had taken more pleasure in writing it]."[22]

At the beginning of 1858, Saint-Saëns moved from rue du Jardinet to lodgings on rue du Faubourg-St-Honoré in order to be closer to the Madeleine where he had daily duties as organist. Here a circle of the composer's friends and acquaintances gathered regularly on Monday evenings to make music, hold discussions, and present their latest works to one another. Soon this "salon" was a byword all over Paris, as famous as the Thursday socials at the home of singer Pauline Viardot.

After the death on 14 March 1861 of Louis Niedermeyer, founder and director of the music academy named after him, and at the request of his son, Saint-Saëns took over the directorship there. Although he was very comfortable in his role as professor, this turned out to be the only teaching he ever did. His favorite pupil, and soon his closest friend as well, was Gabriel Fauré, 10 years his junior, who subsequently assumed Saint-Saëns's pedagogical legacy as director of the Paris Conservatory.

The year 1861 also saw a strengthening of the friendly relationship-between Saint-Saëns and Wagner. Saint-Saëns was the first in France to play the march from *Tannhäuser,*[23]. He also impressed Wagner with an effortless sight-reading of the complicated scores of *Lohengrin* and *Tristan.*

The five-movement Suite for Violoncello and Piano, Op. 16, was composed in 1862. Incidentally, the combination of this work with the Gavotte, which I rediscovered in the Bibliothèque Nationale, is incorrect.[24]

Saint-Saëns did not have an easy time with contemporary Parisian audiences. He repeatedly reinforced his reputation as an eccentric misfit and wavemaker by including the "despised" Classic composers on his concert programs and by standing up for Berlioz, Liszt, Wagner, and the not-yet-controversial Gounod.[25] He took an isolated position in his own creative efforts as well, by tackling chamber music, which was rejected as an obdurate Germanic musical genre.[26] Thus, his First Piano Trio, Op. 18, composed in 1863, was bound to cause a stir, and although it showed relatively little originality or musical substance, it quickly became one of the composer's most-often-played works.[27]

After the positive experience of working with Sarasate on Op. 20, Saint-Saëns wrote another piece for his friend in 1863, the Introduction et Rondo capriccioso, Op. 28. To this day the work is underrated as a mere virtuoso showpiece, but perhaps for that very reason it stands in high favor with violinists and audiences alike.

Despite all his successes, Saint-Saëns's social position was rather shaky, and Bonnerot maintains that this was the real reason the composer made a second attempt to win the Prix de Rome.[28] The jury, however, gave preference to Victor Sieg's cantata, and a major dispute erupted that was similar to the one that later shook the Paris music world over Ravel's repeated failures. After the decision was announced, Berlioz, a member of the jury and definitely well-disposed toward Saint-Saëns, made the often-quoted remark: "Il sait tout, mais il manque d'inexpérience [He knows everything, but lacks inexperience]."[29]

The subsequent years mark the heyday of the composer's career as a pianist. His numerous concerts at home and abroad and the evening chamber music gatherings with Sarasate, Aimé Gros, Jules Lasserre (to whom Op. 43 is dedicated), and Alfred Jaëll were not so much devoted to his own works as to those of other Classic and contemporary composers.

At a concert in the Salle Pleyel on 4 April 1867, two of Saint-Saëns's works that had been written quite a while earlier were first performed publicly: Sarasate played the A-Major Concerto, Op. 20, and Louis Dorus and Adolphe Leroy performed Op. 6. The reaction from audience and press was totally positive:

> Mr. Saint-Saëns knows all the violin effects, all the richness, as well as any violinist, and he also has a knack for making them stand out with an accompaniment that is always interesting.[30]
>
> The real plum of the concert, however, was a new violin concerto in A, which Mr. Sarasate performed masterfully. . . . Suffice it to say that Mr. Saint-Saëns, in our opinion, has never before soared to such heights. The violin was treated here as if the composer were a Joachim.[31]
>
> The program of works by Mr. Saint-Saëns culminated with the performance of a very pretty Tarantella for flute, clarinet, and orchestra. Messrs. Dorus and Leroy undertook the solos, thereby demonstrating their enthusiasm for the work and its composer. . . . The minor section is especially charming.[32]

> The Tarantella for flute and clarinet was encored. Here one can sense a master's hand. The piece is founded almost entirely on a ground bass that is repeated by various instruments in a most original way. The only part that seemed to us not to harmonize with the rest of the work was the cantabile in the middle, with its somewhat theatrical aura.[33]

On the occasion of the great Paris World Exhibition, which Napoleon III had organized to glorify the Second Empire, the French government sponsored a composition contest. Saint-Saëns was proclaimed the winner with his cantata *Les Noces de Prométhée,* Op. 19, a victory that not even the squabbling over its first performance could diminish.[34]

Saint-Saëns was a longtime friend of the Russian pianist, composer, and conductor Anton Rubinstein. In April 1869 Rubinstein asked him to arrange a concert at which he [Rubinstein] would make his Paris debut as conductor. The Salle Pleyel would not be available for three weeks, however, so Saint-Saëns decided on the spot: "C'est bien, j'écrirai un concerto pour la circonstance [Very well, I'll write a concerto for the occasion]."[35] The result was the Concerto in G Minor, Op. 22, which he himself played in the Rubinstein concert on 13 May 1868. As Saint-Saëns was poorly prepared, only the Scherzo revealed its full charm.

> The piano concerto, whose premiere he [Saint-Saëns] played last Wednesday in the Salle Pleyel, may not be a perfect work, but it contains two movements that deserve special attention. The first movement is the kind that tends to defy analysis and seemed to us to be more along the lines of a brilliant improvisation; the Scherzo that followed, in 6/8 time, is charming from start to finish. With its zest, its vivacity, its rapid tempo, the main theme builds and increases with power during the interesting developments. Consequently, this [Scherzo] is an exceptional piece, where everything, piano and orchestra alike, is shaped by the master's hand.[36]

The misconceptions engendered by the weaknesses of the premiere were soon forgotten, and Op. 22 won a permanent place in the repertoire. "What originality, what life, what strength, what flourish, and what color in this work, which has justifiably come to be the most-performed piece of our time."[37]

Another special admirer of this concerto was Franz Liszt, who wrote in a letter to Saint-Saëns:

> I must thank you again for your Second Concerto, which I enthusiastically applaud. The form is innovative and a most felicitous choice. The interest builds throughout the three movements, and you showed the pianistic effects to good advantage without sacrificing any compositional principles, a basic rule in this genre. . . . I played it again the day before yesterday for Sgambati, who Planté will tell you is above average as an artist—in fact, he even rates above the usual celebrity.
>
> He plans to perform your concerto in public next winter, and it is certain to meet with worldwide success.[38]

Another 1868 composition that should be mentioned is the Romance, Op. 27, for violin, piano (or harp), and organ, which Saint-Saëns arranged for orchestra over half a century later. In August of that year, the composer became a member of the Légion d'Honneur.

The year 1869 began with a sad event for Saint-Saëns: His friend Berlioz, who had been ailing for months, died in Paris on March 8. Saint-Saëns also had to struggle with many defeats as a composer. His work on *Samson et Dalila,* Op. 47, which he had begun so enthusiastically the previous year, met with major resistance from the opera directors, and even his friends reacted coolly. Therefore, the project was temporarily moved to a back burner.

At his seventh concert at the Leipzig Gewandhaus in December, when the composer first performed his new Piano Concerto in E-flat Major, Op. 29, a full-blown battle broke out in the audience:

> The instrumental solo performances were in the hands of Mr. Saint-Saëns of Paris. This artist, who is highly regarded in the French capital, did not succeed in gaining our favor with his new piano concerto. It belongs totally to the "interesting" genre and issues mainly from a combinatory talent rather than from genuine creativity. Occasional eloquent beginnings do not deliver what they promise, and despite heavy orchestral effects, which leave a distinct futuristic aftertaste, the work remains trite. The last movement made the best impression, with its terse form and a certain fiery vitality. Under the hands of Mr. Saint-Saëns, the piano took up the fight with the demons he

himself had conjured up from the orchestra. . . . Without exception, the rest of the solo pieces he performed suffered from a certain contrived pretentiousness that may well be able to dazzle but not to inspire.[39]

The Paris premiere the following spring went over better, at least with the critics:

The principal attraction of this evening, however, was the premiere of the Concerto in E-flat, interpreted admirably by its composer, Mr. Saint-Saëns. This is a very noteworthy work, with an extremely innovative opening, charming, and at the same time, bizarre in its clashes and stark contrasts. The passionate admirer of the great German masters is recognizable in every measure of this glowing music: in the tremolos of the strings, the dark and mysterious melodies, and the gleaming flash of the brass.[40]

How little this review represented the general view, of course, is shown in the scathing review that appeared seven years later, after the performance by Elie-Myriam Delaborde, to whom the work was dedicated:

For the gentlemen virtuosos, no matter how talented they are, there is every reason to fear that the good days of the solo concerto in the Salle Bergère are gone forever. The orchestra of a solo concerto cannot come close to competing with even the lowliest symphony, if the composer decides to sacrifice as much as possible of the solo part. Yet this is precisely what Mr. Saint-Saëns has done in his Third Concerto.

In spite of the forceful performance and clever orchestral effects, the work failed. It should also be said that this piece, conceived in the style of the new school and subtitled "The Last Judgment" in the concert hall, is probably destined to hasten the death of virtuosity at the conservatory. Mr. Saint-Saëns did not hit upon ideas here that could rescue him from his musical audacities.

His symphonic poems allow us to forgive him this third concerto, but the Société des Concerts made a mistake in accepting it, nevertheless. The wise Société would do better to remain classical and leave these experiments to the Pasdeloup or Colonne concerts.[41]

In Weimar, meanwhile, Liszt had expressed his interest in *Samson et Dalila* and promised to give the first performance without having seen even one note of the work. But the plan was temporarily foiled by the outbreak of the Franco-Prussian War on 19 July 1870. Saint-Saëns became a soldier in the Fourth Battalion of the Garde Nationale de la Seine.[42]

The armistice was signed on 28 January 1871, and Saint-Saëns then devoted his full energy to the realization of his long-contemplated plan. The date 24 February marked the founding of the Société Nationale de Musique, which according to its thesis, *Ars gallica,* was intended to give younger French composers an opportunity to have their works performed.[43] The proclaiming of the Commune on 18 March prevented any activity at first. Saint-Saëns evaded the unrest in Paris by going to London, where he made his debut as a pianist. When he returned to France, he prepared the opening concert of the Société Nationale, which took place on 17 November in the Salle Pleyel.

Inevitably, his compositional work languished somewhat: a Gavotte in C Minor for Piano, Op. 23, attests to the clash with traditional forms, while *Le Rouet d'Omphale,* Op. 31, the first of his four symphonic poems, emulated Liszt with a form that was a total departure from French tradition.[44] The Romance in D-flat Major for Flute (or Violin), Op. 37, is more of an occasional work.

On 18 January 1872, the composer's great aunt, Charlotte Masson, died at the ripe age of 91. Thereupon Saint-Saëns cancelled all his concert engagements and did not appear again until 10 March, when he gave the first performance of his friend Alexis de Castillon's Piano Concerto in D Major in the Pasdeloup concerts.[45]

The premiere of Saint-Saëns's first opera, *La Princesse jaune,* Op. 30, at the Opéra-Comique on 12 June, was disparaged by the critics as cold and unmelodious, and the exoticisms befitting the subject were rejected as anarchistic. After five performances, the work disappeared from the repertory. This failure slowed progress on *Samson et Dalila,* which had occupied Saint-Saëns since 1868; *Le Timbre d'argent* had also been waiting months in vain for its premiere.

The First Cello Sonata in C Minor, Op. 32, and the First Cello Concerto in A Minor, Op. 33, were written during this period in direct succession.[46] Saint-Saëns may even have worked on both pieces at the same time.[47]

On 19 January 1873, Saint-Saëns enjoyed a privilege that was seldom bestowed on a living composer, as Bonnerot notes.[48] His Op. 33 had its first performance by the Société des Concerts du Conservatoire. The artist, to whom the concerto was also dedicated, was Auguste Tolbecque. The premiere was praised in an extensive review:

> If Mr. Saint-Saëns should decide to continue in this vein, which is consistent with his violin concerto, the Trio in F, and other works of lesser significance, he is certain to recover many votes that he lost with his all-too-obvious divergence from classicism and the tendencies [toward modernism; presumably this assertion refers to Op. 29] in a number of his recent works. In conclusion, we must say that the Concerto for Violoncello seems to us to be a beautiful and good work of excellent sentiment and perfect cohesiveness, and as usual the form is of greatest interest.
>
> It should be clarified that this is in reality a *Concertstück,* since the three relatively short movements run together. The orchestra plays such a major role that it gives the work symphonic character, a tendency present in every concerto of any significance since Beethoven.
>
> The opening Allegro is brilliant, with a distinct momentum; the runs are not overdone but always marked by clever design and good taste. The minuet that follows is most delightful; the main theme, introduced with muted violins, could have the character of a march, were it not for the triple meter; then the violoncello solo comes in with a contrapuntal melody, and the whole piece makes a most felicitous impression. The beginning of the final Allegro is rather bland, but the ending is warm and interesting.[49]

Two things about this review should be noted. First, in labeling it a "concertstück," the author of this review has made the same error with Op. 33 as was made with Op. 20. The text implies that any concerto whose movements run together *attacca* is a "concertstück." The definition of "concertstück" (fragment of a concerto) as a one-movement composition, regardless of its inner structure and form, had of course already been used on de Bériot's First Violin Concerto, Op. 16, and also applies to Saint-Saëns's Op. 62, 94, and 154.[50] Furthermore, there is a distinction between "Konzertstück" (concertino) and "Konzertsatz" (concerto movement).

Second, the reviewer designates Op. 33 as a symphonic concerto because of the important role of the orchestra, and he even goes so far as to draw a connection with Beethoven. If this is not a case of confusing the symphonic concerto with the "sinfonia concertante," which seems unlikely, then it could be inferred from this stance that the term "concerto" applied primarily to virtuoso works, while any representative of this genre that showed a certain degree of independence in the orchestra part was defined as "symphonic." The sequence and structure of the movements do not seem to have been criteria.

The countless concerts, social engagements and compositions had put a great strain on Saint-Saëns's health, so he left Paris for two months (October and November 1873) to relax in the Mediterranean climate of Algiers. He is said to have felt drawn there again and again, where he could find the peace and quiet he needed to outline the third act of *Samson.* Meanwhile his second symphonic poem, *Phaëton,* was premiered by Edouard Colonne in a Concert National; audience and critics were of divided opinion, though not so much over the work as over the new genre.

In the Concert National of 28 March 1873, Marie and Alfred Jaëll gave the first performance of *Variations sur un thème de Beethoven pour deux pianos,* Op. 35. The work is based on the trio from Beethoven's Piano Sonata No. XVIII in E-flat Major, Op. 31, No. 3. The two Romances, Op. 36 (F Major, for Horn or Violoncello) and Op. 48 (C Major, for Violin), like Op. 37, are relatively insignificant occasional pieces. On the other hand, the private performance of the second act of *Samson et Dalila,* which Pauline Viardot had arranged for August 20, must be regarded as a small triumph. This time, the enthusiasm of the audience, including Henri Halanzier, director of the Paris Opéra, was unanimous.

The premiere of the orchestral version of *Danse macabre,* Op. 40, one year after the poem by Henri Cazalis was set to music, was the subject of heated debate. Colonne is supposed to have played the work against the will of the orchestra, and critic Adolphe Jullien wrote: "[It is] a baroque composition that has everything but a musical idea, good or bad. . . . It can only be defined in two ways: as an aberration or as a hoax."[51] Saint-Saëns's Op. 40—which established the composer's world fame, incidentally—was the first Classic work in musical history to include the xylophone. This proved to be one more cause for disquiet among those who attended the premiere on 3 February 1875!

In 1875, in collaboration with Miss Fanny Pelletan, the composer also began editing a complete collection of the works of Gluck. The massive project, which was left in Saint-Saëns's hands alone after the early death of his collaborator on 1 August 1876, dragged on into the present century. After a short trip to Brussels, where he played his Concerto in G Minor, the composer gave a concertante performance of parts of the *Samson* in the Concert du Châtelet on Good Friday, 16 March. The devastating verdict from audience and press which followed, dashed all plans for a scenic performance for the present.

Just prior to that performance, a personal event occurred in the composer's life which must be mentioned here. A marriage between Mr. Camille Saint-Saëns and Miss Marie-Laure Truffot, sister of his friend Jean Truffot, was solemnized on 3 February in Le Cateau. Although the marriage soon foundered because of tragic circumstances to be detailed later, it can be seen as a substantial argument against Saint-Saëns's alleged pederasty. The rumor that the composer indulged his homosexual tendencies, especially during his sojourns in North Africa, was started by hostile, jealous persons and lacks any factual basis.

Georges Bizet, a close friend of Saint-Saëns and his comrade-in-arms in the fight for the stage of the Palais Garnier [the Paris Opéra], died on 3 June 1875; he did not live to see the triumph of his *Carmen.* Bizet's death may possibly explain Saint-Saëns's relatively low compositional output that year. Works of particular note are the Piano Quartet in B-flat Major, Op. 41—a fresh tribute to the "disdained" chamber music of German-Austrian tradition, whose extreme seriousness is reminiscent of Schumann and Brahms—and the Allegro Appassionato in B Minor, Op. 43, for violoncello and piano (or orchestra). The Gavotte in G Minor probably belongs to this period as well.[52]

On 31 October 1875, the Concerts de l'Association Artistique opened with the successful premiere of the Fourth Piano Concerto in C Minor, Op. 44, by Saint-Saëns and Edouard Colonne. It was the high point of Saint-Saëns's career as a composer of concertos. Though Liszt had already succeeded in establishing a new form with his E-flat Major Concerto, the Frenchman's Op. 44 signifies a perfect union of Classic intellect with the structural freedom of Romanticism that makes the work seem like an improvisation:

Mr. Saint-Saëns's Fourth Concerto for Piano, played by the

> composer, contains passages of great beauty, especially in the introduction and the Andante. It is a known fact that this artist is an expert at molding his orchestra. Like Litolff, Mr. Saint-Saëns makes the piano an instrument of the orchestra in his concertos, instead of reducing the orchestra to the subordinate function of accompanist for the piano.
>
> The scherzo was equally pleasing; however, the interlude and the finale too often revert to those aberrations of modern style that Mr. Saint-Saëns adores, and of which he is one of the high priests.[53]

At the end of the year, the composer made an extended concert tour in Russia and did not return to Paris until mid January 1876. Meanwhile, his opera *Le Timbre d'argent* had been accepted by the Opéra-Comique and the premiere was scheduled for October. On 4 March, *Le Déluge* was premiered in the seventh Châtelet concert, along with the Choral Fantasia Op. 80 by Beethoven. Subtitled *Poème biblique en trois parties,* Op. 45, the Saint-Saëns work was based on a text by Louis Gallet, librettist for *La Princesse jaune.* At the premiere, a veritable battle broke out in the audience; while one part tried to boycott the performance by whistling and shouting, the other demanded that the work be played again.

Le Déluge is a rather inconsistent piece, partly reminiscent of Handel's Baroque oratorio, partly springing from the utterly romantic world of Italian bel canto. The opening section contains an extended violin solo, but, as mentioned in the Introduction, it is not included in this study. On the occasion of its premiere in Leipzig in 1892, it was said:

> One has the impression that, in this work more than in others, the composer embraces the "dual souls" theory. In the first part he fancies himself in the dignified role of an academic who prefers to satisfy his musical conscience and skill in a more strictly contrapuntal form, in a fugato. In the continuation, the second part, he sets his academic garb aside and gives free rein to his sense of modern melody; a solo violin becomes an interpreter of tender feelings, which admittedly conform much more to the mode of expression of a sentimental aria in French-Italian style than to biblical simplicity. We commend the composer for his wise restraint in settling for the simple apparatus of a string orchestra and not unleashing all the chaos of orchestral noise to illustrate the billowing waters. It goes without saying

> that the brilliant practitioner handles the string orchestra superbly. The novelty was appealing.[54]

On 2 May 1876, Léonce Détroyat founded a new periodical, *Le Bon Sens,* and Victorin Joncières was given the responsibility for musical reporting. However, the latter's dry commentaries were not well-received by the readers, and soon after, on 2 June, Saint-Saëns was named as his successor:

> The composer Camille Saint-Saëns made his debut as music critic last Sunday in the newspaper *Le Bon Sens.* The article is written with an ironic verve somewhat reminiscent of the style of Berlioz. There are few writers in the field of music who know the first thing about it; we are happy to have one more among those who know whereof they speak.[55]

It was also here that Saint-Saëns's reviews of the Bayreuth premiere of the *Ring* appeared from 19 to 24 August, vehemently disputed and often misconstrued.

Of further interest in connection with the Wagner festival productions are the following lines:

> A striking thing about this audience [at Bayreuth] is the fact that none of the great and esteemed musicians of modern Germany are encountered here, whereas France is or will be represented by Messrs. Saint-Saëns, Guiraud, Joncières, and undoubtedly many others, whom we do not know but who will attend the remaining performances. Brahms, Raff, Hiller, Joachim, Wolkmann [probably should read Volkmann], and Max Bruch are nowhere to be seen. Is it a protest against Wagner's enormous pride, jealousy over his success, or apathy?[56]

Meanwhile, there were enough anti-Wagnerians in Paris that they became Saint-Saëns's undoing. After countless difficulties, *Le Timbre d'argent* was finally premiered on 23 February 1877, at the Théâtre-Lyrique, but it disappeared from the program after only 18 performances. Even before the premiere, a press campaign was initiated against the "Wagnérien" Saint-Saëns, whose objective, neutral report on the *Ring* had caused such a stir.[57] Subsequent performances in Brussels (1879) and Monte Carlo (1907) failed to rescue the work from oblivion.

It was also in 1877 that the last of the four symphonic poems was written, *La Jeunesse d'Hercule,* Op. 50, followed by another romance, which was never orchestrated, Romance in D Major for Violoncello and Piano, Op. 51, and the first of six volumes of Etudes for Piano, Op. 52, which continue the tradition of Chopin and Liszt.[58]

Meanwhile, Liszt was preparing for the first performance of *Samson et Dalila* in Weimar. The work premiered 2 December at the Grand Ducal Theater, in a German translation by Richard Pohl, with Danish conductor Edouard Lassen on the podium.[59] The performance was a huge success, and the news soon reached Paris:

> Saint-Saëns has victoriously planted the flag of the French school in the middle of Germany. Though our military prestige may be low at the moment, our artistic and literary prestige shines gloriously once again. Not only must Germany turn to our playwrights to keep its theater alive; now the fatherland of Beethoven, Weber, and Mozart is calling for our composers as well.[60]

Growing success had also secured a source of livelihood for Saint-Saëns, so that he could afford to give up the organist's position that he had held for nearly 20 years:

> Mr. Camille Saint-Saëns has resigned from his position as organist at the Madeleine, which he held for nearly twenty years. Tied to Paris by the regularity of his duties, he had rarely been able to accept engagements that called him into the provinces or to foreign countries as virtuoso and composer.[61]

Saint-Saëns wanted to write a requiem on the occasion of his friend Albert (Le) Libon's death on 20 May 1878, so he retreated to Bern, Switzerland, to find peace and quiet. The work premiered 22 May in the Eglise Saint-Sulpice in Paris, with Charles Marie Widor at the organ and the composer on the conductor's podium. His Requiem, Op. 54, made a deep impression on the listeners; it seems doubly absurd, in light of this work, to label Saint-Saëns a salon composer.

A few days later, catastrophe descended upon the composer's family. In an unobserved moment, André, the elder of Saint-Saëns's two sons, leaned too far over the balcony railing and plunged to his death on the street. The child was only 2½ years old, and the accident hit the family hard. As if that weren't enough, Mrs. Saint-Saëns went to Reims to stay with her mother and to recover from this blow. She took her other son, Jean-François, with her. There, only six weeks after André's death, the second child died of pneumonia at the age of seven months.[62] Saint-Saëns never got over this dual tragedy. Three years later, after accompanying his wife to a health spa in La Bourboule, he left the hotel and informed her in a short letter that he would not return. They were never legally divorced, but the separation was permanent.[63]

Outwardly, however, Saint-Saëns kept his composure. For instance, he closes a four-page letter to a friend, which is peppered with innuendos and teasing remarks:

> You expressed your heartfelt sympathy to me, and I return the same. I have lost both my children in the space of a month, and I assure you that my happiness is very much subdued. Permit me to embrace you, though I am not a dog. C. Saint-Saëns.[64]

The cantata *Les Noces de Prométhée,* Op. 19, which had won first prize in a contest 11 years earlier, was finally performed for the 1878 World Exhibition. "Justice walks with a slight limp," noted *Le Journal de Musique.* By October the new opera *Etienne Marcel* had been completed and was scheduled to premiere at the Grand Théâtre in Lyon on 8 February of the coming year.

In the wake of a highly successful premiere, the composer undertook an extended concert tour through Germany, Austria, and Switzerland, from which he returned to Paris in mid April. Here, commissioned by the city of Birmingham, he composed his ode *La Lyre et la harpe,* Op. 57, for solos, chorus, and orchestra (based on a poem by Victor Hugo), which premiered 28 August. Meanwhile Saint-Saëns had quit his job as reviewer for *Le Bon Sens,* which had since become *L'Estafette* through a merger. He joined the staff of a journal founded by Laffitte called *Le Voltaire,* where he performed the same function.

On 13 February 1880, his Violin Concerto in C Major, Op. 58, had its premiere in the Pasdeloup concerts:

> The Violin Concerto by Mr. Saint-Saëns is a remarkable work. The theme of the finale could perhaps be faulted for lack of originality; yet the piece is well-styled, and the beautiful rendition by Mr. Marsick was a credit to it.[65]

Also dating from this year are the Third Violin Concerto in B Minor, Op. 61, again dedicated to Sarasate, and the *Morceau de concert,* Op. 62, for violin, as well as the acclaimed *Suite Algérienne,* Op. 60, which was completed in Boulogne-sur-Mer and successfully premiered 19 December at the Châtelet in Paris.

Henri Reber, professor of composition at the Paris Conservatory for many years, had died unexpectedly on 24 November 1880, and Saint-Saëns, Léo Delibes, Ernest Guiraud, César Franck, Edmond Membrée, Félix Clément and Edouard Lalo were under consideration to succeed him. On 19 February of the following year, Saint-Saëns's appointment as Reber's successor was confirmed. Around that time, a survey was taken among the musical giants of France to solicit their views on the past, present, and future of their art. Saint-Saëns's reply seems almost prophetic:

> The last word is certainly not to be found in our enharmonic half-tone system. The latter is only an approximation, and the time may come when our ear, having become more discerning, will no longer be content with it.
>
> Thus another art will be born; the present art will be like a dead language, whose masterpieces remain though the language is no longer spoken. What this new art will be like is impossible to foresee; for if it should appear before us suddenly, we would be just as incapable of appreciating it as an [untrained] person from [a culture with a different musical tradition] is incapable of understanding a Beethoven symphony.[66]

In another place, Saint-Saëns develops this idea further:

> Tonality, which has provided the basis for modern harmony, is in the throes of death. The exclusive use of the major and minor modes is over and done with. Ancient modes are reentering the scene, and following in their footsteps, Oriental modes, in which the variety is immense, are invading art. All this will inject new life into worn-out melody; harmonies will change as well, and rhythmics, scarcely explored, will develop. From all this a new art will be born.[67]

Concerning the nature of music, Saint-Saëns says:

> I have said before and will not cease to repeat, because it is the truth, that music, like painting and sculpture, can exist for its own sake, independent of any emotion; in such cases, the music is pure. . . . The more that feeling develops, the further music

> and the arts move away from their pure state; and when nothing but emotion is sought, art vanishes; we have examples of this staring us in the face.[68] *L'art est un mystère* [Art is a mystery].[69]

The *Hymne à Victor Hugo* for chorus and orchestra, Op. 69, was written in 1881 as a tribute to the celebrated poet. And while Saint-Saëns was already working on his new opera, *Henry VIII,* he fulfilled a request from Emile Lemoine's instrumental ensemble, La Trompette, by writing the Septet for Piano, Trumpet, and String Quintet in E-flat Major, Op. 65, the prelude of which had already been performed successfully in January 1880.

Saint-Saëns devoted almost all of 1881 to completing the score of *Henry VIII,* which was supposed to have been ready much earlier. In March 1882 he directed the first three performances of a new production of *Samson* in Hamburg, which Hans von Bülow praised enthusiastically as "the most significant musical theater work of the last two centuries."[70] Meanwhile the Paris Opéra had accepted *Henry VIII* for the opening of its winter season, so rehearsals began in September. They dragged on for six months under the greatest of difficulties, until the date of the premiere was finally set for 6 March 1883. The opera was a huge success. Edmond Hippeau devoted a whole book to it, and Gounod praised it as "l'une des plus étonnantes organisations musicales [one of the most amazing musical productions]."[71]

After the premiere, Saint-Saëns went to Algeria again to recover from the strain of the rehearsals. Upon returning to Paris, he was forced to suspend nearly all activity because of a serious illness, which plagued him until the beginning of 1884. He wrote the *Rapsodie d'Auvergne,* Op. 73, for piano and orchestra in March, while attending the rehearsals for *Henry VIII;* the Allegro appassionato, Op. 70, had just been completed, as had the Album, Op. 72, for solo piano. Not until November of that year was he able to resume his concert tours. On 15 March 1885, in the Châtelet, Louis Diémer gave the premiere performance of Op. 73, which had been dedicated to him.

Next Saint-Saëns composed his first Sonata for Violin and Piano in D Minor, Op. 75, for Pierre Marsick, who had launched Saint-Saëns's C-Major Concerto in Paris and undertaken the violin solo of the *Déluge* in Geneva in 1884. As a wedding gift for his friend Caroline Montigny-Rémaury, now Caroline de Serres, Saint-Saëns wrote the famous caprice-valse *Wedding Cake,* Op. 76.[72]

The volume *Harmonie et Mélodie,* consisting of the most interesting essays from *L'Estafette* and *Voltaire* and edited by Saint-Saëns, was published by Calmann-Lévy. Meanwhile, heated discussions over the "Wagner issue" had erupted anew, and Saint-Saëns reiterated: "I deeply admire the works of Richard Wagner, despite their bizarre qualities. They are stunning and powerful, and that is enough for me. But I never was, I am not now, I never will be a Wagnerian fanatic."[73]

In November 1885, Saint-Saëns embarked on a concert tour through the provinces with the violinist Raphaël Diaz Albertini. At the beginning of 1886, he went to Berlin, where the press had set the stage for a hostile reception even before his concert:

> During the *Lohengrin* controversy in Paris, Saint-Saëns displayed his hatred of the art and music of the fatherland, a hatred expressed in both spoken and written word, in a form offensive to Germany.[74]

As was to be expected, violent scenes erupted:

> When the French composer Saint-Saëns appeared in the philharmonic concert, expressions of disapproval issued from the audience. The weak applause that greeted the guest aroused opposition, which was manifested again at a place in the piano concerto that was reminiscent of Wagner. Only later did the auditorium calm down, so that when the composer made his second appearance, peace prevailed. Saint-Saëns used to visit Germany often and even premiered several of his compositions here. But lately several of his anti-German remarks have been circulating. He was also an avid participant in the agitation against the *Lohengrin* performance in Paris.[75]
>
> The effects of the Berlin fiasco were far-reaching:
>
> One by one, Saint-Saëns's concert engagements in Germany are being canceled. The latest to follow the examples of Kassel and Bremen is Dresden, so we hear. The Nikodé concert to be held on February 19 in the Saxon capital will forgo Mr. Saint-Saëns's participation, and pianist Emil Sauer will perform in the French musician's place.[76]

The only ones to stand up for Saint-Saëns were Eduard Hanslick and Angelo Neumann, director of the opera house in Prague.

In order to get his mind off this affront, the composer withdrew for a while to a small Austrian village, where he produced in a short time what is probably his most famous work, *Le Carnaval des animaux.* Saint-Saëns adamantly refused to allow publication of this "grande fantaisie zoologique," because he feared—and rightly so—that the musical jest might be regarded as representative of his work in general.

His main work for the year 1886 was his third and last symphony, the Symphony in C Minor, Op. 78, which became famous as the "organ symphony" because of its solo part. Dedicated to the memory of his friend Franz Liszt, the work matured slowly. The premiere on 9 January 1887, was a colossal triumph, and the composer was celebrated as a French Beethoven. Saint-Saëns himself said of Op. 78: "I gave everything to it I was able to give. . . . What I have done, I will never do again."[77]

In addition to the regrettable events in Germany, Saint-Saëns had another debacle in 1886 to lament. A rift had gradually been forming between his "school" and that of César Franck. The altercation was carried over by Vincent d'Indy into the Société Nationale, and a public protest arose against the founder of the organization. Finally Saint-Saëns, along with Romain Bussine, was more or less given a *consilium abeundi* (advice to leave); both tendered their resignations.

On 14 March 1887, Saint-Saëns's new theatrical work *Proserpine* was premiered successfully at the Opéra-Comique, albeit critics panned the work as usual, because they thought they could detect traces of Wagner. A fire at the opera house on 25 May, from which the score of *Proserpine* was barely rescued, provided a welcome excuse to cancel the piece for the time being, since the costumes and scenery had fallen victim to the flames.

The Palais Garnier wanted to stage a new opera, *Ascanio,* for the 1889 World Exhibition. With the libretto in his suitcase, Saint-Saëns retreated to Algiers at the end of 1888 to work on the score. He had just completed the *Havanaise,* Op. 83, for violin and orchestra, dedicated to Diaz Albertini, and the Morceau de concert for horn and orchestra, Op. 94, which was not published until 1893. Shortly before his departure on 18 December, his mother had succumbed to pneumonia at the age of 79. Saint-Saëns returned to Paris in the middle of May to find that preparations for the opera's production had progressed very little. Commissioned by the journal *Le Rappel,* he wrote three long reports on "Les Instruments de musique à l'Exposition."

During this waiting period, Saint-Saëns arrived at a momentous decision. After the death of both his children, the breakup of the family, and the death of his mother, there was nothing and no one left to hold him in Paris. Therefore he broke up his entire household on rue Monsieur le Prince and sent everything—furniture, works of art, sculptures and engravings, his manuscripts, his extensive library—to his cousin Léon in Dieppe. The inner conflict he suffered is documented in his only composition from this period, the Scherzo for Two Pianos, Op. 87.

Since he was also in very poor physical health, Saint-Saëns decided at the end of November to burn all bridges behind him and "find the means, far away and in another climate, for becoming a different self."[78] He left Europe after giving his librettist final instructions for *Ascanio,* whose premiere on 21 March 1890, he never saw. This "flight" set tongues wagging in Paris; some said the composer had died at sea; others claimed he was in a mental institution in Ville-Evrard. In reality, Saint-Saëns had "fled" to the Canary Islands and was allowing nothing to disturb him during his voluntary exile at Las Palmas.

He returned to Paris at the end of May, somewhat recovered. In July, the Musée Saint-Saëns opened in Dieppe. At this time the composer was primarily engaged in literary pursuits. A series of essays entitled "Souvenirs," from which the philosophical treatise *Problèmes et Mystères* issued, was running in the *Revue Blanche.* Saint-Saëns was also revising his book of poetry, *Rimes familières,* for publisher Calmann-Lèvy.

César Franck died on 8 November 1890, and d'Indy succeeded him as director of the Société Nationale. Increasingly restless, Saint-Saëns left Paris again at the beginning of December and boarded a ship bound for Ceylon. Later he went to Cairo and Alexandria, where he wrote *Africa,* Op. 89, a fantasia for piano and orchestra, which was premiered by Mrs. Roger Miclos on 25 October 1891, in the Colonne concerts:

> *Africa!* A fantasia based partly on Eastern themes. Like everything this master musician produces, it is exquisite in its intellectual refinement, its stylistic perfection, and that enormous charm; yet it is quite whimsical, and we would not go so far as to assert that piano and orchestra play well-balanced roles in *Africa.*
>
> Indeed, it seemed to us that the piano was treated in the

> pleasant, smooth style of the old masters, while the orchestra availed itself of all the profusion of modern music.[79]

Another reviewer said:

> It is a sort of African banter, in which the little desert birds seem to play an important role. It might be said that the piano is handled a bit too flippantly, but this is offset by the clever detail exhibited in the orchestration.[80]

Meanwhile the Paris music world had become an almost unbearable burden to Saint-Saëns. The old spirit had been superseded by that of the pupils of César Franck and the young Debussy, and whereas Saint-Saëns was once rejected as a revolutionary, he was now cast aside as scrap iron. Though the Grand Opéra was still reluctant to produce *Samson et Dalila,* the composer was already busy writing the music for a new libretto. The text for *Phryne* was authored by Lucien Augé de Lassus, who later was one of Saint-Saëns's biographers. The Piano Suite, Op. 90, represented a renewed examination of the Baroque period.

In resignation, the composer retreated to Point Pescade near Algiers in March 1892, where he composed the Second Piano Trio in E Minor, Op. 92. This monumental work, created 30 years after Op. 18, is one of the highlights of French chamber music. The triumphant premiere of *Samson* on 23 November compensated Saint-Saëns for many disappointments. The opening performance of *Phryne* on 24 May 1893, was also a great success, thanks in part to Sibyl Sanderson, an audience favorite, who played the title role.

In June 1893, Cambridge University conferred honorary doctorates on Arrigo Boito, Max Bruch, Edvard Grieg, Peter Tchaikowsky, and Camille Saint-Saëns. Fourteen years later, Saint-Saëns would receive the same honor from Oxford University. Ernest Guiraud had died in May 1892, having turned over his opera *Brunehilda* (which later became *Frédégonde*) to Saint-Saëns to complete. Then in October 1893 came the death of his long-time friend and patron Charles Gounod. Once again Saint-Saëns fled to the Canary Islands to escape all that was depressing him in Paris.

Again, very few works were written during this period. The composer turned more to literature and penned a "philosophical essay of 100 pages about the future of society, in which nature is the foundation, independent of any creed."[81] The work was published in July 1894 by

Flammarion under the title *Problèmes et Mystères.* Saint-Saëns attended rehearsals for *Proserpine* in Toulouse until the end of November. Then, traveling by way of Spain and Egypt, where his *Souvenir d'Ismaïlia,* Op. 100, was written, he went to Saigon.

At the request of his publisher, Durand, Saint-Saëns agreed to edit Jean Philippe Rameau's complete works and to convert the scores to contemporary notation. Meanwhile *Frédégonde* had a rather successful premiere. Saint-Saëns returned to Cairo in January 1896. Here, in the seclusion of a hotel room, along with his Second Violin Sonata, Op. 102, he composed his fifth and last Piano Concerto in F Major, Op. 103. It was premiered upon his return to Paris on 6 May, as part of the festival concert celebrating the 50th anniversary of his artistic career—together with the violin sonata, played by Sarasate and accompanied by the composer.

The press greeted the new concerto enthusiastically:

> Never have we heard a more colorful and gripping work. It has the force of Rubens, Raphael, and Michelangelo behind it, for it contains caprice, grace, and power. At the same time, the listener marvels at the incomparable workmanship, the chief quality of this greatest musician of our time, and that prodigious imagination that conveys new and strangely captivating artistic impressions.[82]

> Saint-Saëns awakens Eastern mirages in me, with a feeling of sensuous bliss and the impression of something infinite like sadness or emptiness, the vision—or better yet, the dream—of a flock of storks and great pink ibises against a blue sky, sparkling in the sunlight and reflected in the fleeting mirror of the Nile.[83]

The Eastern color soon earned the work the epithet "Egyptien," and even Saint-Saëns himself confirmed the exotic influence:

> The second movement is a kind of journey eastward, which in the F-sharp episode actually extends to the Far East. The passage in G is a Nubian love song that I heard boat operators sing on the Nile as I traveled downriver on a *dahabieh.*[84]

With the anniversary concert it appeared that Saint-Saëns had weathered his personal crisis and won back the Paris audience as well. His ballet *Javotte* was greeted enthusiastically at its premiere in Lyon on

3 December 1896, and the composer's apparent decision to end his musical career with this work was all the more surprising. He told the press that the *Javotte* was "le postscriptum de ma carrière musicale" [the postscript of my musical career].[85]

It was soon evident that this decision had been reversed, if it was ever meant seriously at all. After extended concert tours, the composer returned to Las Palmas in the winter of 1897–98. In his bag was Louis Gallet's libretto to *Déjanire,* which was premiered in the Bèziers arena on 28 August of the following year. The extravagant production—120 strings, 18 harps, and 25 trumpets!—was an enormous success in the realm of ancient theater. But the triumph was soon overshadowed. Gallet, whom Saint-Saëns valued as a genuine friend after their collaboration on six operas, died a few weeks later. Shortly before his departure to the Canary Islands, the composer had completed his second cycle of piano études, whose brilliant finale constituted the solo in the final movement of Op. 103.

In May 1899, Saint-Saëns traveled to Buenos Aires, where his First String Quartet in E Minor, Op. 112, was premiered. The concert in Argentina's capital, which also included numerous older chamber music works, was a great success. Saint-Saëns spent the transition from 1899 to 1900 in Las Palmas, where he edited his new book *Portraits et Souvenirs.* In March, while still in Las Palmas, he was invited by Victorien Sardou and P. B. Gheusi to compose music for the libretto *Les Barbares.* Saint-Saëns returned to Paris to confer with the librettists, but with the flurry surrounding the new World Exhibition, he hardly got any rest. Honors were conferred on him in quick succession: honorary member of the International Music History Congress, Knight of the Legion of Honor and, thanks to Kaiser Wilhelm II, the order "Pour le Mérite." Saint-Saëns was pressed for time, and for the next few months he was occupied almost exclusively with *Les Barbares.*

But the work came to a standstill when the Orange arena was forced to close in March 1901 because of its unsafe condition. Like *Déjanire, Les Barbares* was designed for spacious, open-air staging, and the facilities available at the Paris Opéra were hardly adequate. Moreover, Saint-Saëns's health had degenerated to the point that he needed complete bed rest. Despite the many setbacks, the premiere took place on 23 October in the Palais Garnier. Its success soon faded:

Amid all its niceties and weaknesses, Saint-Saëns's music seems to advocate the principle: *spiritus flat ubi vult* [The spirit (wind) blows where it wills. John 3:8]. Of course, this lack of system is also a system, but whether it is the best remains an open question[86]

At the beginning of March 1903, the Second Cello Concerto, composed during the previous year, had its premiere. Neither the form, which resembled that of the Piano Concerto in C Minor, nor the unusually virtuosic treatment of the solo part was greeted with much appreciation:

A curious study of certain effects and artful vocalises on the violoncello. Applause from an audience that had held its breath, a simple tremor, and involuntary, poorly restrained sighs were the discreet reactions that greeted the felicitous completion of each of these dangerous feats.[87]

It was said of a later performance:

Mr. Joseph Hollmann played Saint-Saëns's Second Concerto for Violoncello masterfully and with a conviction that we admired without qualification. This work is full of dangerous acrobatics, despite a *Romance-Larme* that tries to be suave and yet would have remained trite, if Mr. Hollmann's violoncello had not sung it so exquisitely. Of course, this concerto shows undeniable craftsmanship on the part of Mr. Saint-Saëns; it is skillful and ingenious, with logical effects; nevertheless, I prefer the accomplished juggler who rarely misses; the fear of a "miss" upsets me too much. So here we have bad music that is well written, and isn't that much more disastrous than good music that is badly written?[88]

Saint-Saëns's incidental music to Racine's *Andromaque* had premiered in the Sarah Bernhardt Théâtre shortly before, and the one-act opera *Hélène,* based on his own libretto, was in the development stages. The latter premiered in Monte Carlo on 18 February 1904, together with Massenet's *Navarraise.* Summer brought new concert engagements, and the *Caprice andalous* for violin, Op. 122, was performed for the first time in November.

The *Caprice andalous,* which I confess I like less than the Rondo capriccioso by the same master, is almost exclusively a virtuoso

> piece. It is the signature stamp, so to speak, on everything the author of *Samson* has written recently about and in favor of the concerto form and with regard to virtuosity in general.[89]

> The *Caprice* seems a little skimpy: brilliantly arranged folk melodies where gaiety and sentiment alternate, but without crassness or emphasis. Mr. Saint-Saëns excels at these simple little compositions, whereby he rescues himself from the brink of triviality with that certain something that is second nature to him; one gets the feeling that an obstacle has been skillfully dodged.[90]

> It seems to me that Andalusian folk music has prettier themes than those the master chose. It also seems to me as if the great symphonist mainly wanted to have fun writing something pretty, rather than to call forth a vivid exotic vision, as Berlioz did in *Harold* and as Charpentier did in *Impressions d'Italie,* or indeed as he himself did in the splendid *Suite algérienne.*
>
> But he scattered delightful pearls throughout the orchestra and wove exquisite harmonies into the melancholy *malagueñas.*[91]

For the first time, Saint-Saëns is criticized in these reviews as basically a composer of modest, pleasant pieces who barely keeps from sinking to triviality. Yet it was not so much his style of writing that had changed, as popular taste, which had cast Romanticism aside and was now confusing lyricism with sentimentality.

That winter Saint-Saëns wrote the Second Sonata for Violoncello and Piano in D Minor, Op. 123. It is remarkable that his First Sonata was composed in direct conjunction with his First Concerto and that now, some 30 years later, the Second Concerto and the Second Sonata also were written in close succession.

Gustave Charpentier's *Louise,* written in 1900, was France's first veristic opera; for a short time it jarred the influence of Wagnerian musical drama. One of the most significant Italian works in the new style was Pietro Mascagni's *Cavalleria Rusticana,* which had premiered in 1890 in Rome. The new trend was also reflected in Saint-Saëns's new opera *L'Ancêtre* (text by Augé de Lassus); the work, which admittedly shows little verism in its musical language, has a Corsican family vendetta as its central theme. The opera premiered 24 February 1906, in Monte Carlo.

The composer spent the spring of 1906 in Italy. His summer was taken up with numerous concert engagements, and on 20 October he boarded the ship *Provence,* bound for North America. But the strains were too much for his already failing health, and a serious case of diphtheria nearly cost him his life. He had not yet fully recovered from the illness when he returned to Europe in mid December, and in January 1907 he withdrew to Cairo to convalesce. It was here that he composed the Fantasia for Violin and Harp, Op. 124, which reveals a distinct impressionistic influence.

Saint-Saëns ailed throughout the year 1907. His few concert appearances left him exhausted, and even a stay at a health resort in Switzerland brought little improvement. Again he spent the winter in Egypt, where Mohammed Ali Pascha, brother of the khedive, had placed a house at his disposal on the Island of Rodah in the Nile. In August 1908, he set Psalm 150 to music, the only one of his works that he never got to hear, as the enormous size of the ensemble made performance prohibitive.

One of the earliest films in the newborn art of cinematography, *L'Assassinat du Duc de Guise,* premiered on 16 November in the Salle Visions d'Art. Henri Lavedan had staged the historic event of the murder of the Duke of Guise, and Saint-Saëns had written a score expressly for the production, thereby becoming the first film composer.

At the time of the film's premiere, Saint-Saëns was already in Las Palmas and he did not return to Paris until the middle of March 1909. Most of that year was taken up with various opera productions, which Saint-Saëns attended. In December he retreated to Luxor, where he wrote *La Muse et le poète,* Op. 132. In its original version, it was for piano, violin, and violoncello, "a dialogue between the two instruments rather than a contest between two virtuosos."[92] Saint-Saëns was already planning a concertante version, which was to be much better than the chamber music version.[93] Eugène Ysaye and Joseph Hollmann played both the London premiere on 7 June 1910, and the Paris premiere on 20 October in the Sarah Bernhardt Théâtre.

This new poem by the great French master, whose name can be

> found on all concert posters at the beginning of this season, impressed me as very beautiful. I disagreed with A(lfred) Bruneau—a good critic, nonetheless!—in his claim that there is a rather large dose of "virtuosity" in this composition. If by this he means that the piece is well-suited to the instruments and that it demands virtuosos of high caliber, then yes! But if we are to understand by this [word] that the composer often abandoned the psychological essence of the work just to take up an ingenious form that is supposed to throw sand in the listener's eyes, then no, no, a thousand times no! What amazes me about this duet which is accompanied by a symphony is that it is full of conviction and feeling, without lapses and without flagging interest. A work of tenderness, which seems to me to actually be a bit painful, or at least somber, in which, despite the diversity of the movements, tones, and rhythms, and without being diverted by superficial things, the listener is caught up in the vibrant unity of an inner drama.[94]

Saint-Saëns had performed Mozart's complete piano concertos in a concert series in London in the spring of 1910. Upon returning to Paris, the tireless composer moved into his last apartment, at 83a, rue de Courcelles. Here he completely rewrote *Déjanire,* which premiered in its new form on 14 March 1911, in Monte Carlo. After almost three-quarters of a century of activity as a composer, his creative powers were beginning to show signs of fatigue. As Saint-Saëns himself put it, "la lyre est désaccordée [the lyre is out of tune]."[95] Once again he turned his attention to literary tasks and wrote bimonthly articles for the *Echo de Paris.*

Not until the end of January 1912 was Saint-Saëns able to muster enthusiasm for a new composition. His piano duet partner, Caroline de Serres, asked him to write a cycle of études for the left hand, since her right hand had been temporarily stilled by surgery. On 29 February, he sent her his Op. 135 from Cairo.

Meanwhile, Saint-Saëns was busy with plans for a new oratorio. In collaboration with Hermann Klein, he produced *La Terre promise,* completing the instrumentation in Egypt during the winter of 1912–13. On 2 April 1913, he participated—along with Debussy, d'Indy, Fauré, and Dukas—in the "Concert inaugural consacré à la musique française [first concert dedicated to French music]," which Gabriel Astruc had organized for the grand opening of the Théâtre des Champs-Elysées.

On 2 June, a festival concert was held at the Queen's Hall in London honoring Saint-Saëns's 75th anniversary as a pianist. There was renewed interest in the composer on the international music scene in general, and he made countless concert appearances throughout Europe. Again his winter domicile was Port Said, and when he returned from there in mid February, new concert invitations already awaited him.

This productive period was interrupted in September by the catastrophe of World War I, whose full impact Europe hardly recognized at first. Saint-Saëns expressed his patriotic convictions in a very dubious series of article entitled "Germanophilie," which were published in *Echo de Paris,* and showed him in a rather unfavorable light abroad as well as in France.[96] On 30 April 1915, he embarked on a trip to America with his newly completed cantata *Hail California,* to participate in the San Francisco World's Fair Exhibition as France's musical ambassador.

Meanwhile he had become France's most famous and celebrated musician, and honors were heaped upon him everywhere. Though he longed for quiet seclusion, he had to undergo the strains of a veritable triumphal procession through all the major cities of France: "It is sure to be said that I am simply unable to sit still; yet I would much prefer to stay at home and work in peace, but fate will not allow it!"[97] At the end of April 1916, Saint-Saëns traveled to Brazil, Argentina, and Uruguay.

Understandably, this constant movement left little time to write longer compositions. Saint-Saëns's output was limited to a few songs, shorter chamber music compositions, and occasional works, except for a rather lengthy essay, "Les Idées de Monsieur Vincent d'Indy," in which Saint-Saëns's basic views on rhythm, form, meter, and so forth are expressed. The composer had spent the past four winters in the unhealthy Paris climate, so his trip to Cannes in the middle of December 1917 was truly a chance to recuperate. Here he prepared a new edition of the book *Problèmes et Mystères* under the title *Divagations sérieuses.*

After returning to Paris at the beginning of August 1918, Saint-Saëns began composing the Morceau de concert, Op. 154; his second string quartet in G major had just been completed. He devoted a stay at a health resort in Hamman R'hira to composing the monumental fantasia, *Cyprès et lauriers,* for organ and orchestra, Op. 156, in which he celebrated the end of the war and France's victory. The premiere at the Casino in Ostende was a great success, as was the Paris performance in the Trocadéro at the end of October 1920:

> An unpublished work for organ and orchestra by Mr. Saint-Saëns was unveiled for us, *Cyprès et lauriers.* The first part in D minor for solo organ was well played by Mr. Gigout. The second part, a dialogue with the orchestra, where the tremendous sonority and harmonic skill of Mr. Saint-Saëns are encountered, gives rise to a grandiose, clear, and wonderfully developed fugue. The hymn [national anthem] bursts forth in pure and noble strains, and victory appears in the triumphal key of D major. This work will endure as one of the most powerful of its kind.[98]

Meanwhile, the aged composer was suffering increasingly from shortness of breath and high blood pressure; the Paris climate was very hard on him. The fact that he could still keep his many concert engagements borders on the miraculous—they must have totally exhausted him. Even Algiers afforded him little rest, where, in the winter of 1920, he wrote his last chamber music works: three sonatas for oboe, clarinet, and bassoon, with piano. Possibly a fourth sonata for English horn was planned, but it never materialized.[99] Shortly before that he had completed *Odelette,* Op. 162, a concertino for flute and chamber orchestra. When he returned to Paris, his chronic bronchitis broke out in full force and restricted him to his bed, from where he kept an eye on the preparations for the reopening of *Ascanio* at the Paris Opéra. The premiere took place on 9 November 1921.

On 4 December the composer took lodging at the Hôtel de l'Oasis in Algiers, where he orchestrated his Violin Romance, Op. 27, which was more than 50 years old. It was his last work. Camille Saint-Saëns died peacefully and painlessly on 16 December at 10:30 P.M. After a memorial service on 19 December in the cathedral of Algiers, his mortal remains were transported to Paris, where a state funeral was held at the Madeleine on Saturday, 24 December. A huge procession accompanied him to his final resting place in the Montparnasse cemetery.

> His example and his work remain. The man is no more, but his spirit hovers over the world, alive and glorious, and will continue to hover as long as we have orchestras and instruments.[100]

The Concertante Works of Camille Saint-Saëns

2

The Form of the Concertos and Concertinos [Morceaux de Concert]

2.1. Movement Sequence

Unlike Germany, Austria, and Italy, France never had a clearly defined solo concerto tradition of its own. When the spread of virtuosity in the nineteenth century awakened interest in concertante compositions throughout Europe, Paris fell back on models from the Viennese Classic period and tried to adapt these forms to the popular tastes of French Romanticism.

The basic structure of the Classic solo concerto was the sequence of a fast first movement in sonata form, a slow movement in three-part song form or occasionally in variation form, and a fast rondo as finale.[1] After Beethoven, the solo concerto had broken away from this three-movement concept almost everywhere, but in France it stood as a binding rule until far into the nineteenth century. In Germany, for instance, symphonic and chamber works of that period show a much stronger relationship to Classic forms and developments than does the solo concerto.[2] This is primarily due to virtuoso trends beyond the Rhine: when the composers, usually their own interpreters, broke into an extremely intricate solo part, they broke away from the form as well.[3]

There had already been efforts in the pre-Romantic era to at least blur the Classic concept, if not to cast it aside completely. Typical of this trend was the attacca connection of the second and third movements, as found in a few of Beethoven's concertos.[4] This soon led to the connection of all movements, not just through attacca junctures but often through unified themes or motifs as well.[5] A further step led to a one-movement form in which the three-part structure could still be detected, and finally to the concertino in free form, which became a typical nineteenth-century genre under various labels (fantasia, rhapsody, introduction, and morceau de concert, etc.).

This development applies especially to the virtuoso concertos, which give prominent exposure to the solo part. The opposite tendency is found in the symphonic concerto, where the traditional form is often supplemented with a scherzo and the solo instrument is integrated with the orchestra to a large extent. Characteristic of this structure are the "symphonic treatment of themes" and the omission of an extended solo cadenza.[6]

In France, on the other hand, the virtuoso concerto flourished in the second half of the nineteenth century in emulation of Niccolò Paganini, who in turn had built upon Giovanni Battista Viotti.[7] While the Classic three-movement form was retained, the technical substance of the solo parts continued to evolve. The traditional form finally became a mere skeleton, bereft of content but still retaining some degree of balance between solo and orchestra.

This led to a series of organized boycotts at the famous Colonne concerts of Paris in early 1904. Supporters of a school of thought that considered itself progressive hissed at solo concertos by Beethoven, Saint-Saëns, and Paderewski to demonstrate their rejection of this genre in general. They claimed that the future belonged to opera, that the concerto was a relic of the past, and that it was high time it disappeared from concert programs. The result was a long press battle in which Camille Saint-Saëns also took a stand as one of those directly affected.

I would like to begin my examination with the following extensive text, because it is probably the most informative and important key to understanding the concertante works of Saint-Saëns.

> Several rather strange explanations have been voiced recently about the history of the solo concerto.
>
> For instance, I was astonished when the following reached my ears: When the solo concerto was introduced by [Johann]

Sebastian Bach and Handel in the seventeenth century, a manifestation of the marvelous genius of these two great masters, it gave expression to the whole spectrum of emotional battles: in the concerto, each instrument of the orchestra set one of the strings of the soul vibrating, such as love, faith, compassion, tenderness, or hate. The most important emotion was assigned to the solo instrument, but the other instruments accompanied it in a way that made the concerto a magnificent harmonious whole, a synthesis of all emotions, magnificently blended into a supreme thrust. But the solo concerto began to weaken and break down with Mozart, who was led astray by the Italian influence; the orchestra was reduced to a purely accompanist function, which was only supposed to allow the skill of the soloist to stand out; the soloist, in turn, was permitted fantasies all the more pernicious in the cadenza.

The description errs in only one point, but it is a crucial one: Namely, in the period when J. S. Bach and Handel wrote their concertos, there was no orchestra in today's sense of the word. Bach was a grand master of color; he used a great many instruments in his marvelous cantatas, often combining them in a very clever fashion, but this was not yet the orchestra as we know it. As for his concertos, their accompaniment is limited to strings. What is meant by "Italian influence" anyway? It may be that rearranging a Vivaldi concerto for three violins into one for three harpsichords inspired Bach to write his own concertos for three harpsichords—of which one, the D Minor, is an admirable masterpiece. But the human emotions, the strings of the soul, hardly vibrate here. This is a decorative art, as it were, whose beauty is in its form and style.

Let no one think that virtuosity has been eliminated here. Nothing is so relative as virtuosity, and even the humblest students of our conservatories accomplish in their playing that which seemed unachievable to our forefathers. But if anyone wants to see this relative virtuosity in its fullest form, it is only necessary to look at Handel's organ concertos. One would think that for the most part they were written for harpsichord; one of them is written for organ or harp ad libitum, and all contain runs and stereotyped phrases of very doubtful interest. From time to time there is a gap, with the instruction "ad libitum" above it—at this point the musician may play whatever comes to mind.

Far from breaking down, the solo concerto takes on form with Mozart. He wrote concertos for several instruments, but the most interesting are those for piano, which he composed for his own use. In these concertos one can see how the orchestra develops and sometimes becomes even more important than the solo; often the latter holds back, so that the orchestra, which is truly symphonic, can be heard. Here is where one can feel all the strings of the soul vibrating, from marvelous lightheartedness to deeply tragic feelings, in an endless variety of delicate nuances and totally surprising effects.

Mozart wrote concertos for his own concerts from day to day, in the space of a few hours, even while he traveled. He could have reused the same material because his audience changed, but he was driven by an irresistible urge to create. Sometimes his haste forced him to perform his concertos without any rehearsal. Yet, upon reading these marvelous scores, upon studying these elegant, impeccable, so marvelously polished manuscripts, one is astounded by so much genius and so much talent and by that prodigious fluency comparable only to that of Sebastian Bach.

Like the string quartet and the symphony, the solo concerto also reached its pinnacle with Beethoven. The description that we have read above could apply to his concertos in C Minor, G Major, and E-flat Major, but it is totally incomprehensible why it is applied to the concertos of Bach and Handel, which are of a completely different nature. The three Beethoven concertos just mentioned and his violin concerto are lovely creations and immortal works of art.

Schumann held the concerto in such high esteem that he entrusted his declaration of love to this form, the story of his liaison with Clara Wieck, his famous life companion.[8]

Ten of the twenty-nine concertante works by Camille Saint-Saëns are identified as "concerto" in the title; they are framed chronologically by Op. 58 (1858) and Op. 119 (1902).[9]

Op. 58
1. Allegro moderato e maestoso
2. Andante espressivo (attacca)
3. Allegro scherzando quasi allegretto

Traditional three-part form, modeled after that of the Ecole Liégoise.[10]

Op. 17 1. Andante—poco più—allegro assai
2. Andante sostenuto quasi adagio
3. Allegro con fuoco

The three-part form is retained but interpreted more or less symphonically. It is important to remember that Saint-Saëns's first three symphonies—A Major (1850), E-flat Major, Op. 2 (1853), and F Major *Urbs Roma* (1856)—were written before his first concertante work. All three begin with a slow introduction before the actual main subject, a practice that was common primarily in classic symphonic composition and found in solo concertos only in isolated instances.[11] Op. 17 also begins with a slow introduction; its relationship to Saint-Saëns's first symphonic works is further emphasized in that he returns to the main theme of the introduction and the first movement in the coda of the finale, just as he did in his *Urbs Roma* Symphony.

Despite these features, it would be incorrect to label Op. 17 as a "Symphonic concerto" in the sense, for instance, of Henri Litolff's Concerto Symphonique in D Minor, Op. 102 (1851) or Brahms's Second Piano Concerto in B-flat Major (1878–81). Neither do Op. 22, 44, nor 119 follow the symphonic concerto form, in that Op. 22 dispenses with the slow movement, replacing it with a scherzo, while the addition of a scherzo section in Op. 44 and 119 results in a concealed four-movement form.

Op. 20 Allegro—andante espressivo—tempo I.

The three-movement form is reduced to one sonata movement in which a slow section with new musical material replaces the development. After the tradition-bound Op. 58, Saint-Saëns looked around for other concerto form possibilities. In this regard, Op. 17 represents a formal extension, whereas Op. 20 takes the opposite route, approaching the morceau de concert form.

Op. 22 1. Andante sostenuto
2. Allegro scherzando
3. Presto

Op. 22 illustrates yet another type of approach to form: According to its tempo marking, the first movement would be slow, but the mass of fluent 32d-note piano runs and the vaguely suggested sonata form give it the Classic character of a main concerto subject. The second movement is a scherzo with two trio sections, which are identical, incidentally—in contrast to those of Schumann, who used this structure frequently (e.g., *Spring Symphony* in B-flat Major, Op. 38; the second movement of *Kreisleriana,* Op. 16; and Piano Quintet in E-flat Major, Op. 44). Op. 22 has often been criticized for the stylistic disparity between the Baroque clarity of the first movement and the playfulness of the last two.[12] The term applied here, "mélange," typifies the dualism of Saint-Saëns, which is especially evident in the prelude to the oratorio *Le Déluge,* Op. 45, for solo violin and strings (see related discussion in Chapter 1). The composer never denied his ingrained traditionalism, and the influence of Mozart and Beethoven especially, whose three-part form he adopted as binding for most of his concertos. But the substance with which he fleshed out this skeletal framework is entirely a reflection of the lyrical tastes of Romanticism that molded the Paris music world of the nineteenth century.

Op. 29
1. Moderato assai—più mosso (allegro maestoso)—moderato assai—più mosso—molto allegro—allegro animato—allegro maestoso—animato
2. Andante
3. Allegro non troppo

While the second and third movements adhere closely to the Classic solo concerto form, Saint-Saëns totally abandons the structure of the traditional sonata movement in the first movement. Here the slow introduction that begins the work is repeated before the development, and the cadenza is inserted between this repetition and the development.[13] Thus, the structure of the first movement has a rather disjunct effect; its only unity lies in the repeated use of motifs and themes belonging to each part.

Op. 33 Allegro non troppo—animato—allegro molto—tempo I.—allegretto con moto—tempo I.—un peu moins vite. a tempo—più allegro comme le premier mouvement—molto allegro

Op. 33 continues the formal design of Op. 20. Here again the three-part structure of the sonata movement is abridged; only the development section is retained, followed by a minuet inserted before the extensive recapitulation.[14] Also interesting in this context is the fact that this minuet was sometimes played as a separate piece.[15]

Op. 44 1. Allegro moderato—andante
2. Allegro vivace—andante—allegro

The structure of Op. 44 has been subjected to very contradictory interpretations in various biographies and analyses. For instance, Cooper speaks of three movements that are to be understood as segments of a single whole, while Lyle discerns five segments in two movements, thereby coming closest to the composer's own division.[16] Hervey shares Lyle's view but also points out formal parallels with the Third Symphony in C Minor, Op. 78.[17] Neitzel speaks of a "variation principle that tends toward improvisation."[18] All these views are summarized by Baumann, who presupposes a three-part whole similar to Op. 78 and emphasizes the improvisatory element.[19] Totally false and incomprehensible is Harding's claim that Op. 44 is laid out much like Op. 33; this reveals his obvious misunderstanding of the structure.[20]

Op. 44 breaks down into two movements of two parts each: I.1 the Allegro moderato with two variations, which corresponds to the concertante main movement; I.2 the Andante, as the slow movement in which the material of II.2 is anticipated; II.1 the scherzo Allegro vivace—the adjoining Andante is merely a transition to the finale, an intermezzo of sorts; II.2 the Allegro in which the theme of I.2 in altered rhythmic form is the basis for variationlike changes. There are also places throughout this last section reminiscent of statements or phrases from I.1 and II.1.

Of all Saint-Saëns's concertos, Op. 44 is certainly the one most nearly corresponding to the symphonic form as Paul Mies defines it.[21] Even the contemporary review by Henry Cohen stresses the unusual balance between solo and orchestra and the concerto's symphonic structure (see Chapter 1).

In addition, my theory is confirmed by a highly interesting manuscript in the Bibliothèque Nationale.[22] Here the Andante section between II.1 and II.2 appears again in full and in the same key but marked "Lento assai." Daniel Fallon has interpreted this sketch as a slow introduction to an unfinished symphony, which breaks off after 9 manuscript pages where the actual first movement would have begun. Penciled on the first sheet is the almost illegible note, "19 mai 1854," so more than 20 years separate this draft from Op. 44. This reworking of a symphonic sketch as part of a solo concerto—Brahms's First Piano Concerto in D Minor, Op. 15, was a similar case—suggests that Saint-Saëns intended to realize a symphonic idea with his Op. 44, which would also corroborate the concealed four-movement form.

Op. 61
1. Allegro non troppo
2. Andantino quasi allegretto
3. Molto moderato e maestoso—più mosso—allegro non troppo—più allegro

After the strict form of Op. 58 and the compressed form of Op. 20, Op. 61 is a reversion, so to speak, a return to the clearly structured three-movement form. Of course, such a structure only appears simple on the surface; Saint-Saëns gives it a very personal interpretation. The orchestral prelude is omitted, the violin—even though its cadenza is not written out—becomes a "prima donna assoluta,"[23] and the finale is preceded by a slow, quasi-recitative introduction reminiscent of an operatic vocal scene, as Mies also observes.[24]

Op. 103
1. Allegro animato—sempre accelerando al prestissimo (quasi cadenza)—a tempo (allegro)—agitato—a tempo poco meno mosso—a tempo primo—sempre accelerando al presto—a tempo, allegro—senza rigore—a tempo ma tranquillo
2. Andante—quasi recitativo—allegretto tranquillo quasi andantino—poco più mosso—andante—più mosso—ritenuto—a tempo primo
3. Molto allegro

For Op. 103, Saint-Saëns modified the traditional movement sequence and structure in a totally different way, but just as cleverly as in Op. 44. The first two movements have the improvisatory character of a fantasia or rhapsody with no set form. In the first movement, the sonata form is faintly distinguishable in that it has two dominant themes, though they are given novel treatment. Only the finale is a clearly structured, toccatalike rondo. Op. 103 compares more to Op. 89 than to the other concertos. Both works are based on programmatically vague musical interpretations of travel impressions, which in some respects correspond to the spirit of impressionism.

Op. 119 1. Allegro moderato e maestoso—andante sostenuto (le double plus lent)—più mosso—accelerando—tempo primo (andante sostenuto)—ritenuto

2. Allegro non troppo—Cadenza ad libitum. très modéré—récit—allegro—récit—allegro—récit—allegro—récit—allegro—mouvement du premier morceau—quasi ritenuto—molto allegro

This last solo concerto of Saint-Saëns is still overshadowed today by Op. 33, although it is far more interesting from the standpoint of form as well as substance. The movement structure is much like that of Op. 44; again we detect a hidden symphonic form—four sections in two movements—which Lyle also recognizes.[25]

I.1 is faintly recognizable as a three-part Allegro moderato e maestoso, and I.2 Andante sostenuto could be regarded as the slow movement. The scherzolike II.1 Allegro non troppo leads into a highly virtuosic cadenza, and the finale II.2 consists of a repetition of I.1 movement du premier morceau and an extended coda.

In addition to the symphonic interpretation, there is yet another possibility. The return to the first theme in the finale could justify a comparison to Op. 20 and 33. However, what happens musically between I.1 and II.2 seems too substantial to be interpreted as merely the development section of an oversized sonata movement. Furthermore, the formal structure and thematic material of I.2 and II.1 stand entirely on their own.

Compared to the solo concertos, Saint-Saëns's concertinos have little in the way of special form features. They tend more to reflect French tastes of the period.

Op. 6 1. Presto, ma non troppo—più mosso, da qui si stringe il tempo poco sine al prestissimo—prestissimo

Three-part dance form with coda; the trio section is set off by a modulation from A minor to A major rather than by a tempo change.

Op. 28 Andante malinconico—animato—allegro ma non troppo—più allegro

By the very fact that it has two parts, slow and fast, Op. 28 is typical of the form used predominantly by the virtuosos.[26] To attribute its origin to the structure of a symphonic first movement with slow introduction would be inaccurate, since there are two criteria for the latter that are rarely found in two-part concertante works. First, the fast part is in sonata form—at least as a rule; and second, the theme of the introduction is used in the main section.

A more likely influence was the sequence of recitative and aria in Italian opera, which in any event had a considerable impact on nineteenth-century French instrumental music. In the opera, the recitative serves to carry the plot forward, while the bel canto aria is only a contemplative elaboration on a particular emotion or moment in the story, during which action is suspended. We are reminded here of Louis Spohr's Eighth Violin Concerto in A Minor (in modo d'una scena cantante), Op. 47 (1816).

In the instrumental adaptation of this form, the first part is normally slow and meditative, distinctly lyrical, and frequently recitativelike; runs or longer ornamental passages are rare.[27] The fast part, on the other hand, is often developed from a single thematic element, embellished and varied in virtuoso style (e.g., Sarasate's *Gypsy Airs,* Op. 20, 1878). Therefore, the preferred form is the rondo, which corresponds to the strophic aria.

Another influence could conceivably have been the attacca bonding of the second and third (slow and fast) movements in the solo concerto. In numerous works, even in sonata literature (e.g., Beethoven's *Waldstein Sonata* in C Major, Op. 53, 1803–04), the middle movement dwindles to become merely a transition to the finale; the result is close to the two-part concerto in form.

Op. 27 Andantino

Op. 36 Moderato—un peu plus de mouvement—a tempo

Op. 37 Moderato assai

Op. 48 Allegretto—animato—Tempo 1°—All°—Tempo 1°

Mendelssohn's "Songs without Words" (1829–45) must be considered direct forerunners of the instrumental Romance. However, the practice of presenting vocal compositions without text as instrumental pieces is mentioned as early as 1736 in the song collection "Sperontes Singende Muse an der Pleisse."[28]

The formal structure of the instrumental Romance, which I define as a setting for a "vocal" (woodwind or string) solo instrument with piano or orchestra accompaniment, corresponds to that of three-part song form. In its capacity as melody carrier and substitute for the human voice, the solo instrument above all has a lyric, cantabile quality.

Op. 43 Allegro appassionato

Op. 70 Allegro—andantino—allegro

While Saint-Saëns's Romances are grounded in the three-part song form, Op. 43 and 70 are based on the three-part scherzo form; a double trio can be identified in Op. 43, as in the corresponding section of Op. 44, which was discussed earlier in this chapter.

Gavotte Allegro non troppo

Like Op. 6, the Gavotte follows the three-part dance form, and the trio section is set off by a change in instrumentation.

Op. 73 Lento ad libitum—andantino espressivo—allegretto con moto—allegro molto—quasi recitativo—andantino (tempo primo)—presto

Even the title Rhapsody suggests that Saint-Saëns did not have a definite form in mind when he conceived Op. 73; one could make a case for a three-part structure by regarding the Lento ad libitum as a recitative introduction and the Presto as a coda.

Op. 62 Largamente—allegro—poco meno allegro—lusingando poco rubato—animato—a tempo—poco meno allegro—animato—meno mosso—(tempo primo)—Cadenza. allegro

Presumably because of its direct proximity to Op. 61, Op. 62 has been assumed to be the first movement of an unfinished Fourth Violin Concerto.[29] Marnat even sees a correlation between Op. 62 and the first movement of Op. 22, but this is doubtful, especially since he presupposes a monothematic structure in both works that does not exist.[30]

Op. 94 Allegro moderato—ritenuto—adagio—allegro non troppo—cantabile—a tempo

The Morceau de concert for Horn is a series of variations.[31] Aside from the variation element in Op. 44, I know of only three other works in which Saint-Saëns used this musical form: "Variations pour deux pianos sur un thème de Beethoven," Op. 35; "Thème varié pour piano," Op. 97, wherein the chronological proximity to Op. 94 is noticeable; and the second movement (Scherzo con variazioni) of the Second Sonata for Violoncello and Piano, Op. 123. The strict form of Op. 94—relative to Op. 154, for instance—demonstrates the broad range of possibilities offered by the title Morceau de concert.[32]

Op. 154 Allegro non troppo—animato—allegretto—moderato—ritenuto—andante sostenuto—molto allegro quasi presto—allegro non troppo—animato—molto allegro

Like the Fantasia for Solo Harp, Op. 95, Op. 154 has a free form resembling the rhapsody or fantasia and is based mainly on two themes. The return to the main theme as a recapitulative closing followed by a coda could be interpreted as unconventional sonata form.

Op. 89 Molto allegro—cadenza—stringendo—andante espressivo—allegro—sans presser—meno allegro—tranquillo—animato—molto allegro (tempo I°)—animato

This "carte postale musicale" shows striking parallels to Op. 73, and the two works also have a folkloric basis in common.[33] Op. 89 is a good example of the compressed form that the composer used increasingly in his later works. After a rhapsodic beginning—with frequent tempo changes and motivic themes that remain undeveloped—a basic tempo is gradually established. The second part, the return to the tempo primo, takes up more than half the score. Here the presentation of the thematic material is clearly structured, and the arrangement shows a certain similarity to the two-part form.

Op. 132 Andantino—stringendo—poco allegro—poco a poco ritenuto—andantino—stringendo—allegretto—allegretto moderato—animato—poco a poco animato—allegro—sempre più animato—le double plus lent—andante—più animato—poco a poco ritenuto—andante—stringendo—ritenuto—andantino—stringendo—allegretto—stringendo—allegro

There have been attempts to interpret the title of Op. 132 programmatically and use it to explain the formal structure. In refutation of such claims, however, I have succeeded in proving beyond a doubt that the title was added later, at the request of the publisher Durand, to make it more salable.[34] The work is completely free in form; if a structure can be identified at all, then it is in five parts (slow—moderately fast—fast—moderately fast—slow) with an extended, fast and brilliant coda.

Op. 156 Poco adagio—poco a poco stringendo—tempo I°—adagio—moins lent—andantino—poco a poco ritenuto—adagio—allegro non troppo

Though it is divided into two movements connected attacca, Op. 156 clearly corresponds to Op. 28 in its two-part structure, slow—fast.

Op. 162 Andantino

This last concertante work of Saint-Saëns (aside from the orchestration of Op. 27) is in rondo form—not in the sense of a brilliant rondo finale, but as a separate concert piece of a more melancholy character.

Saint-Saëns established his musical language relatively early—around 1852, with his Symphony in E-flat Major, Op. 2—and did not change it significantly up to the time of his death. He was interested more in giving form to the material at hand than in seeking new possibilities for expression; in this regard he was like Johannes Brahms or Gabriel Fauré. This overview of the movement sequences in his concertante works provides a basis for the detailed discussions of form which follow.

2.2. *The Orchestra Introduction*

Until well into the nineteenth century, it was customary to begin the first movement of a solo concerto with an extended orchestra introduction in which the main themes of the sonata movement were presented. This often resulted in a duplication of the exposition. To be sure,

Mozart, in his Ninth Piano Concerto in E-flat Major, K. 271 (1777), had moved the solo entrance up to the second measure of the Allegro first movement, and Beethoven, in his last two piano concertos, had also set aside the traditional exposition.[35] Of course, one should bear in mind that such exceptions to the Classic tradition were in no way a basis for the French concerto. Saint-Saëns was one of the first in France to break away from the traditional solo concerto introduction and experiment with other forms. His efforts met with resistance in Paris for a long time. Outside of France, however, Saint-Saëns found many emulators.

The departures from tradition can be classified according to three features. First, there is the recitativelike solo introduction, almost a cadenza, which is sometimes followed later by an orchestra introduction. This occurs in Beethoven's Op. 58 and 73, for example; in the Violin Concerto in D Minor by Jean Sibelius, Op. 47; and in the Double Concerto in A Minor, Op. 102, by Johannes Brahms. Next, there is the slow introduction, almost as in a symphony, with or without solo, before the actual first movement begins, as found in Busoni's Violin Concerto in D Major, Op. 35, and other works.[36] Mies interprets this not as a variation of the orchestra introduction, however, but as a special way of connecting movements, and he illustrates it with the exceptional example of Bruch's *Scottish Fantasy,* Op. 46.[37] Finally, especially with Saint-Saëns, there is the reduction of the orchestra introduction to an incisive tutti chord or other nonthematic element (tremolos, sustained chords) that can continue as tonal background even after the solo has begun. In this context, I would particularly call attention to Paul Mies's examination of the shortening and omission of the first tutti section.[38]

The virtuoso solo concerto, as it was preferred by the French Romantics, retained the Classic orchestra introduction automatically for the most part, following in the footsteps of Paganini and giving little heed to the modifications of Beethoven just mentioned. They were mainly interested in the solo part and how it could be made most effective. The retention of the extended introduction may have been related to the idea that the main task of the orchestra part was to introduce; after that it functioned only as accompaniment.

This disparity is felt especially keenly in the two piano concertos by Chopin. Hector Berlioz was right when he wrote: "In Chopin's compositions, all the interest is centered on the piano; the orchestra in his concertos is nothing but a cold and almost useless accompaniment."[39]

When the introduction is omitted, the orchestra becomes a major component of the concerto and assumes a position of equality beside the soloists—an "emancipation" not at all in keeping with virtuoso concertos.[40]

In Saint-Saëns's first and still relatively unoriginal solo concerto, Op. 58, we can already detect a break with tradition. Over a C-major chord in repeated eighth-note triplets, the violin enters with the main theme as early as m. 3, and the second theme follows soon after. The full orchestra introduction comes in later, however, beginning at m. 32, so that we have here another case of double exposition. Beethoven's Op. 58 may have served as a model.

In Op. 17, the actual main subject is preceded by a clearly structured 24-measure introduction, in which each 12-measure section is subdivided into an andante and a poco più. The first 10 measures present a fanfarelike horn motif, which bears a striking resemblance to a motif in the last movement of Chopin's Op. 21, and which is reinterpreted as the main subject of the first movement without modification, beginning at m. 25 (Example 2.1). In both the Chopin and Saint-Saëns pieces this motif appears the second time as an echo. The last two measures of the first theme in the introduction to Op. 17 are expressed as a unison piano run.

Example 2.1. *Top,* Saint-Saëns, Op. 17/1, m. 1f; *Bottom,* Chopin, Op. 21/3, m. 406f.

The theme of the poco più turns up again in m. 102 (letter E of the score) as a second theme; in the introduction it breaks down into four orchestra measures, two solo upbeats (this time two-part), two orchestra measures, and four measures in which orchestra and soloist are combined. The symmetry of this introduction becomes clear in a diagram (Figure 2.1.).

Orchestra	10	–	( )	–	4	–	( )	–	2	–	4	
												Measure
Piano	( )	–	2	–	( )	–	2	–	( )	–	4	
			Unison				Two-part				Two-part	

Figure 2.1. Symmetry in Saint-Saëns, Op. 17, introduction.

As in Op. 58, a traditional orchestra introduction follows, but here an essential feature of Saint-Saëns's solo concertos becomes apparent: Unlike representatives of the virtuoso style, Saint-Saëns was concerned about a balance of power, which is established already in the slow introduction of Op. 17. Here again I would point out the symphonic element in Op. 17 (discussed earlier in Section 2.1) and the fact that Brahms was following a similar course at about the same time. His First Piano Concerto in D Minor, Op. 15, started out as a symphony, and this affected the character of the work substantially.[41]

With Op. 20, Saint-Saëns turned to a very individualistic interpretation of the solo concerto form, which to my knowledge had never been tried before. Concentration of the musical material in a single sonata movement precluded an introduction in the traditional sense from the outset, since all nonessentials, including the solo cadenza, had to be deleted.

Op. 20 begins with a quarter-note tutti attack, followed immediately by the solo violin with the massive chords of the main theme. Nor is the bypassed introduction retrieved at any later point—the tutti attack functions somewhat like the final chord of a traditional introduction. Besides the one-movement form, this may have been another reason for the work's designation as a "Concertstück." A model for this type of opening may have been Robert Schumann's Piano Concerto in A Minor, Op. 54 (1841–45); but the startling effect of an incisive opening chord attack can also be felt in Brahms's Op. 15, where the volume of the thudding *ff* chord is immediately cut back, before the main theme sounds forth again in *fortissimo*. The virtual end of this development is the slapstick tone with which Maurice Ravel opens his Piano Concerto in G Major (1931). It is significant that Ravel looked to Saint-Saëns as his model for this work.[42]

Op. 33 also begins a tutti attack, again a consequence of the concentrated form. Other examples are the Capriccio for Violin and Orchestra by Niels W. Gade (1878) and, with qualifications, the Piano Concerto in A Minor, Op. 16, by Edvard Grieg (1868).[43]

Op. 22 begins with a lengthy solo introduction which appears to be modeled after the toccatas of J. S. Bach.[44] Virtuoso cascades offer relief from the sequential character and rather strict writing, and the key of G minor remains unchanged. The movement is marked Andante sostenuto, but with the "ad libitum" instruction and the unmeasured notation, the introduction becomes almost a cadenza. However, it has a more recitative character here, since at a later point (m. 68ff.) Saint-Saëns expressly marks a longer solo passage "Cadenza ad lib." In his review of the premiere (see Chapter 1), Albert L'Hôte refers to the improvisatory style of the composition, which is already manifest in the introduction.

Another notable feature in Op. 22 is the transition from the introductory solo to the main subject. The last five *fff* chords of the piano, D–C–B–B-flat–A, lead logically into G minor; the chord is played by the full orchestra without the soloist, leads to D major, and finally, after two prominent tutti measures, settles into soothing, subdued piano arpeggios. They interrupt the harmonic sequence (Example 2.2), which

Example 2.2. Saint-Saëns, Op. 22/1, transition from introductory solo to the main subject.

does not resume until two measures later, with the pizzicato B-flat/F-sharp. Spanning the break is a cantilena by the solo oboe. Then the G (minor) that logically follows (letter A of the score) is carried by the solo and marks the actual beginning of the main subject. Not until the orchestra entrance does the composer designate the tempo with the metronome setting ♩ = 54.

At the end of the movement, the first four measures are repeated, this time supported by piano runs and chords. Now the harmonic con-

Example 2.3. Saint-Saëns, Op. 22/1, end of introductory solo.

nection is finally concluded (Example 2.3). Directly before this *moins lent* coda, Saint-Saëns restates the solo introduction (fifth measure after letter F of the score), supported harmonically by subdued chords in the strings. The resulting frame for the developmentlike middle section of this almost monothematic movement could be interpreted as exposition and recapitulation.[45] With an improvisation as starting point, the treatment of the musical substance is compressed, only to end again with an improvisation.

The main subject of Op. 29 is preceded by a slow introduction (Moderato assai), as in Op. 17; but in these 31 measures the piano, with its rushing arpeggios and cascading chords, supplies the tonal background, while the orchestra comes in with the main theme in m. 3. Hervey correctly points out the similarity of this theme to the "Great" C Major Symphony (1828) by Schubert (Example 2.4).[46] Here again, we

Example 2.4. *Top,* Saint-Saëns, Op. 29/1; *Bottom,* Schubert, Symphony, D. 944.

cannot speak of an anticipated cadenza, since the actual cadenza appears later, albeit at an unusual spot (see Table 3.1).

With Op. 44, it is hard to characterize the introduction in precise terms, since the Classic solo concerto structure is indistinct here. However, the main theme and variations that follow can be divided into two groups of sixteen measures, each of which subdivides into eight orchestral and eight solo measures; all four groups begin with an upbeat (see Section 5.1). It was this clear symmetry that was interpreted as academicism by Saint-Saëns's opponents.[47]

Just as the solo entered over a repeated eighth-note chord in Op. 58, so it is a B-minor chord in the 32d-note tremolo of the strings in Op. 61. Over this dense tonal background, the solo comes in with the prominent main theme in m. 5, and the omitted orchestra introduction is not recovered later. Again we have a compressed structure, which makes the extended introduction seem disproportionate.[48] Here, more than in other works, the omission of the first tutti proves to be a fundamental structural principle in the balancing of solo and orchestra.

The introduction to Op. 103 is also symmetrical: eight orchestra measures (sustained tonic chord in the woodwinds and rising pizzicato in the strings) are followed by sixteen piano measures—the main theme—which appear as two distinct eight-measure periods. This theme, which Engel characterizes somewhat imprecisely as "rocking," is actually more like a chorale melody.[49]

On the whole, the formal structure of Op. 119 is similar to that of Op. 44. While the main theme is hinted at in the six introductory orchestra measures, it does not appear in its definitive form until the solo entrance in m. 7. Nevertheless, this is really the only solo concerto by Saint-Saëns in which the orchestra assumes a relatively important role in the introduction.

In summary, we see that in none of the composer's concertos is the traditional orchestra introduction taken over without modification. Cooper correctly points out that in all Saint-Saëns's more mature concertante works the solo entrance comes at the very beginning.[50] The problem that Schröter sees in the coordination of sonata-movement form and orchestra introduction exists for Saint-Saëns only to a limited degree, since his formal plan also often deviates from the sonata form.[51] For Saint-Saëns, shortening or omitting the first tutti is mainly a way to achieve better balance between solo and orchestra parts.

Since the overall form affects the first tutti passage only in exceptional cases (in the concertos Op. 20 and 33), a look at the introductions to the shorter concertante works would also seem worthwhile.

Op. 6 opens with a 24-measure introduction with a 4-measure ostinato in the bass that serves as foundation for the entire first section. The theme is suggested here but does not appear in its definitive form until the unison entrance of the two solos.

In Op. 28, as in all other representatives of the above-mentioned two-part form, the entire opening must be regarded as an introduction. In the 36 measures of the Andante malinconico, the theme appears in m. 3 with the solo entrance, and the orchestra functions only as rhythmic-harmonic support. On the whole, this section has the character of recitative.

In the orchestrated version of Op. 27, the solo (main theme) and orchestra part (harmonic support) begin at the same time. In this regard, it corresponds to the 1868 chamber music work on which it is based.

The four-measure introduction to Op. 37 is organized as follows: two F-minor measures with a transition to D-flat major, the main key; and two measures of 16th-notes, which prepare for the solo entrance with the main theme in m. 5 and serve as an accompaniment figure throughout the main section.

Op. 37, like Op. 36 and 48, has a lyrical character as suggested in its title. The solo-accompaniment relationship is already evident in the introduction, which is similar in form and function to the piano introduction of an art song. In Op. 36, the basic rhythm and main key of the piece are established in two introductory measures; the same is true of Op. 48.

In Op. 43 and 70, the orchestral openings correspond to their respective solo versions and cannot be considered representative of Saint-Saëns's concertante style. The same is true, incidentally, of works like Chopin's Op. 22, Liszt's arrangement of Schubert's *Wandererfantasie* for piano and orchestra, and Busoni's orchestration of Liszt's *Rhapsodie espagnole.*

Op. 62 has an eight-measure Largamente introduction, which begins with one measure for the solo violin. The same measure is also exposed at the beginning of the Allegro main section, turns up again at the beginning of the Poco meno allegro, and has an almost monothematic influence on the entire work.[52] The introduction as a whole can be divided into two four-measure phrases with identical structures; central theme/cadenzalike run backed by pedal point in the orchestra/two-measure cadence with solo and orchestra.

True to the free form of the rhapsody, Op. 73 begins with an 11-measure solo cadenza (Lento ad libitum) resembling recitative.

Like Op. 28, Op. 83 is in two parts, though this is not expressed in the title.[53] A 73-measure Allegretto lusinghiero introduces a theme (solo entrance in m. 8), which recurs at a key point in the Allegro main section (letter C of the score). This introduction differs from the one in Op. 28 in that it anticipates major elements of the main section. Because of its length, it is close to being a separate movement.

The four introductory measures of Op. 94 are what might be called a musical colon (this term could also be justified for Op. 43), after which the solo comes in with the variation theme in m. 5.

In the eight-measure introduction of Op. 154, the orchestra is dominant, while the solo only echoes with afterbeats. In m. 479 (number 23 of the score) this theme is carried by the orchestra alone; then a turnabout follows (m. 487), with the afterbeats coming from the orchestra. Here, as in Op. 62, Saint-Saëns makes the introduction an integral part of his structure.

In the Gavotte, the orchestra's function is reduced to that of the continuo in a Baroque concerto. This also accounts for the upbeat entrance of the solo.

The complexity of Op. 89 makes it hard to define the introduction precisely. The best solution, as I see it, is to interpret the 38-measure Molto allegro section as an introduction preparing the way for the actual solo entrance, the cadenza ad lib. Although the soloist does have an earlier entrance on the last eighth-note of the first measure, the soloist can only be regarded as support for the orchestra throughout the introduction. At no point does the soloist have a phrase of his/her own.

A similar case is Op. 132, where solo and orchestra are tightly interwoven. Preceding the violin entrance are 15 orchestra measures that could just as well have been the beginning of a symphonic composition.

In Op. 156, the two-part form is much more clearly defined than it is in Op. 28 or 83. Here the two parts become two movements, the first of which is even left entirely to the solo. This division has a forerunner in Chopin's Op. 22, though the relationship should not be overestimated. After all, the Chopin work was not orchestrated until later and is not regarded unquestionably as a concertante piece. Probably the most famous example after Saint-Saëns is Maurice Ravel's *Tzigane* (1924), but there the lavish solo opening functions as a cadenza.

In Op. 122, nine measures precede the solo, which introduces the 18-measure main theme beginning with an upbeat in m. 9. Op. 162 also has three measures preceding the six-measure main theme of the solo.

In examining the various orchestral introductions and openings, both by themselves and in conjunction with the solos that follow, we discover a symmetry that is characteristic for Saint-Saëns. Despite the frequent unconventionality of his introductions, the composer adheres to the Classic laws of periodicity and thematic regularity. Often this is also true of the first solo passage that follows, even when it does not actually introduce a theme. Table 2.1 may clarify this.

Incidentally, more will be said later about Saint-Saëns's symmetry as it applies to his melodies. One last point seems worthy of mention: With the exception of Op. 44 and the Gavotte, none of his concertos or concertante pieces begins with a clear upbeat.

In conclusion, it can be said that the novelty in the openings of Saint-Saëns's concertante works lies mainly in the early solo entrance rather than in their internal structures.

Table 2.1. Symmetry in the orchestral introductions and solos that follow in the concertante works of Saint-Saëns.

Opus No.	Introduction/Opening	Solo
Op. 6	24 measures, divided by the ostinato into 6 × 4 measures.	1st solo has 16 measures, divided into 2 × 8 or 4 × 4 measures.
Op. 17	24 measures, divided by tempo change into 2 × 12 measures, set apart from main movement; segments of 2 and 10 measures, and 4 + 2 + 2 + 4 measures.	
Op. 58	2-measure opening.	
Op. 28	36-measure slow introduction, 1st 2 measures assigned to orchestra.	16-measure melody follows introduction, divided into 2 × 8 or 4 × 4 measures, as in Op. 6.
Op. 43	4 measures that seem to end with a "colon."	8 measures, follows introduction, subdivided into 2 × 4 measures.
Op. 44	32-measure highly structured introduction; 2 segments divided into 16 measures each, with 8 measures assigned to solo, and 8 to orchestra.	
Op. 61	4 measures.	16 measures, divided into 2 × 8 measures.

Opus No.	Introduction/Opening	Solo
Op. 62	2 identically structured groups of 4 measures preceding main section of piece.	Despite "unclassical" periods, 10-measure melody is given a corresponding symmetry through its 2 × 5 division.
Op. 94	4 measures precede theme, and 4 follow; overall structure (including theme) is 6 × 4 measures.	16-measure theme, divided into 2 × 8 or 4 × 4 measures.
Op. 103	8-measure orchestra introduction.	Solo follows introduction with 2 × 8 measures of main theme.
Op. 119	6-measure introduction.	Asymmetrical solo follows introduction, with 20 measures divided into groups of 7 and 13.
Op. 122	9-measure introduction.	18-measure solo follows introduction.
Op. 154	8 striking measures begin the work, and are picked up again as exposition.	
Op. 162	3 measures.	6-measure solo theme, divided into 2 × 3 measures.

2.3. *Form of Individual Movements*

Just as Saint-Saëns rarely applies Classic structures to the movement sequence in his concertos and concertante works without modification, neither does he adhere closely to these structures within the individual movements. Though he usually proceeds from the three main forms—sonata movement, song, rondo—he tries to vary them through rearrangement of the elements, change in emphasis, or subdivision. Especially important in this context is the role of the solo instrument, which in the traditional solo concerto is frequently used to define the subdivisions of the movement. For example, the positioning of the cadenza between the recapitulation and coda is characteristic of the sonata form; the division into first tutti and first solo results in an extension of the exposition section; the alternation of solo and orchestra determines the structuring of a rondo.[54]

Tobin states that the concerto grosso, the prototype for the solo concerto, was superseded by the development of sonata form in the concerto in the Classic sense (Haydn, Mozart, and Beethoven being its chief representatives).[55] Ansermet sees symphonic style, which comes from the Italian forms of the instrumental sonata and the concerto, as premise for the sonata form.[56] Very important, it seems to me, is Mellers's observation that "sonata form" is more accurately regarded as a principle of composition rather than as a form.[57] These authors agree with Robertson and Stevens that the essence of the sonata form lies in thematic contrasts and dramatic key changes.[58]

Basic to the sonata form is its division into exposition, development, and recapitulation.[59] In the concerto, the coda becomes essential because of the position of the solo cadenza mentioned earlier, whereas it remains optional in the symphony or in chamber music compositions. The exposition begins with the first or main theme in the tonic, and after a modulation, the second theme follows either in a relative key or in the parallel major (if the main theme is in a minor key). In their contrasting character (e.g., dramatic/lyric), these two themes anticipate the treatment in the development section. A codetta leads back to the main key and ends the exposition section. This section was usually duplicated in the classic solo concerto; that is, the exposition was heard in the first tutti and then had to be repeated when the solo came in. This structure proved unsatisfactory mainly because the soloist was forced into the role of an echo, merely repeating the musical material of the tutti rather than standing on its own.[60]

The two themes of the exposition are elaborated upon in the development section. Its key feature is the wealth of modulation, as found, for instance, in Mozart's Piano Concerto No. XXVII in B-flat Major (K. 595, 1791). The composer may segment the two themes and derive new motivic material from them, fall back on the themes of the codetta, or even (especially in the Romantic period) introduce completely new themes. An example of the latter practice is Tchaikovsky's First Piano Concerto in B-flat Minor, Op. 23 (1875).

The recapitulation that follows is essentially a repetition of the exposition. The main difference is that now the second theme also appears in the tonic, and the dramatic tensions of the development are thus resolved. The return to the main key can be reinforced by a coda, which uses material from either the first theme or the codetta. But one particular rule remained in effect far beyond the Classic period: A sonata movement in a minor key had to lead to a major in the recapitulation (either the parallel major or a relative major key) and could not end in the minor tonic—a remnant from the Baroque theory of key characteristics and the doctrine of affections. The sonata form can be diagrammed (see Figure 2.2).

For the traditional solo concerto, the diagram changes (Figure 2.3).

ne 1 Theme 2 Codetta Development Recapitulation Coda

Theme 1 Theme 2

onic dominant tonic free tonic tonic tonic

Most of this diagram is found in Robertson and Stevens 1960–1968, 61.

Figure 2.2. The sonata form.

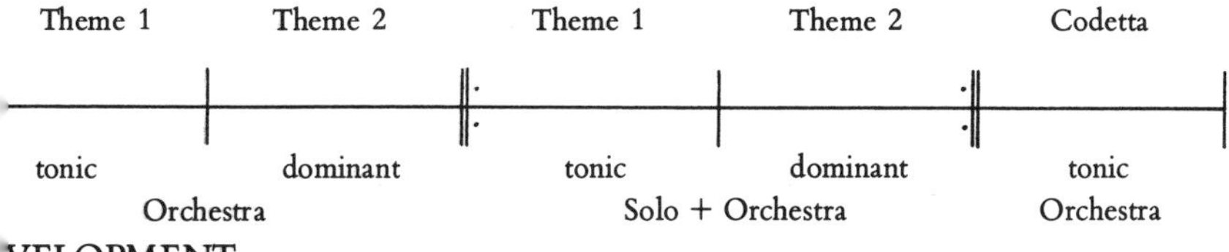

VELOPMENT

tment of the thematic material with copious modulations, whereby the basic themes are often mented by the solo instrument.

CAPITULATION

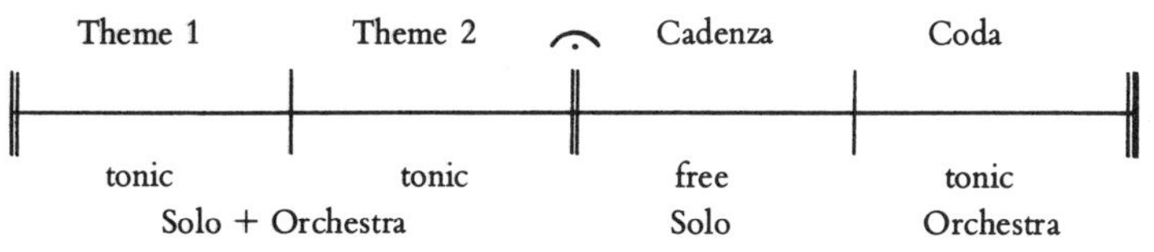

Figure 2.3. Structure of the traditional solo concerto.

Beethoven in his concertos was one of the first to try making the cadenza into a new and independent movement section, so that recapitulation and cadenza correspond to the tutti/solo part of the exposition.[61] It should also be pointed out that at the second occurrence of the first theme in the exposition, the solo often comes in without the orchestra, and that in the recapitulation, the second part of the second theme is usually reserved for the orchestra. This allows for an especially effective solo entrance in the cadenza, frequently after a six-four chord with fermata.[62]

Saint-Saëns uses this Classic pattern as a basis for all his concertos but gives it his own personal stamp from one work to the next. In his early works (up to about Op. 33), the modification is often no more than a rearrangement of individual components, as in Op. 58, where the first two blocks of the exposition are reversed, or in Op. 29, where the solo cadenza appears at a highly unusual place (see Table 3.1). An especially interesting and characteristic example is the first movement of Op. 22, which I would now like to examine in more detail.

After an unmeasured ad libitum cadenza (see discussion in Section 2.2)—which could have been written metrically, as it indeed was in its later occurrence (m. 98ff.)—and two solo measures in 4/4 (A, in Figure 2.5), there are four marcato orchestra measures, two measures with subdued piano arpeggios over a solo by the first oboe, and a transitional pizzicato measure in the strings (A′). With the cadenza counting as one measure, A and A′ form a 10-measure introduction to the actual sonata movement.

The first theme of 2× 4 measures begins with the solo alone in m. 11 (letter A of the score) and is accompanied by the orchestra (B^{1}) in the second half (Example 2.5). In dialogue with the tutti, a motif follows in

Example 2.5. Saint-Saëns, Op. 22/1, m. 12f.

m. 19 (letter B^{1} of the score) whose rhythmic structure is derived from the accompaniment figure of the first theme ($B^{1\prime}$) (Example 2.6). Two

Example 2.6. Saint-Saëns, Op. 22/1; *Top,* m. 11; *Bottom,* m. 19.

transitional (tr.) measures lead to another four-measure phrase ($B^{1\prime\prime}$); these two elements ($B^{1\prime}$ and $B^{1\prime\prime}$) are developed later in the middle section of the cadenza. Finally, the second theme (B^{2}) is heard in m. 29; it is in a different key (here, the parallel B-flat major), as Classic form dictates, and has a different character (Example 2.7).

Example 2.7. Saint-Saëns, Op. 22/1, m. 29f.

This completes the exposition section of the movement. The development begins in m. 38 (letter C of the score). With one exception (m. 65), the soloist now participates only with virtuoso embellishments; treatment of the thematic substance is reserved for the orchestra. The first three measures must be regarded as transitional, based on several criteria: one is that the final three measures of B² are repeated by the first clarinet and the first violins; also, a clear break is created at m. 32 by the tempo mark un poco animato. The development consists mainly in a constant intensification, which leads to sempre piü animato (m. 40) and molto animato (m. 48), then back to tempo primo (m. 52, letter E of the score). Here the tutti begins with B¹; the second half is carried by the piano for 1½ measures, then the orchestra picks up the theme again, supported by dazzling solo arpeggios. The tempos and structuring result in a highly symmetrical buildup and release of tension (Figure 2.4). The ratio of buildup to release is 2.5:1. There is also a concentration of the theme in the last eight measures.

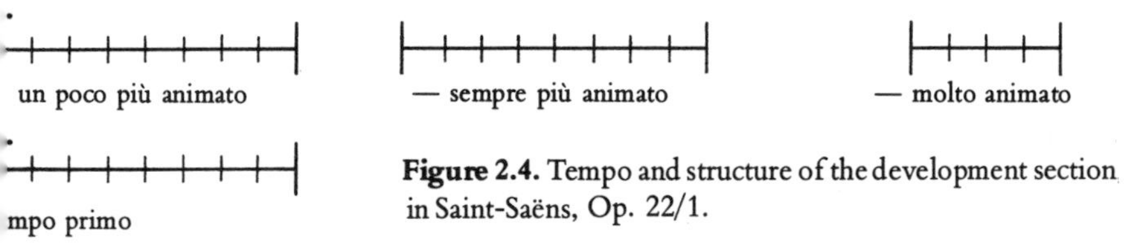

Figure 2.4. Tempo and structure of the development section in Saint-Saëns, Op. 22/1.

The cadenza, written out metrically by Saint-Saëns and marked più mosso ad lib., is faster than the preceding section. The accompaniment figure in the opening measures is patterned after the middle section of the introductory cadenza in its structure and interval sequence; above it we hear a modified element from B¹ (Example 2.8).

Example 2.8. Saint-Saëns, Op. 22/1; *Top,* m. 12f.; *Bottom,* m. 69f.

Then B¹′ is taken up again in m. 74 (tempo primo), this time by the piano alone; three transitional measures (one more than in the exposition) lead to B¹. The treatment of this theme takes up seven measures, the last of which is again transitional. After the instructions *cresc. e stringendo* and *agitatissimo,* the composer returns in m. 88 to the tempo primo and B¹, which appears here in modified form as two five-measure phrases. The entrance of the orchestra in m. 93 (letter F of the score) corresponds to the symmetrical concept of the exposition section.

The cadenza seems to lead into a recapitulation that continues until m. 97, but this would mean interpreting mm. 98 to 116 as a coda. It makes more sense to me to place the beginning of the recapitulation at m. 98, the return to theme A—this time supported by sustained chords in the strings and (m. 109f.) flutes. In my view, the actual coda is the five-measure *moins lent* restatement of A′, in which the harmonic change to G minor, left open in the introduction, is carried to completion. The whole movement comprises 116 measures, whose organization is illustrated in Figure 2.5.

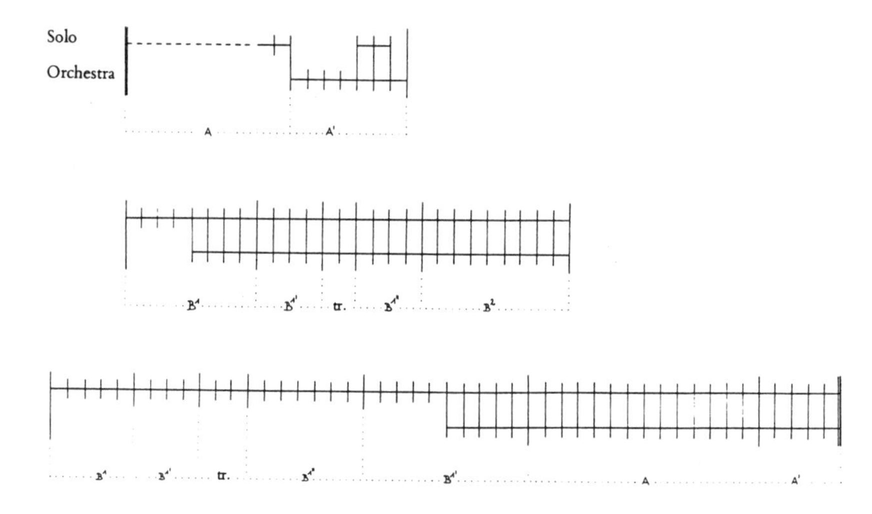

Figure 2.5. Structure of Saint-Saëns, Op. 22/1.

Besides the symmetry within the development section, as discussed above, additional symmetries emerge among the various sections. For instance, if the three transitional measures leading into the development (letter C of the score) are regarded as the closing phrase of the exposition, then the ratio of introduction to exposition is 1:3 and the ratio of solo cadenza to movement finale is 1:1. The climax of the development, the molto animato of mm. 57–60, comes in the exact middle of the movement, so that the intensification must be understood as applying not only to the development but to the movement as a whole. The symmetry is even more amazing if we disregard the 10-measure introduction and 19-measure repetition at the end of the movement. This puts the ratio of exposition to development (up to the cadenza, including the last five measures of B^1, solo with orchestra) in an exact 2:1 ratio. These symmetrical relationships are characteristic of all Saint-Saëns's works. They provide evidence of how firmly the composer was committed to the great Classic models. Furthermore, his departures from traditional sonata form suddenly seem not at all whimsical, but precisely calculated.

Another departure that stands out is the absence of a repetition of the second theme (B^2). But it would be incorrect to label the movement monothematic on this basis, as Cooper does.[63] Instead, the structure could be reinterpreted, so that the whole introductory section, A and A′, is seen as the first theme and parts B^1 and B^2 as the second. Then the cadenza would mark the beginning of a reversed recapitulation, within which the substitution of B^1 for B^2 would hardly be of any consequence. Another possible interpretation would be to regard $B^{1\prime}$ and $B^{1\prime\prime}$ as the second theme and reduce B^2 to a mere transition. Two points in support of this interpretation are the curious nine-measure phrasing (6 + 3) and the use of the last three measures as a bridge to the development.

It is difficult to analyze the harmonic structure of this movement because the development section is almost exclusively chromatic. However, this much is certain: by omitting the repetition of B^2, Saint-Saëns locks the movement firmly into the minor tonic.

In none of Saint-Saëns's three-movement or three-part (e.g., Op. 20 and 33) concertos can any great departures from traditional form be identified in the two final movements or parts. The only exception is the middle movement of Op. 17, whose unique structure merits special attention.

While neither the first movement nor the finale of this concerto calls for a cadenza, the middle movement consists almost entirely of unmeasured virtuoso piano passages, which in many ways seem to anticipate Maurice Ravel's famous *Jeux d'eau* (1901) (see Chapter 4). The movement has four basic elements: a main theme in G minor, the main key of the movement (Example 2.9), a rhythmic motif, which breaks down into four segments (Example 2.10), a subsequent unmeasured cadenza, which also breaks down into several segments,

Example 2.9. Saint-Saëns, Op. 17/2, m. 2f.

Example 2.10. Saint-Saëns, Op. 17/2, m. 11f.

and finally a second theme in the relative B-flat major (Example 2.11).

Example 2.11. Saint-Saëns, Op. 17/2, m. 15ff.

Of these, motif a is especially clear as a structural element, since it is stated four times and forms a harmonic-dynamic contrast to what precedes it. This is also clarified in Figure 2.6.

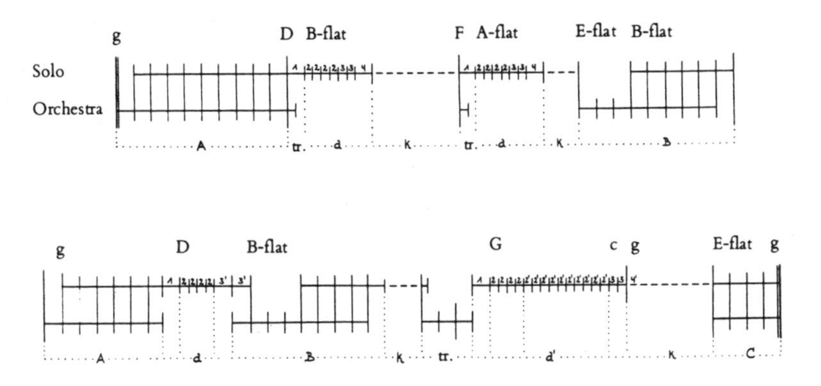

Figure 2.6. Structure of Saint-Saëns, Op. 17/2.

The middle movement of Op. 17 also shows a clear symmetry. If the four-measure coda is disregarded, the recurrence of theme A in m. 25 clearly marks the halfway point. Whereas segment a^3 occurs in simple form the first time, Saint-Saëns deviates from this the second time, replacing it with a new segment $a^{3'}$ in m. 32, and doubling it to $2 \times a^3$ in m. 47; the resulting intensification is reinforced by an extension of a^2 to four identical and ten sequential units, whereas in mm. 11/12, 13/14, and 31, a^2 consists only of four identical units. The symmetry of the k segments is also twofold. While 21 units (m. 12) and 12 units (m. 14) are recognizable in the first part, the k sections in the second part break down into two units (m. 40) and 31 units (m. 48); thus, the total is 33 units both times.

Also striking is the fact that in the repetitions of both A and B, only the first measures are retained, and then the themes continue in altered form. Thus, the ostinato accompaniment figure of the orchestra lasts for nine measures in A^1, but only for six in A^2. With Saint-Saëns, such modifications follow a symmetry in every case.

With Op. 44 and 119, Saint-Saëns successfully incorporated the traditional three-part form into a larger four-part (symphonic) form. Thus, it is difficult to analyze individual movements. Having made some general observations (see Section 2.1), let us now examine the special features of this structure, using Op. 44 as an example.

First, in several of his works (e.g., *Urbs Roma* symphony, Op. 41, 102, and 132) the composer strove to establish connections between movements through restatement of the thematic material or its individual elements, and the resulting forms were often almost cyclic. Op. 44 is an especially clear example. The practice found little general acceptance in the Romance countries (probably the most significant exception is César Franck's D Minor Symphony in 1889), whereas German Romanticism (e.g., Schumann's D Minor Symphony, Op. 120, in 1841) showed a stronger tendency toward this type of unity. The key to Saint-Saëns's formal specifications could be "the logical context that gives every creation its aesthetic value."[64] In other words, if an internal and external balance is to be maintained, the disregard of a given form determined by movement structure (namely, that of the sonata) must be supplanted by a formal principle inherent in the work.

As already mentioned, Op. 44 is divided into two major sections. Looking beyond thematic-motivic relationships, we note the repetition of forms. The introductory variation sequence has a symmetry consisting of four eight-measure phrases for the theme and the two variations together. The first and third phrases are carried by the orchestra, the second and fourth by the piano. The theme of the variation sequence at the end of the second section divides into four groups of 16 measures each. This time the solo carries groups one and three; the orchestra, groups two and four. Another link is the fact that an element (mm. 100–

105) of I.1 becomes the basis for the scherzo section (II.1) and the theme of II.2 has already been suggested in I.2. This can be illustrated by a diagram (Figure 2.7).

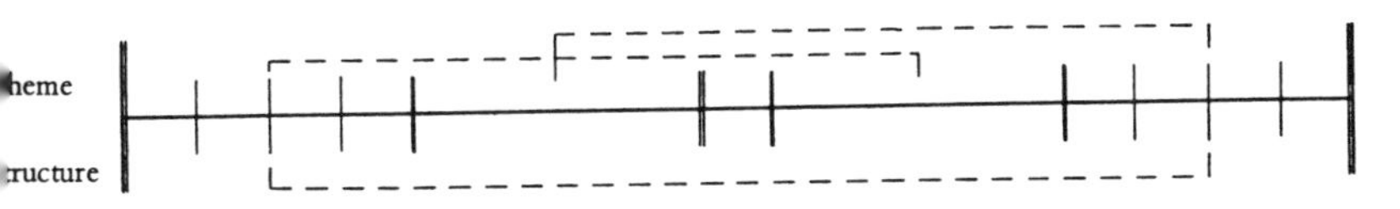

Figure 2.7. Relation of theme and structure in Saint-Saëns, Op. 44.

The theme of the second part of I.2 (mm. 139–146, and even more clearly, mm. 179–186) is also picked up again in the second section, namely in the transitional andante, whose early version as a symphonic composition was already mentioned (see Section 2.1). A part of I.1 is restated in II.1, as shown in an overview of the thematic and motivic parallels of Op. 44 (Examples 2.12–2.15).

Example 2.12. Saint-Saëns, Op. 44; *Top,* I. 1, m. 1ff.; *Bottom,* II. 1, m. 34ff.

Example 2.13. Saint-Saëns, Op. 44; *Top,* I. 1, m. 100ff.; *Bottom,* II. 1, m. 2ff.

Example 2.14. Saint-Saëns, Op. 44; *Top,* I. 2, m. 129ff.; *Bottom,* II. 2, m. 295ff.

Example 2.15. Saint-Saëns, Op. 44; *Top,* I. 2, m. 179f.; *Center,* I. 2, m. 210f.; *Bottom,* II. transition, m. 259f., and Saint-Saëns, MS. 909(1), m. 1f., Bibliothèque Nationale, Paris.

The examples given here include only the longer corresponding passages; the abundant repetitions of shorter or minute elements in Op. 44 were disregarded. These parallels prove that Saint-Saëns began with a clear overall concept and that the often improvisatory character is not arrived at arbitrarily but follows a master plan. This also explains the symmetric relationship of the first main section (225 mm.) to the second (675 mm.), a 1:3 ratio—which could be regarded as coincidental, were it not for the fact that such symmetries are the rule in Saint-Saëns's works.

Figures 2.8–2.10 will help the reader to visualize the structure of Op. 44. The basic structure of both main sections consists of symmetrical eight-measure periods, which can either be divided into two groups of four measures (e.g., variation 3) or expanded as needed into two groups of eight measures (e.g., variation 10). Saint-Saëns always

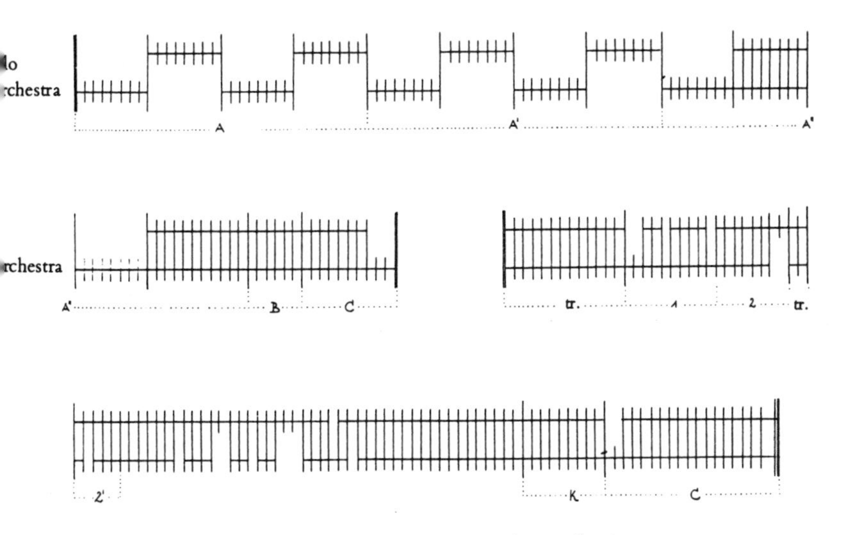

Figure 2.8. Structure of Saint-Saëns, Op. 44/I.1 and I.2.

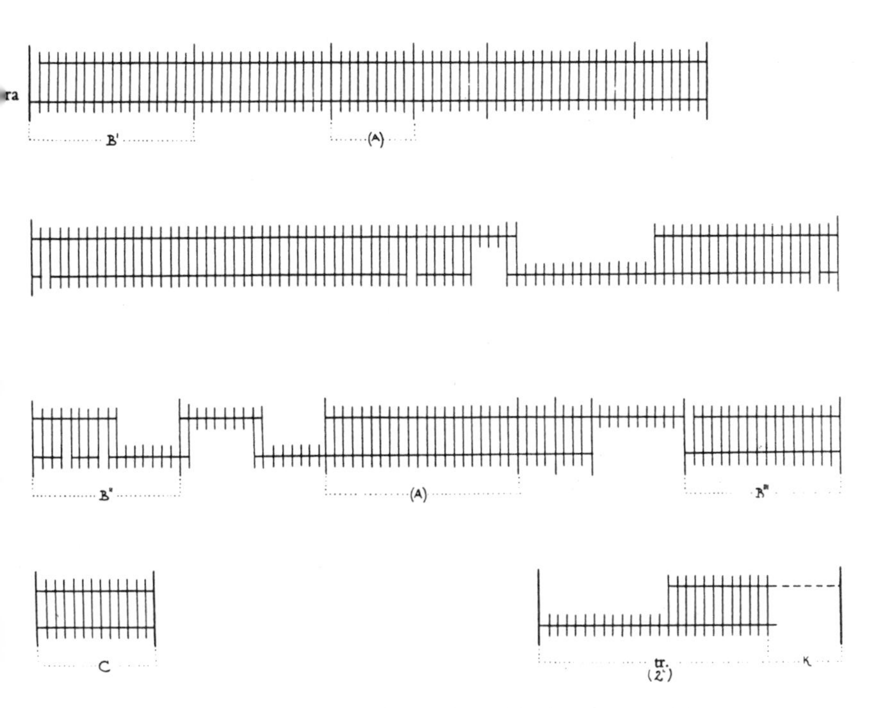

Figure 2.9. Structure of Saint-Saëns, Op. 44/II.1 and II.transition.

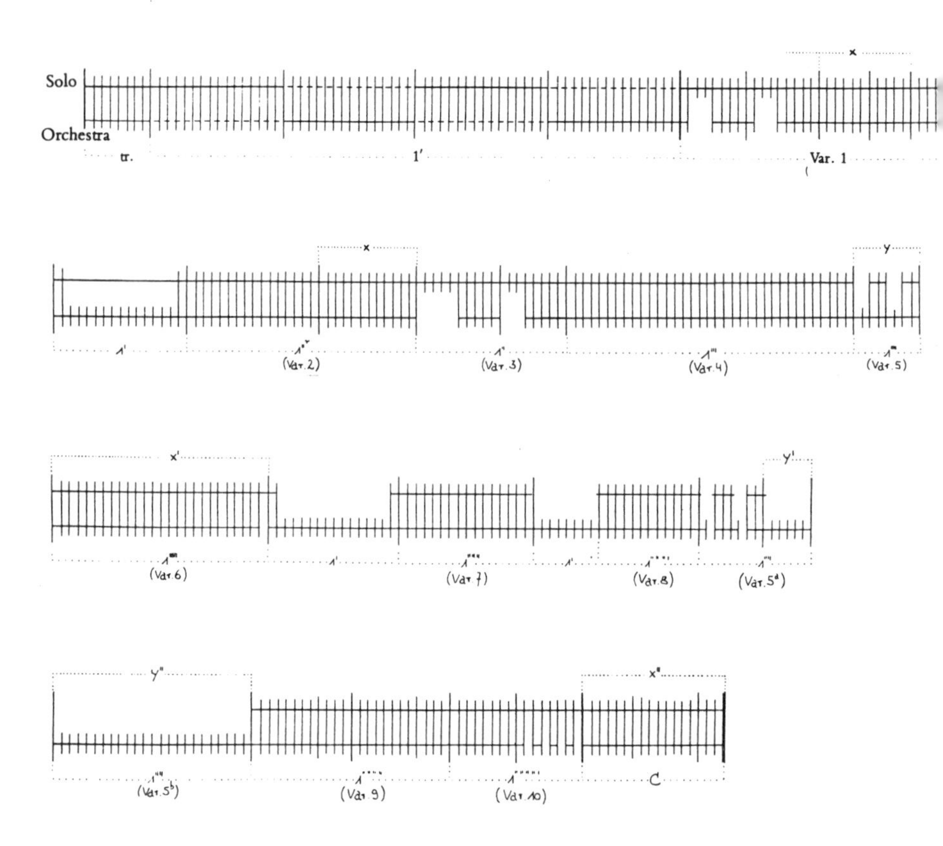

Figure 2.10. Structure of Saint-Saëns, Op. 44/II.2.

proceeds symmetrically in other subdivisions as well (e.g., variation 9, two groups of eight-plus-four measures). Even the transitional part of section II has a clear division: 14 orchestra measures, followed by 14 measures of solo with orchestra.

Also worth noting is the unusual variation technique that the composer uses in II.2 (Figure 2.10). The theme in its basic form (1′) is inserted repeatedly like an intermezzo, so that it would not really be accurate to speak of a strict variation principle. It is also extraordinary that the ascending figuration in the first variation is reversed to a descending figuration in the second. The variations are linked intrinsically, e.g., by elements x and y in the orchestra, which are derived from the solo parts of the first (y) and second (x) variations.

At the time that Op. 44 was written, variation was a totally new concept in the solo concerto context. There were, of course, earlier attempts, such as in Mozart's piano concertos, No. 27 (G Major, K. 453, 1784) and No. 24 (C Minor, K. 481, 1786). Mozart structured the final movement of both these concertos as a theme with variations, and Beethoven used variation form for the middle movement of his violin concerto (D Major, Op. 61, 1806). But since the variation sequence is limited to one movement in each of these examples, it really represents a borrowing of formal principles from chamber music, which strictly speaking do not apply to the basic concerto form.

Numerous composers, especially in the first half of the nineteenth century, created variations for solo instrument and orchestra (e.g., Chopin, *Là ci darem la mano*—si bémol majeur—varié pour le piano avec accompagnement d'orchestre, Op. 2, 1827; Liszt, *Hexameron* morceau de concert—Grandes Variations de Bravoure, 1837, and *Totentanz* 1849). These variations reflected the flourishing virtuoso instrumental style and the fondness for brilliant paraphrases associated with it, but had no significant impact on the concerto form.

A characteristic of French variation technique is the insertion of ritornello sections between the individual variations.[65] However, this applies to the finale of Op. 44 only to a limited extent, since the restatement of 1' is used not to separate the individual variations but to complement variation sections.

The form of Op. 44 has no parallel in the music of the nineteenth and early twentieth centuries and certainly had a decided influence on what is probably the most significant concertante variation work by a French composer: César Franck's *Variations symphoniques* for piano and orchestra (1885).[66] However, the Franck work differs from the Saint-Saëns in that the variation principle is followed consistently in the former; the concerto form is a product of the (sonata form) dualism of the two varied themes on the one hand, and of the traditional fast-slow-fast arrangement on the other. The main body of the work is preceded by a slow introduction, which affirms the symphonic character expressed in the title.[67]

Without going into detail here on the other concertos and concertante works of Saint-Saëns, I offer the following overview of their formal arrangements (Table 2.2).

Table 2.2. Formal arrangement of the concertos and concertante works of Saint-Saëns.

Opus No.	Structure
Op. 6	D^3
Op. 17	^1S (I) F (II) R (III)
Op. 58	S (I) L^3 (II) R (III)
Op. 20	S^v
Op. 28	^1R
Op. 22	$^1S^v$ (I) Sch^3 (II) D^3 (III)
Op. 27	L^3
Op. 29	$^1S^v$ (I) L^3 (II) R (III)
Op. 37	L^3
Op. 33	S^v
Op. 36	L^3
Op. 48	L^3
Op. 43	Sch^3
Gavotte	D^3
Op. 44	V (I.1) S^v (I.2) Sch^3 (II.1) V (II.2)
Op. 61	S (I) L^3 (II) $^1S^v$ (III)
Op. 62	^1S
Op. 70	Sch^3
Op. 73	F
Op. 83	^1R
Op. 94	V
Op. 89	F
Op. 103	S (I) F (II) R (III)
Op. 119	S^v (I.1) L^3 (I.2) Sch^3 (II.1) S^v (II.2)
Op. 122	F
Op. 132	F
Op. 154	F
Op. 156	^1F
Op. 162	L^3

S = strict sonata form
S^v = varied strict sonata form
^1S, $^1S^v$ = sonata form with slow introduction
L^3 = three-part song [Lied]
D^3 = dance
Sch^3 = scherzo form
V = variation or arrangement resembling variation
R = rondo
^1R = rondo with slow introduction
F = free form, close to the rhapsody or fantasia

In conclusion it can be said that Saint-Saëns deviated considerably from established French tradition in fashioning his concertos and concertante works, but that he always oriented himself to Classic forms. He undoubtedly was the "spiritual father" and initiator of unusual form features, on several accounts (e.g., the "tutti stroke" opening and the three-part single-movement sonata form in Op. 20 and 33). All the works discussed have a characteristic symmetry, which often transcends the individual movements. The significance of periodicity will be discussed in Chapters 5 and 7.

Saint-Saëns's efforts to find new formal arrangements that depart from traditional concerto form spring from his concern for balance between solo and orchestra: "But neither the formal structures nor the balance of sound fall victim to a superficial striving. Saint-Saëns goes back to the 'unity' he has previously established."[68]

This very feature, the blurring of distinct forms, refutes one of the main arguments of Saint-Saens's critics, as formulated by Parker, for instance: "in comparison with some of the moderns, he seems obvious and easy because he is intelligible at all points."[69] Also of interest in this context is the following observation by Prod'homme:

> Often, it is true, Saint-Saëns has been reproached by some for being too faithful to classic form, for sacrificing too much to its requirements, for being "too cold," or not sufficiently a "man of the theater"; while others, on the contrary, have praised him for the same qualities. He himself spoke out about this a number of times. For him music, indeed art, did not exist without form, form that evolved out of centuries of experience, in every branch of human activity. He did not refuse to recognize that form is, beyond all doubt, subject to variation according to its epoch; but he preferred the classic form handed down to us from Greco-Roman antiquity, for it corresponded to his temperament, his education, his aesthetic sense, that is to say, his feelings and sensibilities.[70]

3

The Relationship of Solo and Orchestra

3.1. The Orchestra—Independence and Balance

> The orchestra may be considered a large instrument capable of playing a great number of different tones simultaneously or in succession; its power is moderate or gigantic according to the proportionate use of all or only part of the resources available to the modern orchestra, and according to the more or less propitious application of these resources in relation to acoustic conditions of various types.[1]

This passage from Hector Berlioz's *Treatise on Instrumentation* was certainly familiar to all French composers in the second half of the nineteenth century, and most of them strove to comply with the laws of expenditure and effect drawn up by Berlioz. However, very few realized that a vital orchestral treatment could spring only from the combination of historical techniques with contemporary possibilities, that effect alone was no sign of quality, that extravagance did not automatically equal colorfulness.

Camille Saint-Saëns was certainly one of the first in France, and possibly the first worldwide, to pay heed to the musical past and to the authenticity of performance practice in regard to the instruments: "The French 'Société de Concerts d'instruments anciens,' under the direction of Camille Saint-Saëns, recently gave concerts in Berlin performed on early instruments."[2] Naturally this interest in history had a decided influence on the composer's own works, especially since tonal refinement had largely disappeared in the nineteenth century (aside from the great exception, Berlioz) because of fatal circumstances to be discussed in Chapter 8.

The solo concerto, especially, had reached rock bottom.[3] The reason, as mentioned earlier, was that composers were intent predominantly on highlighting the solo part and the soloist's virtuosity. If the soloist was not the composer himself, the soloist was at least the immediate reason for the composition. Therefore, the function of the orchestra was to provide as restrained an accompaniment as possible. There was no attempt to create an original tone color suited to the individual work, just as there was no effort to balance solo and orchestra when the two elements were combined. It was not at all uncommon for the remark "avec accompagnement d'orchestre ou de piano [with orchestra or piano accompaniment]" to be printed on the title page.

The efforts of the Ecole Liégoise to do away with this underrating of the orchestra met with only limited success. A work like the Violin Concerto in D Minor (1866) by Victorin Joncières is a sad example of a superfluous and trite orchestral treatment.[4] In over half the work, the violin is supported by tiresome string tremolos whose harmonies rarely change.

The fact that Niccolò Paganini was frequently referred to in this context shows complete ignorance of the actual reason for the admittedly rather simple orchestration of his concertos. Since no legal protection of author rights existed in his day, Paganini had to worry about competitors "stealing" his compositions. Concert rehearsals were especially opportune occasions for such theft, so Paganini tried to limit opportunities as much as possible by providing extremely simple orchestrations.[5] Orchestra players would read their parts at sight, and Paganini would collect the music immediately after a rehearsal or performance.

On the other hand, Saint-Saëns strove for a balance between solo and orchestra that was remarkable for the France of his day. Despite the diversity of opinion concerning his music, even his opponents were filled with respect for the sensitivity of his instrumentation, as revealed in several quotations:

> His clear and lucid instrumentation, in which there is not one

> superfluous note, can serve as a model for generations to come.[6]

> His lucid, simple, uncluttered orchestration gave his musical thought every opportunity for free expression.[7]

> In the colorfulness of instrumentation, Saint-Saëns ranks close to the great classic masters, Mozart and Mendelssohn.[8]

Probably the best acknowledgement of his orchestration skill comes from Adam Carse:

> The segregation of the function of each instrument or group of instruments at any particular moment, the clear distinction between the tone-colour [sic] of instruments employed for melodic and for accompanying purposes, the judgment which governs the choice of the moment of entry and cessation for a particular tone-colour [sic], the spacing of change of colour [sic], the knack of using very few notes effectively, and of avoiding combinations in which one tone-colour [sic] cancels the individuality of another; all these give variety, clearness, and balance to the work of Saint-Saëns, and place his work at the extreme opposite pole to that of Brahms and many of his German contemporaries. His light touch and restraint served Saint-Saëns particularly well when orchestrally accompanying solo instruments or solo voices; almost the only quite satisfactorily scored violoncello concerto by a nineteenth-century composer is his well-known work in A minor. In enterprise and invention Saint-Saëns must be credited with having made some advance on the orchestration of his immediate predecessors, and on that of some of his French contemporaries.[9]

Before the special features of this orchestration are taken up individually, the reader is referred to Table 3.1, which shows the scoring of Saint-Saëns's concertos and concertante works. Table 3.2 shows the scoring of six nineteenth-century concertos. A comparison of the two tables reveals how much Saint-Saëns's scoring differed from the scoring of other nineteenth-century composers who wrote concertos.

With the exception of Fauré's Op. 19, in which the teacher Saint-Saëns shows through, all the works listed in Table 3.2 have considerably larger orchestral settings than comparable works by Saint-Saëns. Yet despite their more extensive use of sonority, Paganini and Vieuxtemps in particular—Lalo and Debussy should really be viewed as representing symphonic form—are overshadowed by Saint-Saëns, since the actual accompaniment to the solo is extremely sparse; only in the purely orchestral passages are the capabilities of the large instrumentation fully utilized. They could almost be seen as imitations of the Baroque concerto grosso, with its division into concertino and ritornello.

Table 3.1 brings out yet another characteristic that illustrates Saint-Saëns's concern for tonal balance. In his works for wind instruments (Op. 6, 37, 36, 94, and 162), the composer avoids the overlapping of solo and orchestra by omitting the solo instruments from the accompaniment. As far as I have determined from studying other concertos, this practice is almost unprecedented in French concertante music (see Chapters 9–11).

In his concertos and concertante works, Saint-Saëns strove for the classic ideal of balance. His orchestra has absolute independence without diminishing the concertante character of the work, and in no case can it be replaced by mere piano accompaniment, except in the works originally written as chamber music.[10] To this end, Saint-Saëns used a mixture of timbres similar to the medieval "Spaltklang" (use of distinct sonorities); in contrast, his French contemporaries frequently had the orchestra play "en bloc"—that is, woodwinds, brass, and strings comprised separate instrumental groups and were never mixed. Incidentally, similar orchestral scoring can be detected in the two piano concertos by Felix Mendelssohn-Bartholdy; significantly they exemplify the virtuoso concerto.

A thorough examination of Saint-Saëns's scores reveals certain procedures to be characteristic. For instance, formal segments are often defined by a change in timbre or orchestra disposition. This is especially clear in Op. 33, where a decisive change takes place in the orchestra at the beginning of the minuetlike middle section (letter F of the score): Horns, trumpets, and timpani are not used, nor are the woodwinds until the second part, after the modified theme has been played by the cello. In the strings, the use of mutes produces a timbre that sets this section off from the two outer ones.

Before delving further into the characteristics of Saint-Saëns's orchestration, I need to say something about the French orchestra of this period, which, according to the scathing opinion of Hector Berlioz, could be considered totally unworthy of discussion.[11]

Table 3.1. Orchestration of Saint-Saëns's concertos and concertante works.

Opus No.	6	17	58	20	28	22	27	29	37	33	36	48	43	G	44	61	62	70	73	83	94	89	103	119	122	132	154	156	162
	◆	■	■	■	■	■	◆	■	◆	■	◆	◆	◆	▲	■	■	■	◆	◆	◆	■	■	■	■	■	◆	■	■	■
Piccolo	●																												
1st Flute		●	●	●	●	●	●	●		●	●	●	●	●	●	●	●	●	●	●	●	●	●	●	●	●	●	●	
2d Flute		●	●	●	●	●	●	●		●	●		●		●	●	●	●	●	●	●	●	●	●	●	●	●	●	
3d Flute																			●									●	
1st Oboe	●	●	●	●	●	●	●	●	●	●	●	●	●		●	●	●	●	●	●	●	●	●	●	●	●	●	●	●
2d Oboe	●	●	●	●	●	●	●	●	●	●			●		●	●	●	●	●	●	●	●	●	●	●	●	●	●	●
English horn														●															
1st Clarinet		●	●	●	●	●	●	●	●	●	●	●	●	●	●	●	●	●	●	●	●	●	●	●	●	●	●	●	
2d Clarinet		●	●	●	●	●	●	●	●	●	●		●	●	●	●	●	●	●	●	●	●	●	●	●	●	●	●	
1st Bassoon	●	●	●	●	●	●	●	●	●	●	●	●	●		●	●	●	●	●	●	●	●	●	●	●	●	●	●	●
2d Bassoon	●	●	●	●	●	●	●	●	●	●			●		●	●	●	●	●	●	●	●	●	●	●	●	●	●	●
3d Bassoon																												●	
1st Trumpet	●		●	●	●	●		●	●	●					●	●	●	●	●	●				●	●	●	●	●	
2d Trumpet	●		●	●	●	●		●	●	●					●	●	●	●	●	●				●	●	●	●	●	
3d Trumpet																												●	

Opus No.	6	17	58	20	28	22	27	29	37	33	36	48	43	G	44	61	62	70	73	83	94	89	103	119	122	132	154	156	162
	◆	■	■	■	■	■	◆	■	◆	■	◆	◆	◆	▲	■	■	■	◆	◆	◆	■	■	■	■	■	◆	■	■	■
1st Cornet																						●							
2d Cornet																						●							
1st French horn	●	●	●	●	●	●		●	●	●		●	●		●	●	●	●	●	●		●	●	●	●	●	●	●	
2d French horn	●	●	●	●	●	●		●	●	●		●	●		●	●	●	●	●	●		●	●	●	●	●	●	●	
3d French horn		●							●										●				●	●				●	
4th French horn		●							●										●				●	●				●	
1st Trombone	●		●						●							●	●		●		●	●			●	●		●	
2d Trombone	●		●					●							●	●			●		●	●			●	●		●	
3d Trombone								●							●	●			●		●	●			●	●		●	
Tuba																												●	
Harp			●				●																		●	●		●	
Timpani	●		●	●	●	●		●	●	●					●	●	●		●	●	●	●		●	●	●	●	●	
Percussion																			●			●						●	

◆ Original composition for solo and orchestra
■ Orchestrated version of a chamber-music work (i.e., originally with piano accompaniment)
▲ Unknown origin
G Gavotte

Table 3.2. Orchestration of six nineteenth-century concertos.

	Op. 6[1]	Op. 7[2]	Op. 31[3]	Op. 21[4]	Fantasie[5]	Op. 19[6]
Piccolo				●		
1st Flute	●	●	●	●	●	●
2d Flute	●	●	●	●	●	●
3d Flute					●	
1st Oboe	●	●	●	●	●	●
2d Oboe	●	●	●	●	●	●
English horn					●	
1st Clarinet	●	●	●	●	●	●
2d Clarinet	●	●	●	●	●	●
Bass Clarinet					●	
1st Bassoon	●	●	●	●	●	●
2d Bassoon			●	●	●	●
3d Bassoon					●	
Contrabassoon	●	●				
1st Trumpet	●	●	●	●	●	
2d Trumpet	●	●	●	●	●	
3d Trumpet					●	
1st French horn	●	●	●	●	●	●
2d French horn	●	●	●	●	●	●
3d French horn				●	●	
4th French horn				●	●	
1st Trombone	●	●	●	●	●	
2d Trombone	●	●	●	●	●	
3d Trombone	●	●	●	●	●	
Tuba			●			
1st Harp					●	
2d Harp					●	
Timpani/Percussion	●	●	●	●	●	

[1]Niccolò Paganini, First Concerto in D major for violin and orchestra, Ed. 1851.
[2]Niccolò Paganini, Second Concerto in B minor for violin and orchestra, Ed. 1851.
[3]Henri Vieuxtemps, Fourth Concerto in D minor for violin and orchestra, 1849–50.
[4]Edouard Lalo, *Symphonie espagnole* in D minor for violin and orchestra, 1849–50.
[5]Claude Debussy, Fantasia for piano and orchestra, 1889–90.
[6]Gabriel Fauré, Ballade in F-sharp major for piano and orchestra, 1881.

First, as to its disposition: In 1855, the orchestra of the Paris Opéra, for example, had 11 first and 11 second violins, 8 violas, 10 cellos, and 8 basses. In addition, there were 3 flutes, 3 oboes, 3 clarinets, 4 bassoons, 5 French horns, 4 trumpets, and 3 trombones. Two harps, timpani, percussion instruments, and an ophicleide rounded out the ensemble, for a total of 78 musicians. A comparable German orchestra of the same period, that of the Dresden Court Opera, numbered only 65 musicians.

The orchestra of the Société des Concerts Pasdeloup in 1859 was even larger: 16 first and 14 second violins, 10 violas, 12 cellos, and 8 basses, as well as 4 flutes, 2 oboes, 2 clarinets, 4 bassoons, 4 French horns, 2 trumpets, and 3 trombones. Including a harp, the timpani and the ophicleide, it had 85 musicians at its disposal. Again by way of comparison, the Gewandhaus Orchestra of Leipzig in 1865 consisted of only 70 musicians.[12]

For special occasions—the performance of Op. 156 comes to mind—these regular dispositions could be amplified considerably. So in scoring his works, Saint-Saëns could assume an orchestra with a capacity fully comparable to today's ensembles.

But back to the orchestration of his concertos. The practice of using changes in the distribution of the instruments to delineate form, which is especially evident in Op. 33, is found earlier in the Baroque solo concerto. Vivaldi, for instance, in his slow middle movements, frequently calls only for the continuo as accompaniment to the solo. A clearer example yet is Beethoven's Op. 58, where in the slow movement the piano is set opposite an orchestra reduced only to strings. This means of formal delineation was used less and less during the course of the nineteenth century, so Saint-Saëns can be considered an exception in this regard. Incidentally, the omission of trumpets and trombones in the middle movements is encountered frequently and must likewise be viewed as a return to Classic traditions, closely related to the recognition of the solo concerto as a dramatic form.

Saint-Saëns also applies the principle of timbre variation in the repetition of themes, motifs, or segments. For example, the main theme of Op. 33 (m. 1ff.) is stated in the exposition by the cello to the accompaniment of string tremolos; in the recapitulation (letter H of the score), it is picked up by the solo oboe, complemented by clarinets, bassoons and French horns. Then a new rhythmic-melodic element is added by the pizzicato of the cellos and basses.

Here we can identify another procedure typical for Saint-Saëns: With the omission of the first tutti, the task of introducing the main theme at the beginning of the exposition falls to the solo in most concertos. Then in the recapitulation, this theme is often carried by the orchestra, as for instance in Op. 29 (letter D of the score, piano + strings—letter E of the score, flute solo + strings) and in Op. 103 (m. 9, piano—4 mm. after number 9 of the score, violoncello + contrabass). Often the basic character of the theme is also varied dynamically; in Op. 33 and 29, for example, the theme is expressed in a *marcato mezzoforte* (Op. 33) or *forte* (Op. 29) in the exposition, whereas it is toned down to *piano* (Op. 33) or even *pianissimo* (Op. 29) in the recapitulation. In this way, Saint-Saëns manages to veil the formal segments at the transitions.

Timbre variations are especially abundant in the motif from the middle movement of Op. 61 (see Example 3.1). Table 3.3 shows the various combinations of instruments used in this middle movement. The changes in tone color of the motif can be clearly heard. Furthermore, at the very beginning of the finale, the motif is transformed into the main element of the recitativelike introduction.

Example 3.1. Saint-Saëns, Op. 61/2, m. 58.

All the works under study in this book contain countless minor, even minute, elements that are modified in their repeated occurrences. Let me give a few examples, again from Op. 61: Directly after the entrance of the main theme in the first movement, we hear subdued chords from the woodwinds (m. 6); in the corresponding passage at the

Table 3.3. Orchestration of Saint-Saëns, Op. 61/2.

Measure:	58	59	60	61	62	63	64	65	66	67	68	69	70	71	72	73	80	81	82	83	84	85	87	122	123	125	126
Flute							1	1																1	1		
Oboe							1	1																1	1		
Clarinet							1	1																			
French horn																											
Violin solo																	●	●	●	●	●	●	●	●		●	●
1st Violin	●		●		●	●			●		●		●	●	●	●											
2d Violin	●	●	●	●	●	●			●	●	●	●	●		●	●											
Viola	●		●		●	●			●		●		●	●													
Cello																											

beginning of the development (m. 142), the woodwinds are replaced by French horns; and finally, at the start of the recapitulation, the French horns are replaced by trumpets (m. 233). As insignificant as such changes in tone color may appear at first glance, they lend a richness and subtlety to Saint-Saëns's scores that few other French concertante works of his day display.

Especially interesting are the solo/orchestra combinations that the composer manages to construct. Here it is clear that the orchestra never functions purely as accompanist, but rather serves as a logical complement or as counterpoint to the solo. In this context, consider the intensity emanating from the short oboe solo at the beginning of Op. 22/1.[13] Indeed, the combination of piano arpeggios with oboe (m. 8ff.) is enormously effective, especially since the oboe's D serves as an appoggiatura to the C minor piano chord.

A few examples from Op. 103 illustrate Saint-Saëns's method of combining solo and orchestra. For instance, the four-measure piano melody in the first movement (number 4 of the score, m. 102ff.) is repeated exactly by solo woodwinds. Here the composer uses a technique whereby the tone color is divided up: The first part of the melody is carried by the oboe, the second by the clarinet, and the third by the bassoon.

The combination of French horn and piano occurs frequently, whether as mere reinforcement of a pedal-like bass tone, as in mm. 267 and 275 (10 and 2 measures before number 11 of the score), or as an effective countermotion (m. 314ff.) Often—this too is characteristic for Saint-Saëns—the reinforcement of the bass tone just mentioned is sustained in the orchestra after the tone has already faded out in the solo. The result is a blending of various timbres, which Carse expressly praises. An example of this is (in Op. 103/1) the beginning of the rit. molto (4 mm. after number 19 of the score); another is in the second movement in mm. 48 and 52 (9 and 5 mm., respectively, before number 22 of the score). In both cases it is the strings that sustain the tones or chords in pedal-point fashion.

Another interesting passage in Op. 103 is found in the second movement at m. 105 (number 24 of the score). Here the solo melody is doubled by the flutes, which creates a two-octave range and gives the passage great transparency of tone. The same is true of m. 110, where a new hue is achieved through the combination of flute, oboe, and piano.

Seldom encountered, and therefore very effective, is the unison doubling of solo and orchestra, as in mm. 131f. and 147ff., where the piano is supported by the entire wind section. The multilayered contrapuntal fabric is compressed, so to speak; then, after the respite thus won, the weaving continues.

Another figure deserving special attention is found in the middle movement of Op. 61 (see Example 3.2). After this figure is heard in all manner of combinations in the orchestra alone (see Table 3.4), it is carried from m. 140 to the end of the movement by the clarinets, with the ethereal harmonics of the solo violin (m. 140f.). "In the final measures, it dissolves in harmonics, becoming more and more remote, while the clarinet deepens into a voice as pensive as silence."[14] Lyle, too, mentions the very gradual fading of tones.[15]. Cooper speaks of a perfectly written "morceau de salon."[16]

Example 3.2. Saint-Saëns, Op. 61/2, m. 11.

Table 3.4. Combinations of instruments in Saint-Saëns, Op. 61/2 that repeat the figure found in m. 11.

Measure:	11	19	37	45	90	92	93	101	109	128	130
Flute	●	●			●	●	●	●		●	●
Clarinet					●	●	●			●	
Bassoon											●
Violin Solo			●	●					●		
4th French horn				●	●						

Such examples are too numerous to list. In summary, the following observations about the accompaniment function of the orchestra in Saint-Saëns's works can be made: Doubling is rare, and when it occurs, it serves to broaden the color spectrum or provide a respite from polyphonic voice leading. In repetitions of thematic-motivic material, new tone coloring is achieved through a change of instrument combinations. The timbre of the solo is blended with this material through reinforcement of key bass notes by the orchestra, and sustaining a tone or chord longer in the orchestra brings about a blurring of sounds. In these combinations, thematic-motivic complements to the solo are mainly the task of the woodwinds, while timbre-chordal complements are more often assigned to the strings. Among the former we note a decided preference for the oboe, which is given soloistic prominence in six of the twenty-nine works (Op. 6, 22, 61, 89, 103, and 162). Less common, on the other hand, are solos for flute (Op. 61 and 103), clarinet (Op. 29 and 61), and bassoon (Op. 94, 89 and 103). The occasion for which Op. 156 was composed (see Chapter 1) explains the extended solo passages for trumpet and French horn in the work. An effect such as the timpani solo at the beginning of the middle movement of Op. 22 remains an exception.

However, the tonal balance between solo and orchestra in Saint-Saëns's concertos is achieved not only through the combination of instruments but chiefly through a special treatment of the melody line, whereby the melody is often divided between solo and orchestra. The result is a mixture of timbres on a horizontal plane, which is not found again until the advent of expressionism. Various procedures of this type can be ascertained in Saint-Saëns's work.

First, there is the complementing of a melody by the orchestra in the sense of a hocketlike interplay—that is, a broken melody. Examples of this are found in Op. 44 II/2: When the piano comes in with the main theme, the orchestra "fills it out" (m. 295ff.). The reverse occurs in the second and fourth parts of this theme (as discussed in Chapter 2), which are carried by the orchestra (first violin and viola) and complemented by arpeggios in the piano.

We find a similar structure at the beginning of Op. 154, where the orchestra fills out the thematic rests of the harp (m. 1ff.). When the theme reappears as a sort of recapitulation, it is divided in half; the first half is carried by the orchestra alone, while the second corresponds to the beginning of the work.

In Op. 103, this compositional technique is less pronounced, but here too (in the first movement) cellos and basses complement the main piano melody in pizzicato (m. 16ff.) Again, these three examples are merely a representative selection. The abundance of material makes a complete survey impractical.

The second procedure involves the continuation of a solo melody line in the orchestra, or vice versa. In Op. 162, for instance, the 32-note figure of the flutes, accompanied by the first violins, is picked up by the second violins and violas (m. 104). In Op. 83, solo and orchestra (first and second violins) fuse into one line, which is especially charming because of the identical tone colors (m. 102ff.).

A very similar technique is the essential formal principle for Op. 94. Here theme segments are echoed by the orchestra, in a canonical manner, again providing a polyphonic texture. In m. 7f., bassoons and cellos pick up the eighth-note scale of the French horn, and the first and second violins reply in m. 25f.

Finally, the contrapuntal style should be mentioned. An especially beautiful example—though played only by the orchestra—is the transitional andante section in the second movement of Op. 44, that symphonic fragment of earlier date. Another is the dialogue between cello and strings in Op. 33 (m. 248ff.)

No other solo concertos or concertinos in nineteenth-century France compare with the works of Camille Saint-Saëns in coloring, subtlety, and function of the orchestra part. Even outside the Gallic realm, only concertos of symphonic character exhibit comparable mastery. Furthermore, I know of no French composer before Saint-Saëns who achieved a blending of solo and orchestra while still preserving the concertante character of the work.

The reason for this extraordinarily compact and colorful style is on the one hand psychological: "Lyricism . . . was at the heart of his temperament. . . . Episodes of deep intimacy offer relief amid the tumults."[17] But Saint-Saëns's style is also rooted in the form of his concertos:

> The symphonic structural unity of Saint-Saëns's concertos surpasses all that had been achieved by earlier composers. Orchestra and solo instrument are given roles almost equal in importance, so that neither one nor the other could be heard alone without the melody's being robbed of an essential part.[18]

3.2. *The Solo—Virtuosity as Dramatic Function*

"The solo of a concerto is a role that must be conceived and treated like a dramatic character," said Saint-Saëns in response to a journalist's question concerning the boycotts mentioned earlier (see Section 2.1).[19]

Naturally such a central role can issue only from confrontation with others—the instruments of the orchestra—just as it must nevertheless always remain the "leading" role.

Let us stay with the imagery that Saint-Saëns himself chose. The work in which this leading role appears must be as complex as possible without causing confusion: "Music can express all feelings, from deepest calm to extreme agitation; you distort its nature and restrict its domain unnaturally if you only let it express heat and passion."[20] Here, too, Saint-Saëns proves himself a classicist: "The pursuit of novelty at all costs . . . leads, in music, to cacophony and incoherence. And it is a grave error to believe that it produces originality."[21]

Saint-Saëns's basic attitude, evident not only in his concertos, is his concern with expression. "Expression of what? . . . What else but the expression of a musical frame of mind?" Boschot adds.[22] Now it would stand to reason that this task could be accomplished more easily through vocal music, but

> there is a phenomenon prevailing in the modern music world: the emancipation of instrumental music, once a vassal to vocal music, but suddenly taking off, revealing a new world, presenting itself as a rival to its former mistress.[23]

Because solo and orchestra are in opposition, though not necessarily in a "hostile" sense, the concertante form is understood as dualistic per se. Since Mozart, the composer has been identified with the solo part.

> The concerto satisfied his dual tendency, since it pushes lyricism to its maximum intensity and at the same time repeats and restrains the expansion of the soloist within the totality of the orchestral voices.[24]

Despite the dramatic conception of his concertos, we must keep in mind that Saint-Saëns was not trying to impart a "message" to the world—comparable, say, to Beethoven's humanitarian ideal.[25] His purely musical interest is also documented in his playing, which was somewhat controversial in his day.

> People preferred . . . the famous virtuoso in him, though he never sought to win the favor of his audiences with charlatanism at the piano. His playing was always simple, noble, and classically perfect in every respect, which often led to his being labeled cold and unfeeling.[26]

After the performance of Mozart's Piano Concerto in G Major, K. 453, by the 17-year-old Saint-Saëns in 1852, Henri Blanchard wrote: "He is a skilled technician with his fingers but shows little soul, little passion, and as for his instrument: he pontificates at the piano."[27] Eight years later, Adolphe Blotte made this assessment: "A classic pianist of great, though rather cool and dry, talent."[28] And finally, a posthumous evaluation of Saint-Saëns's playing—which is confirmed, incidentally, in several documentary piano-roll recordings by the Welte-Mignon company:[29]

> His technique comes from the great classical tradition. Despite his deep admiration for Liszt, Saint-Saëns does not imitate him. He tries to tailor his playing to the nature of the work being performed, without ever deviating from his principles of clarity and precision, without resorting to the slightest exaggeration. If we were to note the characteristics of his playing, we might first mention the matchless transparency of his strokes, his sense of rhythm, his magnificent power, his talent for infinitely modulating and shading the sound. I should add that this variety of accentuation is mainly due to simple articulation—not arm-work but finger-work. Indeed, Saint-Saëns's talent lies in his extraordinary lightness of touch, in the fact that he avoids hammering and knows how to produce that beautiful legato, which most of today's virtuosos neglect. Thus he elicits orchestral tones from the piano and at times manages to impart to it the charm and persuasive accent of the human voice.[30]

Since Saint-Saëns's compositions were "mental exercises. . . . One cannot gather from his music whether he was good, kind, or capable of suffering."[31] Frequently his compositions were misunderstood as superficial virtuoso works. Yet, if we examine the function of the solo part in his concertos and concertante works, we can clearly see how unfair this assessment is.

First of all, bear in mind that there is a significant dichotomy in Saint-Saëns's concertante works. A few pieces can be regarded as instrumental recreations of vocal writing, namely Op. 27, 37, 36, 48, 162, and, to a limited degree, 132. The solo parts of these works have little relevance to the following investigations. I should also like to disregard the three-part Op. 6, 43, and 70, and the Gavotte, which have little to offer in terms of a dramatic combination of solo and orchestra.

Our attention shall be directed primarily to the ten concertos that document the essence of Saint-Saëns's concertante style in its great variety. The first two concertos are entirely different in nature and quality. Whereas the dismissal of Op. 58 by contemporary critics as a predominantly virtuoso piece is undoubtedly warranted (see discussion in Chapter 1), Op. 17 already exhibits all the features of the composer's later concertos. The middle movement, in particular, merits special attention.

Certainly the cadenzalike piano passages reveal a definite virtuoso attitude, but this virtuosity assumes a dramatic function in its contrast with the orchestra. The main theme, which is really a series of motifs, is called into question by the solo passages. That is, the rhythmically independent chord sequence that introduces each solo passage seems to insist on a position opposed to the theme (for more on the thematic material of this movement, see related discussion in section 2.3). The piano cascades also provide a critical counterweight to the orchestra part, which is predominantly ostinato in nature. In this sense, the virtuosity of Op. 17 was a pioneering effort, as a comparison with a work such as Ravel's *Jeux d'eau* demonstrates—the latter was written about one-half century later (1901). The unmeasured form of the cadenza passages in the middle movement far exceeds anything the nineteenth century had dared thus far within the bounds of the solo concerto. Even Liszt limits the virtuoso figuration in his two concertos, for the most part, by writing out the measures.

At this point I would like to make some observations about the substance of virtuoso passages in Saint-Saëns's work. The elements that he uses repeatedly are essentially these: runs, either chromatic (at least not tonal), as in Op. 83, m. 265, or in the form of scales, as in Op. 103/2, m. 5f.; cascading chords, usually distributed over both hands, as in Op. 29/1, m. 30; trill sequences, as in Op. 119/I, m. 169—especially difficult because of their extreme position; and octave passages, as in Op. 58/2, m. 122. Then there are the frequent position changes in the works for string instruments, which in the case of Op. 119 led to what is probably unique in the cello concerto literature: distribution of the solo part over two staves so that it looks like a piano part; and extremely high stressed notes, as in the cadenza (Op. 119/II, m. 258). But such virtuoso elements should not be misconstrued. Since they take up relatively little space in Saint-Saëns's works, it would be erroneous to classify his concertos as virtuoso on the whole.

Virtuoso figuration can be used for tone color, as in the works of Debussy, Ravel, or Alexander Scriabin. The first composer to use runs, cascades, and trills not as superficial ornamentation but as coloring was Charles Henri Valentin Morhange, known as Alkan. He, along with Liszt, must be regarded as the founder of functional virtuosity—virtuosity that serves a purpose in the overall concept.

Likewise, everything technically difficult in Saint-Saëns's work in some way serves tonal or structural considerations. For instance in Op. 119/II (m. 258), enormous tension is created by a leap spanning four and a half octaves (see Example 3.3). The cascading chords in Op. 29/1 (m. 30), an expanse of sound whose actual tone sequence is no longer discernible, are a logical continuation of the work's hazy beginning.

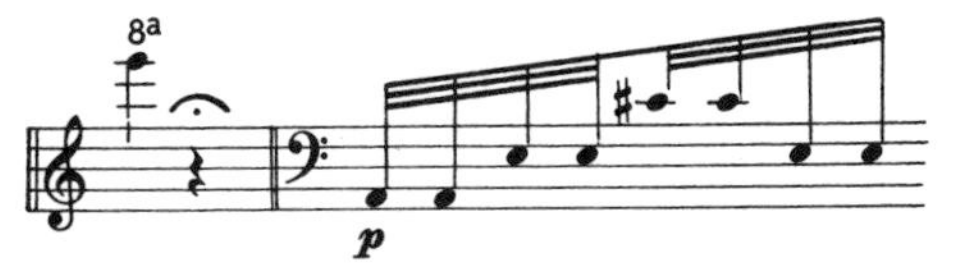

Example 3.3. Saint-Saëns, Op. 119/II, m. 258f.

A special complication occurs in the middle section of the finale to Op. 22. Over a chorale-style chord sequence in the orchestra, the piano has a series of 84 trills covering every range. Here, again, virtuosity produces an expanse of sound that certainly does more than demonstrate the soloist's technical skill.

If we examine the various solo parts closely, we note that Saint-Saëns generally uses the above-mentioned structures over lengthy stretches. This is another argument against labeling his concertos superficially virtuoso, since one of the basic characteristics of, say, Paganini or Litolff is the concentration of many different effects in minimal space—and not only in the cadenza—to create a virtuoso ostentatiousness. Furthermore, virtuoso structures in Saint-Saëns's works are always combined with the orchestra, as illustrated in the example of Op. 22.

Thus, in Op. 83 (m. 265) the chromatic run in thirds begins an eight-measure phrase in which the run is repeated a whole step higher, followed by two runs in sixths; each of these runs is followed by the same motif (see Example 3.4). Even virtuoso passages show symmetry. A similar case is the Moderato assai introduction to Op. 29, which has twenty-one measures of arpeggios, four measures with the same struc-

Example 3.4. Saint-Saëns, Op. 83, m. 102.

ture but with cascading chords in two voices, and finally two measures with cascading three-note chords.

Another procedural characteristic of the purely virtuoso concerto, but rarely used by Saint-Saëns, is the brilliant elaboration of a melody. Even the variation sequences in Op. 44 I/1, II/2, and Op. 94 display only moderate virtuosity.

Because of his eclectic attitude, which he himself admitted to, Saint-Saëns was not nearly so successful in later years with the public that had once glorified him as a musical child prodigy.[32] He had learned long ago to greet the fame of a pianistic career with caution, as he once confessed in an interview.

> His mother feared that the gushing and compliments traditionally paid to child prodigies might turn young Camille's head. Therefore she advised him to beware of flatterers. As a result, the boy gradually came to receive even deserved praise with mistrust, and this tendency never left him.[33]

Organ music in France, more so than in other countries, has always relied heavily on improvisation. In view of Saint-Saëns's long-term position as organist at the Madeleine, a comparison of his organ playing with his piano playing would be in order. On the whole his organ works, written primarily for his own use, show a stronger tendency toward improvisation than do his compositions for piano. Even stricter forms such as the preludes and fugues, Op. 99 and 109, are treated freely, while such treatment is totally lacking in the six piano fugues, Op. 161. Other organ works reveal their natures in their titles: *Three Rhapsodies* (Op. 7), *Three Fantasies* (Op. 101, 157, and one unnumbered) and *Seven Improvisations* (Op. 150).

The structural parallelism between the beginning of Op. 22 and the Préludes Op. 99/3 is interesting. Both works open with a thoroughly Baroque-style introduction over a pedal point that establishes the tonic. Saint-Saëns explained this common ground: "The second (concerto) was originally written for pedal piano. With your keen insight, you will recognize traces of the earlier conception."[34]

Consistent with the clear symmetry and tonal transparency of Saint-Saëns's scores is his regard for the metronome. Most of his works specify exact metronome settings. He explained

> [that] the establishment of the tempo, which old music totally disregarded, is becoming more and more important in modern technique; that in our time, even a small fraction of a second added to or subtracted from the duration of a measure can distort the character of a piece, even in the slow movements, where each measure lasts several seconds.[35]

Elsewhere he wrote:

> In reality, music is the art of combining sounds simultaneously (harmony) or successively (melody). In either case, a sound being composed of a certain number of constant vibrations in a given time, the whole of music is reduced to a relation between numbers. Melody and harmony are nothing more than rhythmical combinations.[36]

Here the scientist Saint-Saëns has offered an extremely interesting analysis of a musician's compositional technique!

The scores of Saint-Saëns's concertos and concertante works basically follow the Classic principle of melody and accompaniment, except in the case of elaborate polyphonic structures. In this regard the Frenchman is fully comparable to Mozart. Whereas in the Classic period the contrast between the first and second theme of a main sonata movement was expressed primarily through a key change, Saint-Saëns frequently uses contrasting technical structures. A typical example is found in Op. 20, where the main theme consists of full violin chords, while the secondary theme has the lyrical nature of a cantilena.

It is also striking that Saint-Saëns's solos are suspended for only a few measures each, which is more a sign of the movement's compactness than of a symphonic tendency. Even in sections in which the orchestra clearly dominates, the solo part often has a contrapuntal function and lends a certain coloring to the overall sound—for instance in the passage of Op. 122 in 5/4-time (m. 251ff.), where it is expressly noted: "Le solo librement—l'accompagnement—très mesuré."

I was unable to identify an actual predilection for particular structures. With chords and chord sequences, especially in the strings, the intervals are frequently kept constant; this is also true of most of the scales, as in the middle section of the first movement of Op. 22. A passage from the middle movement of Op. 103 also takes on special significance in this context, and will be further discussed in Chapter 6.

Unison playing at one- or two-octave intervals leads into the phrase shown in Example 3.5. The similarity of this phrase to a passage from Manuel de Falla's *Nights in the Gardens of Spain* is indeed astounding (see Example 3.6).

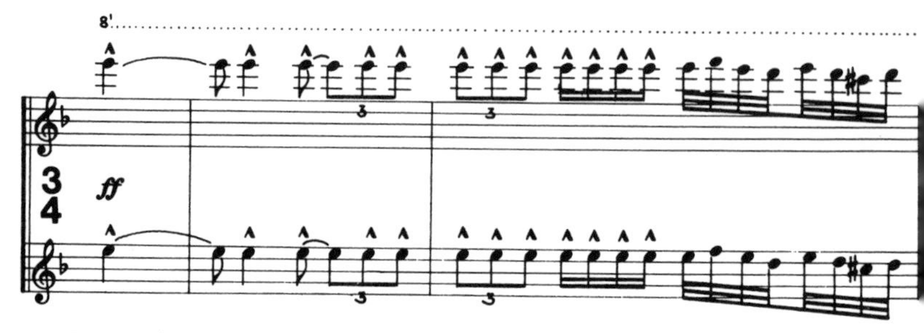

Example 3.5. Saint-Saëns, Op. 103/2, m. 6ff.

Example 3.6. de Falla, *Nights in the Gardens of Spain*/3, m. 41ff.

There are countless other techniques and solo structures in Saint-Saëns's concertos that, as far as I could determine, had never been used before. Several of these seem to me to be especially worthy of mention, in view of the fact that later composers claimed the "copyright" for them (or authorship was attributed to them by pupils and friends). Not surprisingly, the majority of these technical innovations are found in Saint-Saëns's piano works.

First, he adopted from Liszt an advanced technique of the left hand, whose role the latter had expanded to inconceivable dimensions.

> In traditional piano music, each hand has its assigned function, from which it never escapes, so that one can speak of dualistic music with its two planes. This is not the case in chamber and orchestral music. Here the musical structure consists of three planes (obviously only in the theoretical sense): the singing part, the bass part, and a more-or-less complex intermediary layer. Liszt wanted to adapt this tri-level concept to the piano, and he accomplished it by constantly bringing the left hand from the low to the middle range of the instrument. The poor left hand was not used to these kinds of gymnastics, and in order to do justice to its new function, it had to attain a heretofore unaccustomed facility and dexterity.[37]

With Saint-Saëns the accompaniment is frequently split between bass and middle ranges, as in Op. 22/1, m. 11, which requires this same dexterity of the left hand. In other places the accompaniment jumps from the bass into the discant range (Op. 103/2, m. 170f.). The bell-like effect of this passage is also produced by the octaves with grace notes in the discant, which directly follow (m. 183ff.).

Tone (m. 225f.) and chord repetitions (see Example 3.7) have their equivalents in the piano études (Example 3.8). These examples are significant not only because the technique is novel but also because a virtuoso figuration appears for the first time in a solo-concerto context without rendering the piece superficial.

Example 3.7. Saint-Saëns, Op. 89, m. 264f.

Example 3.8. Saint-Saëns, Op. 52/III, m. 1.

The technical demands within the cadenzas are, of course, more an end in themselves. Yet here too Saint-Saëns deviates sharply from the norm of his day in position, structure, and function. This will be discussed in the next chapter.

4

The Cadenza

The cadenza, as "free soloistic ornamentation of the penultima" was, as a rule, the six-four chord before the coda (see Section 2.3). It

> served to reinforce the final effect. This extension of the final cadence, already suggested in the clausula of the Middle Ages, was originally improvised, and in it the main themes of the piece were restated. The vocal and instrumental virtuoso concerto of the eighteenth and nineteenth centuries gave rise to the great concerto cadenza, which was by then also written out by the composer or an arranger, the goal being to [make] the theme repetition appeal to the audience.[1]

Mozart and Beethoven were the first to write out their concerto cadenzas, but these are still far from being virtuoso "cadenza di bravura" or "cadenza fiorita."[2] Beethoven is particularly significant in this regard. In his effort to free the concerto cadenza from its formal irrelevance to the rest of the movement and to develop it as a new section, he invented the solo cadenza with orchestra accompaniment in the rearrangement of his Violin Concerto, Op. 61, for piano and orchestra (1807), which Clementi had commissioned.[3] In Op. 73 he finally dispensed with cadenza and improvisation altogether. The six-four chord with fermata still appeared at the usual place.[4] However, it was followed by the composer's injunction: "non si fa una Cadenza ma s'attacca subito il seguente [there is to be no cadenza; rather the next part should be attacked at once]." The ensuing finale combines elements of the traditional cadenza and coda.

The cadenzalike transition (to formal sections or entire movements) was still common in the works of Mozart and Beethoven—especially in the rondo finale, where

> it is not the actual beginning of the rondo that is important, but rather: How do I get into this familiar theme, this theme that has already been heard for the second and third time? . . . If the composer has not incorporated the transitions into the work, then he indicates this with a fermata.[5]

This transition was retained in the nineteenth century to some extent, but it lost its improvisatory character completely; the composer wrote out such passages.[6] Yet countless examples show that they could still be virtuoso.

With the spread of virtuosity in the nineteenth century, instrumental soloists were no longer satisfied with traditional cadenzas, and it became customary for them to write their own, which frequently far exceeded the musical language of the work. For instance, Alkan wrote a cadenza to Mozart's D-minor Piano Concerto, K. 466 incorporating, among other things, themes from the "Jupiter" symphony (in C Major, K. 551), which was written three years later.[7] Even Camille Saint-Saëns composed cadenzas to concertos written by others, but they at least showed an obvious concern for stylistic unity.[8]

Introductions, transitions, and shorter cadenzalike insertions at nontraditional spots often served a formal function in the nineteenth century. For instance, the chord cascade at the beginning of Schumann's Piano Concerto in A Minor, Op. 54 (1845) must be understood as an introduction to the actual main theme. The same is true of the Piano Concerto in A Minor, Op. 16 (1868) by Edvard Grieg. The cadenza of the Romantic period often is recitative in character, as in the two solos of Brahms's Double Concerto in A Minor for Violin, Violoncello, and Orchestra, Op. 102 (1887). Saint-Saëns's Op. 119 also contains a recitativelike cadenza, which will be discussed presently.

Mies claimed that the virtuoso character of the cadenza was less pronounced in the nineteenth century, even—in fact, especially—in the virtuoso concerto.[9] He maintained that because the entire solo part of the work was so heavily virtuoso, further intensification of technical brilliance in the cadenza was scarcely possible. This thesis is only partly right, however. In the main sections (exposition, development, and recapitulation) accompanied by the orchestra, the soloist to a large extent was governed by the formal development and arrangement of the thematic material, whereas the cadenza offered him a chance to be freely creative with content as well as in the combination of effects.[10] On the other hand, Mies is certainly correct in his observation that traditional cadenzas—those designated by the composer for improvisation—are rare in the nineteenth century.[11]

Before we further examine the position, structure, and character of the cadenza in Saint-Saëns's works, let us consider two examples that illustrate what has been said thus far. First, we will consider the transitions and cadenzas to Mozart's last piano concerto (B-flat Major, K. 595, 1791), which were published as K. 624/34–36.

The cadenza to the first movement stands at the traditional position between the recapitulation and the coda—the latter played only by the orchestra, as customary then. It extends over a total of 37 measures (m. 351 of the score). The first eight measures are comprised of material from the motif that connects the second theme and its corollaries. This is followed by a four-measure closing, ending with a fermata. Then comes a variation of the main theme, six measures followed by a three-measure closing. A run leads into the motif that the strings play as an afterbeat (*Nachschlag*) to the theme in the exposition (cf. m. 77f., and before that, m. 5f. in the winds). The descending run completes this eight-measure phrase, which ends at the second fermata (C minor). A run in thirds, such as Mozart has already used frequently in this movement, leads through three measures of figuration to the third fermata (D-flat), finally followed by the canonically arranged main theme in its original form. An ascending chromatic run ends with the concluding trill characteristic for Mozart, the trilled C, which leads back to B-flat major and the coda.

The remarkable thing about this cadenza is its virtuosity, which for Mozart is relatively great, though of course the thematic work stands at the forefront. Also interesting is the dialogue in the right hand (cf. m. 15 of the cadenza), which clearly seems to be patterned after the relationship between solo and orchestra (see Example 4.1).

Even more dazzling are the transitions (m. 130ff. of the score, labeled by Mozart as "cadenza," and m. 147ff. of the score) and the cadenza (m. 272ff. of the score) in the rondo finale. Here Mozart ingeniously combines figuration with thematic treatment. All the

Example 4.1. Mozart, K. 595/1, cadenza.

Mozart cadenzas handed down are written in measured time—nowhere do we find a performance note such as "ad libitum." However, the latest research in the area of performance practice suggests that performers in Mozart's day followed the time much less strictly than the score would indicate.

The second example we want to consider is found in the two piano concertos by Liszt, E-flat Major (1849) and A Major (1839/61), where the virtuoso element predominates almost continuously. The free form of these two concertos does not allow for a traditional cadenza. In the A-Major work, however, there are three solo sections expressly designated as cadenzas, as well as about twelve cadenzalike solos. The first of these cadenzas (m. 64ff.of the score) is metrically defined by dotted bar lines, the second (m. 289) is unmeasured, and the third (m. 511) is divided into major sections by broken lines. Whereas the first has a run leading into recitativelike motifs, the other two combine only runs and chord chains. Unlike Chopin, Liszt uses such cascades as tone coloring.

Saint-Saëns, who was certainly influenced by Mozart as well as by Liszt, combines the methods of both masters insofar as he stipulates a cadenza at all, or at least allows room for it. He continues Beethoven's practice of integrating the cadenza into the movement as a whole, but he does it in his own special way. He changes the position of the cadenza and, guided by his ever-present consciousness of form, generally makes it an unaccompanied part of the movement whole.

An overview of Saint-Saëns's transitions and cadenzas is given in Table 4.1. All the cadenzas and transitions in this table have been written out by the composer himself. There are no additional places where a cadenza or transition might be indicated by a fermata. All the cadenzas were written into the score, except in Op. 62; here the notation "cadenza ad. lib." appears in the score, and the cadenza "écrite pour

Table 4.1. Overview of the transitions and cadenzas in Saint-Saëns's concertante works.

Opus No.	Movement No.	Cadenza(s)	Transition(s)
Op. 6		None	None
Op. 17	1	None; cadenzalike solo part in introduction	
	2	3 cadenzalike solo parts	
	3	None	None
Op. 58	1	Traditional; coda with solo	
	2	None	2
	3	None	None
Op. 20		Traditional; before beginning of middle section	
Op. 28		Cadenzalike solo part before coda	
Op. 22	1	Cadenzalike solo introduction; traditional cadenza; and cadenzalike solo part before coda	
	2	None	1
	3	None	None
Op. 27		None	None
Op. 29	1	Cadenzalike introduction with orchestra accompaniment; cadenza before beginning of development; 2d cadenza before recapitulation	
	2	None	None
	3	None	None
Op. 37		None; cadenzalike solo part before middle section	
Op. 33		Cadenzalike solo part before recapitulation of middle section	
Op. 36		None	None
Op. 48			Before middle section
Op. 43		None	None
Gavotte		None	None; long unaccompanied solo
Op. 44	I.1	None	None
	I.2	Cadenzalike solo with orchestra accompaniment	
	II.1		
	II.2	Cadenzalike solo follows transitional section	
Op. 61	1	None	None
	2	Cadenzalike solo before coda	
	3	Recitative cadenzalike introduction	

Opus No.	Movement No.	Cadenza(s)	Transition(s)
Op. 62		Cadenzalike introduction; traditional cadenza	
Op. 70		None	None
Op. 73		Recitative cadenzalike introduction	
Op. 83			1 in slow section, 2 in fast section
Op. 94		None	None
Op. 89		1; 1 recitative, cadenzalike solo	1
Op. 103	1	1 (no longer labeled "cadenza" at its 2d occurrence); 1 recitativelike solo	
	2	1 before recapitulation of 1st part; 1 "recitativo"	
	3	None	None
Op. 119	I.1	None	None
	I.2	2 cadenzalike solos	
	II.1	None	None; cadenza
	II.2	None	None
Op. 122		None	1
Op. 132		None	1 for violin; 1 for cello
Op. 154		None	None
Op. 156		None	None; 1st movement solo without orchestra
Op. 162		None	None

Monsieur Jean Noceti" is given in the appendix to the work. I based my differentiation between transition and cadenzalike solo on thematic considerations. That is, if the passage clearly functions as a link between thematic or formal groups, it is called a transition; in all other cases it is referred to as a cadenzalike solo. Not included are solo passages that are completely subordinate to the thematic-formal course of the work and thus not designated in any way (with fermatas, for instance) as expressly soloistic.

Saint-Saëns's cadenzas are distinguished mainly by two features: improvisation, even if the cadenza is written out; and a recitative character, which is fully consistent with the composer's view on the dramatic function of the solo part.[12] The recitative element is expressed not only in the cadenzas, however, but in the entire solo treatment; it is especially clear in the middle movement of Op. 103.[13] His concertos "are as spirited as partially improvised compositions, so that they seem to come into existence under the fingers of the performer as they are played."[14]

As we see from Table 4.1, only four works (Op. 58, 20, 22, and 62) have a traditional cadenza. Of these four cadenzas, only Op. 58 is traditional in the sense of the pre-Romantic concerto form—that is, at the usual place between recapitulation and coda, and based on the Classic six-four chord. In Op. 20, the compact form leaves no room for an extended cadenza. It is reduced to a single solo measure marked "Cadenza," which is actually more transitional in character. The cadenza of Op. 22 is hardly heard by the listener as such, since there are numerous cadenzalike formulas throughout the whole movement. They are much like Mozart's cadenzas in terms of structure and treatment of the thematic material, though the virtuoso element seems to be more restrained here in contrast to the rest of the movement. Finally, the cadenza in Op. 62 has no special features and appears in the traditional position, but it is unusual in a Morceau de concert. This circumstance may partially account for the work's being erroneously classified as an unfinished concerto (see discussion in Section 2.1).

Let us take a closer look at what is probably the most interesting example, the cadenza in Op. 119. If we view the work as a whole, we see that the cadenza functions almost as an independent movement.[15] Notated without measures, it appears between sections II.1 and II.2, beginning at m. 148 of the movement (number 19 of the score) after an E-flat seventh-chord in the orchestra. Its exact marking reads "Cadenza ad libitum. Très modéré," and it serves to link the scherzolike II.1 with II.2, which is the recapitulation of I.1. Thus, the cadenza begins with a motif (Example 4.2) that is derived from the main theme of I.1 (Example 4.3) and ascends chromatically in four repetitions. This beginning marks a break, both structural and thematic, from the material of II.1; the theme (Example 4.3) did not appear in either I.1 or II.1.

Example 4.2. Saint-Saëns, Op. 119/II, cadenza.

Example 4.3. Saint-Saëns, Op. 119/I.1, m. 7.

The next element in the cadenza (Example 4.4) is reminiscent of a passage in I.2 (Example 4.5). At the repetition of this passage, it moves by way of E-flat minor to D major (Example 4.6).

Example 4.4. Saint-Saëns, Op. 119/II, cadenza.

Example 4.5. Saint-Saëns, Op. 119/I.2, m. 62 (number 11 of the score).

Example 4.6. Saint-Saëns, Op. 119/II, cadenza.

The next part in the cadenza (Example 4.7), marked *Récit,* also is vaguely reminiscent of a figure in I.2 (Example 4.8). A gloomy arpeggio figure answers the recitative and proceeds through G minor and G major to E minor and finally to E major (Example 4.9).

Example 4.7. Saint-Saëns, Op. 119/II, cadenza.

Example 4.8. Saint-Saëns, Op. 119/I.2, m. 11f.

Example 4.9. Saint-Saëns, Op. 119/II, cadenza.

A second *Récit* follows, intensifying the first dynamically and agogically (Example 4.10). Two brutal pizzicato chords modulate from E major to A minor (allegro).

Example 4.10. Saint-Saëns, Op. 119/II, cadenza.

The second *Récit* conforms to the new key but leans toward F major; it is considerably shorter and more restrained dynamically than the two previous figures, and the gloomy bass part seems to "win" (Example 4.11).

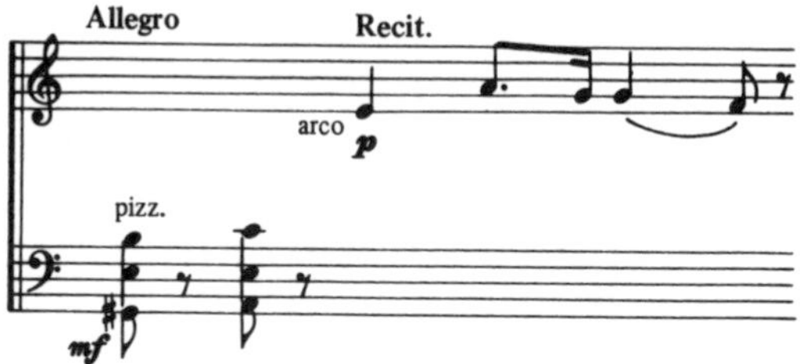

Example 4.11. Saint-Saëns, Op. 119/II, cadenza.

F major is picked up and changed to B-flat major, then forced into G major by the next *Récit* (Example 4.12), and finally led to C major. The intensification of the *Récit* (Example 4.13) leads to a contrary motion (Example 4.14) and a triumphant A minor in the upper part.

Example 4.12. Saint-Saëns, Op. 119/II, cadenza.

Example 4.13. Saint-Saëns, Op. 119/II, cadenza.

Example 4.14. Saint-Saëns, Op. 119/II, cadenza.

Then a brilliant run spanning more than two octaves leads to the concluding allegro, which, with six repetitions of the motif (Example 4.15), leads back to the rhythmic world of the initial motif.

Example 4.15. Saint-Saëns, Op. 119/II, cadenza.

The figure already cited in Example 3.3, appears three times (A major—B-flat major—A major), the last time in the highest discant. This, with its enormous leap from e'''' to the A of the great octave (number 20 of the score), marks the beginning of the opus's closing section, II.2.

If the logic behind Saint-Saëns's unusual practice of notating the solo part on two staves was not obvious before, it becomes clear in this cadenza. Indeed, a dialogue seems to take place here, which Saint-Saëns brings out vividly through alternating ranges and through the alternation between pizzicato and arco. The cadenza of Op. 119 could almost be compared to an opera scene. Even the rugged bass figure at the beginning of II.1 seems to advance the dramatic plot, which is not resolved until the arrival at the main theme five measures later, this time in a radiant D major. The upper part of the cadenza has prepared for this point and made it seem urgent. The virtuosity arising from the dualism is secondary and, as always with Saint-Saëns, serves the dramatic function.

5

Horizontal and Vertical Structures

5.1. *Melody*

In 1885 Calmann Lévy published a collection of essays by Camille Saint-Saëns under the title *Harmonie et Mélodie* (see Chapter 1). This title is as instructive as the quotation cited earlier in which Saint-Saëns defined melody and harmony as mere rhythmic combinations.[1] Furthermore, in view of the composer's classic orientation and his strict consciousness of form, based on traditional periodization, we might also expect him to be largely epigonic with respect to the three basic musical structures: melody and rhythm (horizontal), and harmony (vertical). It may even appear so to the modern observer. However, a look at the customary treatment of these structures in nineteenth-century Paris will confirm that Saint-Saëns was significantly innovative even here and resisted contemporary fashions.

> To the casual listener, melody is the easiest structure of a musical work to comprehend. Thus it was also the first musical element to be legally safeguarded in the nineteenth century—the protection of rhythmic or harmonic ideas from plagiarism seemed impossible at that time. Furthermore, the success of a work with audiences depended mainly on its melodies. Arrangements, rearrangements, paraphrases, fantasias, potpourris, and all the other re-creations inspired by successful

> works spring from melodic thematic material; variations are composed on themes, not on rhythms, harmonies, or tone colors. In this context, I assume melody to be a sequence of tones at various pitches, meaningfully united by the manner in which they move through time and tone range, by their resulting relationships to one another and to the whole, and by the dynamics of their course.[2]

Because of the success of Italian opera in France, popular taste was focused on bel canto melody. At the time Saint-Saëns wrote his concertos, bel canto was also holding its ground in instrumental music, as exemplified in the Ecole Liégoise. Without the catchy lyricisms of the Italians, even virtuosity would have been inconceivable, for it could only be sparked by extremely simple melodies with readily recognizable structures.

The melody was respected and valued as an absolute phenomenon; tone quality and harmony were secondary, and if they obscured the outline of the cantilena, they could even be perceived as disruptive. Furthermore, the melodic happenings were limited to a consistently maintained timbre—in music theater, the voice; in the instrumental realm, a solo instrument. Interrupting a line and continuing it on a different tone level meant rejection on the part of the audience.[3]

Concertante music had submitted to this melodic doctrine heretofore. Saint-Saëns was one of the first to strive for another kind of thematic material and to apply it to the concertante form. This proved disastrous for his musical dramas. His operas did not meet the standards of either the Paris Opéra (Meyerbeer) nor the Opéra Lyrique (Gounod). With the possible exception of *Samson et Dalila,* none was a lasting success.

The essence of Saint-Saëns's melodies

> is so immediate that the primordial element from which they are formed can often be found intact. . . . He speaks a language long cultivated, wherein verve is more and more difficult to achieve. He does not at all try to break with the established relationships of that language. Nevertheless, his melodies are identifiable among all others. . . . They are perfectly clear, but it is a clarity distinct from that of Mozart or Bizet: Their penetrating and concentrated strength calls for reflection. They have a neatness peculiar to them, which is abstract and at the same

> time malleable. The themes of his symphonies move like animate beings. . . . What they express at the most basic level is a clairvoyant conformity to rule, to reason.[4]

Baumann's observations are correct in every respect. Eclectic adherence to existing structures is especially characteristic of Saint-Saëns's melodies. However, the structures he prefers are not the same as those used by the French Romantics. In Op. 20 (m. 1f.), the main theme, with its massive chords, goes against the trend of lyric cantabile, which the composer had still followed in Op. 58. In Op. 20, as in many of his concertos and concertante works, the themes are characterized by prominent and decisive rhythms. Though they were not complicated, they were perceived as complex, as the antithesis of the sweeping bel canto melodies of the Ecole Liégoise. In fashioning his themes, the composer fell back on these rhythms in order to embrace the dualism that is intrinsic to the concertante form and the sonata movement, as the theme of the slow middle section of Op. 20 (m. 128ff.) illustrates.

The large volume of material precludes a detailed study of all the melodies in Saint-Saëns's concertante compositions. Instead, I will document general criteria for his melodies with selected examples.

In the discussion on form (see Chapter 2), I have already alluded to the classic (eight-measure) periods of most of his concertos. Since form issues from the sequence and treatment of melodic phrases, the themes are also periodic for the most part. Especially notable is the internal periodicity: there are further periodic subdivisions within the eight-measure themes. Figure 5.1. shows the structures that are revealed in the themes.

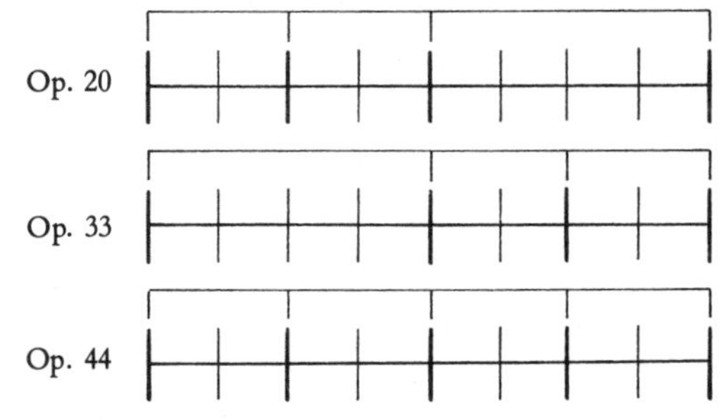

Figure 5.1. Structures within Saint-Saëns's 8-measure periodic themes.

Indeed, the clearly recognizable primordial melodic element mentioned by Baumann is characteristic of most of the themes. It is not only defined by a particular interval sequence, but is often the rhythmic nucleus of the movement as well (as in Op. 44/I.1 and 62).

Another characteristic feature is the opening interval. Saint-Saëns shows a marked preference for small steps, which often define the first phase of the melody (as in Op. 61/1, m. 5). With few exceptions, the melodies begin with an interval in the second-to-fifth range. Larger intervals are also rare within an entire melodic phrase and are related to the formal development of the theme. This is especially clear in Example 5.1. The second of the opening has become a minor third, the dynamics have changed from *mezzoforte* to *forte*, and the continuation of the theme is altered in the reprise (here not meant as part of a sonata movement).

Example 5.1. Saint-Saëns, Op. 89; *Top,* m. 18ff.; *Bottom,* m. 219ff.

The change from major to minor second in Example 5.2 is also as subtle as it is effective. The abrupt change in dynamics from *forte* to *piano* gives this modulation another special accent. Here, at the very beginning of the coda, the B major (corresponding to Classic tradition) seems precarious again, tending toward the actual main key of B minor. Only at the next *forte* (m. 395) does it resolve to the major once and for all.

Example 5.2. Saint-Saëns, Op 61/3, m. 383ff.

To extend the range of a melodic phrase, Saint-Saëns often turns to the principle of diminution (Examples 5.3–5.5). At another place, only

Example 5.3. Saint-Saëns, Op. 162, m. 4f.

Example 5.4. Saint-Saëns, Op. 162, m. 28f.

Example 5.5. Saint-Saëns, Op. 162, m. 32f.

the closing phrase is changed (Examples 5.6 and 5.7), and the range is thus diminished from an octave to a sixth.

Example 5.6. Saint-Saëns, Op. 132, m. 15ff.

Example 5.7. Saint-Saëns, Op. 132, m. 37ff.

The theme from Op. 44/II.2, which Baumann calls "chorale," may possibly be of folk origin.[5] Yet, it has all the typical features of Saint-Saëns's melodies.[6] We shall, therefore, examine it in detail, as a representative example (see Example 5.8).

Example 5.8. Saint-Saëns, Op. 44/II.2, m. 295–311 and 327–343.

The theme from Op. 44/II.2 breaks down into eight symmetrical phrases of four measures each, which begin on an upbeat; the importance of each break is indicated by the slash lines in Figure 5.2. The

a¹ (m. 1–4) / a² (m. 5–8) // b¹ (m. 9–12) / b² (m. 13–16) ///
c¹ (m. 17–20) / c² (m. 21–24) // d¹ (m. 25–28) / d² (m. 29–32)

Figure 5.2. Rhythmic parallels in the theme from Saint-Saëns, Op. 44/II.2, m. 295–311 and 327–343.

figure also shows the rhythmic parallels in this theme: a¹ corresponds to b¹; a² corresponds to b²; c¹ corresponds—except for the last note value—to c² and d¹; d² has its own rhythmic structure. Of course, the rhythmic pattern of the entire theme is extremely simple. The result is a rhythmic unit much like the iambic second mode of medieval music (see Figure 5.3).

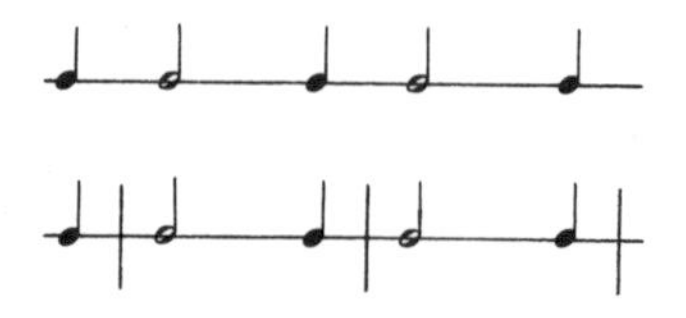

Figure 5.3. Rhythmic unit of iambic second mode in medieval music compared to rhythmic unit of Saint-Saëns, Op. 44/II.

Another instructive and characteristic element is the interval structure of the theme (see Figure 5.4). First of all, we note that the largest interval Saint-Saëns uses is the perfect fifth, and four out of seven of these occur at the transitions between the phrases. Equally remarkable is the fact that phrases a^1, a^2, b^1, b^2, c^1, and c^2 each begin with a perfect prime, so that the rising fourth at the beginning of d^1 receives special emphasis in this position, reinforced by an accent. Aside from the hidden transition from a^2 to b^1, the prime occurs only one other time (m. 31)—to emphasize the tonic.

gure 5.4. Interval structure of the theme from Saint-Saëns, Op. 44/II.2, m. 295–311 and 7–343.

rase	Intervals																
a^1	1^P		3^M+	**2**	2^M-		2^M-	**3**	4^P+		2^m-	2^M-	**4**	2^M+	3^M-	(5^P+)	**5**
a^2	1^P		2^M+	**6**	3^m+		3^m-	**7**	2^M-	3^m-	2^M-	2^M-	**8**	2^M+		(1^P)	**9**
b^1	1^P		3^m+	**10**	2^m-		2^M-	**11**	4^P+		2^M-	2^m-	**12**	2^m+	3^m-	(5^P+)	**13**
b^2	1^P		2^M+	**14**	2^m+		3^m-	**15**	2^M-	5^P-	3^M+	2^M-	**16**	2^M-		$((5^P+))$	**17**
c^1	1^P		2^M+	**18**	2^m+	2^m-	2^M-	**19**	2^M-			2^m-	**20**	2^m+	3^m-	(5^P+)	**21**
c^2	1^P		2^M+	**22**	2^m+	2^m-	2^m-	**23**	2^m-			2^M-	**24**	2^M+		(3^M-)	**25**
d^1	4^P+		2^M-	**26**	2^M-	2^m-	2^M-	**27**	2^M+			2^M-	**28**	2^M-		(2^m-)	**29**
d^2	2^M-	2^M+	2^m+	**30**	2^M+	2^M+	3^M-	**31**	1^P			2^M-	**32**	2^M+			

ld numbers denote measures, which, for simplicity's sake, have been numbered from 1 to
.

1 = prime
2 = second
3 = third
4 = fourth
5 = fifth
^{P} = perfect interval
^{M} = major interval
^{m} = minor interval
+ = rising
− = falling

In the last half of the theme (c^1–d^1), the second takes on special significance—a major change from the melodic shape in the first half. In six cases out of eight, the transition from the penultimate to the ultimate measure of a phrase is a mirrored interval (x^y—/ x^y+). In addition, entire interval sequences are mirrored, such as 2^M+ 2^m+ 2^m-2^M- (m. 17f.) or 2^M- 2^M- 2^m- 2^M- 2^M+ 2^m + 2^M+ 2^M+ (m. 27ff.).

In general, an ascending fourth (d^1) is followed by descending intervals, which strike a balance. The importance of the second is reaffirmed by the fact that this interval falls on the downbeat of the second measure of a phrase seven times out of eight, and on the downbeat of the fourth measure five times out of eight.

The rhythmic breakdown of a quarter note into two eighths is always found at the same spot, namely the last beat of the second measure of phrases c^1, c^2, and d^1; in phrases a^1, a^2, b^1, and b^2, it is the last beat of the third measure that is broken down, and—following the above-mentioned rhythmic parallelism—the second beat as well, in a^2 and b^2. Thus, the final phrase d^2 is the only one lacking these subdivided beats. Instead, the sequence of seven quarter notes, which breaks the pattern of the iambic mode, gives it the separate character of a miniature coda.

All Saint-Saëns's melodies—not only in his concertante works, but in his other instrumental and vocal works as well—are constructed symmetrically. This is evident even in the most minute breakdowns of his periods as well as in the precisely balanced rise and fall of his melodic phrases.

The composer avoids larger intervals wherever possible, while still keeping to diatonic rather than chromatic composition. (Large intervals are typical of the virtuoso style and have this status in his works too—in Op. 28, for instance.) The rhythmic terseness of his themes stands in stark contrast to the sweeping bel canto melodies.

Many of Saint-Saëns's themes are built on mirrored rhythms, intervals, or interval sequences (inversion), so that an "axis" can be identified, as in Example 5.9. In their basic form, most of the com-

Example 5.9. Saint-Saëns, Op. 43, m. 5f.

poser's themes are limited to a relatively narrow range. A theme like the one in the first movement of Chopin's piano concerto (m. 1ff.), which spans a twelfth in the first four measures—typical, incidentally, of the lyric virtuoso style as created by the Ecole Liégoise for the violin concerto—would be unthinkable for Saint-Saëns. His lyrical themes, as in the four romances, are more circular than soaring. Here, too, he clearly renounces the vocal melodic style of instrumental music of his era. Sweeping cantilenas characterized the operatic style of the Italian school and were fostered mainly by followers of the latter.

Saint-Saëns's preference for small intervals in his themes had yet another consequence: A theme with a wide range offers numerous possibilities for embellishment with virtuoso figuration, for insertion of a brilliant run or other ornamentation between two tones that are further apart, without altering the basic nature of the theme. But the smaller the intervals, the more they discourage virtuoso additions.

The bare skeleton of the theme in Saint-Saëns's work has little significance in itself:

> From the great Classic composers, Saint-Saëns adopted the habit of taking a basic idea with little intrinsic charm and developing it into a musical subject of the first order. And this prestigious development is astonishingly simple.[7]

These very qualities of Saint-Saëns, "this master of precision, of discrimination, of perfection, and of taste, whose style is always fashioned with utmost care," were criticized by audiences of his day as weaknesses.[8] It was said that his melodies were not refined enough (Debussy rejected them later as "sentimental"[9]), that they depended too much on artistic treatment, that they did not appeal directly as did the cantilenas of Italian opera. Then, when the latter were forgotten and Wagner's star was also waning, Saint-Saëns was seen as the dangerous proponent of a modernistic trend that opposed melody altogether. The theme of his Scherzo Op. 87 for two pianos (Example 5.10) bears a cer-

Example 5.10. Saint-Saëns, Op. 87, m. 1ff.

tain resemblance to Debussy's *Lindaraja,* also for two pianos, which was written twelve years later (1901) (Example 5.11). This theme gave rise to heated arguments: "Saint-Saëns is crazy. Look at his Scherzo!" versus "He certainly is *not* crazy. Look at his Scherzo!"[10] One thing is certain—

Example 5.11. Debussy, *Lindaraja,* m. 1ff.

the truth lies somewhere in the middle, as the composer himself recognized: "In reality, it is not I who have changed, but the situation."[11]

One final thought on Saint-Saëns's melodies: The unadorned themes of his concertos and concertante works were never tailor-made for the respective solo instruments in the true sense. Consider, for example, the thoroughly nonpianistic nature of the variation theme in Op. 44/II.2 discussed earlier, which perhaps for that very reason is all the more effective. Rarely is the full register of an instrument used—either as tone range or in its extremes. Seldom does the composer call for special fingering or chords which can only be realized on this instrument. All this shows up only in the course of the formal and thematic development.

Again, the reason for this lies in his desire to balance solo and orchestra. Neither of the two should impose the melody on the other and thereby appear to have precedence. This often resulted in parallels to the Classic tradition. In other, mainly virtuoso Romantic solo concertos, compromises in instrumentation can already be sensed in the orchestra introduction; the theme does not emerge in its intended form until the solo begins.

Here I might also mention a special case. Henry Alkan, the formidable pianist, took the opposite route. He rearranged concertos by Mozart (K. 466) and Beethoven (Op. 37) for solo piano and composed a piano concerto—considerably stricter in form and structure than Schumann's sonatalike *Concert sans orchestre,* Op. 14—in which orchestral and solo passages are clearly distinguishable. That Saint-Saëns also exercised tonal freedom in fashioning his concerto themes is evidenced by the alternative solos of the two romances, Op. 37 (flute or violin) and 36 (horn or violoncello), and by the accompaniment of Op. 132, which is certainly orchestral, even though it is taken unchanged from the piano version.

Saint-Saëns never waits long to unfold the thematic material in his concertos. In the works of others—for example, Franck's *Variations symphoniques* (1885) and the *Symphonie sur un chant montagnard français* (*Symphonie cévenole*) (1886) by his pupil d'Indy—the melody is a goal or, as in the virtuoso concerto, the melody is the obvious high point of the thematic content. For Saint-Saëns, it is the inconspicuous nucleus of the whole and needs numerous manipulations for its full richness to be revealed.

5.2. *Rhythm*

For a long time, overestimation of the melodic substance of music resulted in the neglect of the second horizontal structure, rhythm, which was not emancipated until the rise of expressionism at the beginning of the twentieth century. Completely overlooked was the fact that the interval sequence is only as significant as the sequence of time values attached to it, which make up its distinctive character.

Of course, more weight was attached to rhythm in certain musical realms: The dance element is based on rhythmic structures, and the charm of polyphonic style also lies in the artistic treatment of rhythmic patterns. Since concertante music in nineteenth-century France was not concerned with polyphony nor did it aim to be dancelike, rhythmic figures, which seemed meaningless without the melody, were regarded as ornamentation or—in light of the increasing trend toward the exotic—as non-European coloring.

The rhythm instruments of today were not yet fully developed nor were their manifold possibilities recognized, except by Berlioz, who, in his imaginary (i.e., ideal) orchestra, called for 8 timpani, 6 snare and 3 bass drums, 4 pairs of cymbals, 6 triangles, 6 sets of bells, 12 cymbals (in addition to the 4 sets already mentioned), 2 large bells, 2 tom-toms, and 4 half-moons—a group of small percussion instruments set up in a half-moon arrangement.[12] Other than the timpani, an orchestra usually had a triangle, a bass drum, and a pair of cymbals at most. They were mainly used for dynamic intensification or accentuation, as in the concertos of Paganini. Berlioz also was the first to recognize and make use of the rhythmic potential in the traditional array of instruments. Passages such as the combined col legno and pizzicato of the strings in the concluding "Songe d'une nuit du Sabbat" of his *Symphonie fantastique* or in the "Queen Mab" scherzo of *Roméo et Juliette* place him among the artistic avant-garde of his age.

Saint-Saëns is anything but avant-garde in his concertos, as far as rhythm and its effects are concerned. Percussion instruments are specified in the scores of only three of his works (Op. 73, 89, and 156); in nine of his twenty-nine concertante works he even forgoes the timpani (see Table 3.1). And yet, as shown in the quotation mentioned several times,[13] rhythm for him was the nuclear element of music and part of the "espace céleste" with which he was concerned as philosopher, scientist, and astronomer.[14]

His rhythm is generally intrinsic to the melody and issues from the tension in the interval sequences; in very few passages (not only in his concertos but in all his works) is a rhythmic pattern treated independently. Although a disciple—and to some extent also a follower—of pre-Classic polyphonic thought, Saint-Saëns seldom used pure polyphony in his compositions. When he did, it was often isolated (in the Preludes and Fugues for Organ, Op. 99 and 109, and in the Piano Fugues, Op. 161).

However, the importance of rhythmic structures in his work is shown by the fact already mentioned in connection with his melodies—the melodic nucleus is usually also the rhythmic nucleus of the whole (see discussion in Section 5.1).

First of all, we note that the composer seldom begins his themes with an upbeat, the only major exception being Op. 44. This gives the themes a certain immediacy; with the downbeat of the first melodic note, a unique "life" is called into being. Most of the melodies that begin on an upbeat occur in slow passages or movements, such as in Op. 132. This seemingly insignificant stylistic feature is important in that it is also typical of the Classic composers, especially Mozart. Thus, it reaffirms Saint-Saëns's adherence to tradition. Syncopations, such as the one in Op. 28 (Example 5.12), and the numerous instances in Op. 89, where rigid metric patterns are broken (Figure 5.5), are mainly attributable to the folkloric source of the work, which will be discussed in Chapter 6.

Example 5.12. Saint-Saëns, Op. 28, m. 39f.

Figure 5.5. Syncopations in Saint-Saëns, Op. 89, based upon folkloric sources.

Saint-Saëns was skillful at altering the basic meter without changing the time signature, as illustrated in Example 5.13. The melody line does not follow the designated 3/4 time at all. Instead, it can be better represented by the combination of changing meters shown in Figure 5.6.

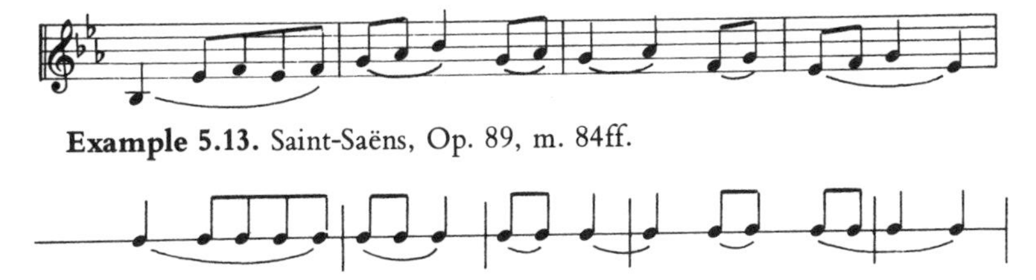

Example 5.13. Saint-Saëns, Op. 89, m. 84ff.

Figure 5.6. Changing meters in Saint-Saëns, Op. 89, m. 84ff.

Another characteristic of Saint-Saëns is that he forms his rhythmic patterns from a very limited number of note values. Here again we cite Op. 44/II.2, this time as an especially clear example. Its 32-measure theme consists only of half notes, quarter notes (two dotted quarters), and eighth notes. Thus, once again the rhythmic flow, which is maintained over long stretches of the score, illustrates the composer's traditional Baroque posture and is in direct opposition to the self-indulgent melodies of the Romantics.

An interest in Baroque and Classic dance and suite forms left its imprint on many of Saint-Saëns's works (e.g., *Suite pour orchestre,* Op. 49; *Sarabande et Rigaudon pour orchestre,* Op. 57; *Suite pour violoncelle et piano,* Op. 16; *Gavotte pour piano,* Op. 23; and *Suite pour piano,* Op. 56). Their influence can also be detected in his concertos and concertante pieces, such as the Gavotte, which was probably part of a suite, as well as in the minuet that comprises the middle section of Op. 33, and in the Sicilienne from the middle movement of Op. 61 (m. 5 f.). The use of dance rhythms, particularly the pre-Romantic forms, was rare in French concertante music. Exceptions include Charles Dancla's *Air de danse brillant,* Op. 148 (1879), though it is virtuoso in nature, Lalo's *Fantaisie-*

Ballet for violin (1885), and Gabriel Pierné's Op. 6 for piano by the same name (1886).[15] On the other hand, *Entr'acte et Rigaudon* for violoncello (1901), by Théodore Dubois, is a reminiscence of the old masters that corresponds to Debussy's orientation.

March rhythms were introduced in French concertante music fairly early with Luigi Gianella's *Concerto militaire* for flute and orchestra (probably written in 1802) and continued successfully by A. François Servais with his cello concerto of the same name, Op. 18 (1862). Apparently these rhythms held little attraction for Saint-Saëns despite their metric strictness, which should have appealed to his aesthetic sense. Aside from the second movement of Op. 156, where the occasion for the composition determined the rhythm (see Chapter 1), none of the composer's concertante works have the character of a march.

An important feature of Saint-Saëns's rhythms is their sequential character, which follows logically from the above-mentioned uniformity of note values. Almost all rhythmic patterns occur in sequence, which gives many passages an ostinato character. The pattern in Figure 5.7. appears 82 times in Op. 132. Thus, movement sec-

Figure 5.7. Rhythmic pattern occuring in sequence in Op. 132.

tions, even entire movements, often resemble toccatas (in the nineteenth-century sense) in their rhythmic disposition.[16] This is especially true of Op. 103/3, as Saint-Saëns expressly designated his Solo Etude Op. 111/VI as "Toccata d'après le finale du cinquième Concerto." Op. 22/1 and 119/II.1 are also close to being toccatas.

Op. 22/2 merits special attention, too. Here we find the only example in Saint-Saëns's concertante works of an almost purely rhythmical opening (Example 5.14). The rhythm of the theme is antici-

Example 5.14. Saint-Saëns, Op. 22/2, m. 1ff.

pated by the timpani, but its relationship to the interval of a fourth is only barely discernible (see Example 5.15). For the trio of this scherzo movement, which occurs twice, the composer turns the 6/8 time into a fast waltz (m. 75ff.). How little Saint-Saëns uses rhythmic change in

Example 5.15. Saint-Saëns, Op. 22/2, m. 5f.

general is illustrated in Example 5.16, where we might expect the variation form to have resulted in more distinct variations. The breakdown of the theme's original rhythmic structure appears to lack originality, but its charm lies in the harmonization and instrumentation of the orchestra accompaniment.

Example 5.16. Saint-Saëns, Op. 94; *Top,* m. 5; *Center,* m. 57; *Bottom,* m. 95.

In summary, it can be said that the rhythmic structures of Saint-Saëns's concertos and concertante works have little about them that is unusual. The composer uses only basic meters for his themes and seldom changes them in the course of the movement. To lend variety, he shifts accents without changing the time signature. The rhythmic form of the themes is simple and therefore easy to remember; rhythmic phrases are strung together in periods. The comment that "the joy of life often pulsates in its rhythmical accents" applies only to his toccatalike works and those inspired by non-European folklore.[17] On the other hand, the comment about the "union de la mélodie et du langage" certainly applies generally.[18] The apt comparison of his rhythms and symmetrical patterns to those of Pindar underscores his Classic orientation once again.[19]

5.3. *Harmony*

"Melody is fundamental to the effectiveness of musical language, but this melody must be permeated with harmony and emanate from the harmony."[20] The chords and harmonic color in Saint-Saëns's work have a subtlety that no other pre-impressionist French composer attained. The rejection in Leipzig that met the bold harmonies of Op. 29/2 shows that Saint-Saëns was by no means eclectic in that regard.[21]

> In their smooth, effortless style, his harmonies shed the weight of the knowledge that conceived them and retain only an element of plastic beauty, color, and emotion. All of his works are testimony to the unspeakable, magical powers of harmony. A chord by itself can sustain a stirring vibration in us for it strikes or caresses our body in the very depths of our unconsciousness and stimulates vague sympathies. But only a great master of harmony such as Saint-Saëns has the gift of creating from a very simple progression the sensation of a tonal sequence that is unique, never before imagined, and as penetrating as a well-crafted song.[22]

Of all the biographers, Baumann deals with Saint-Saëns's harmony in the greatest depth, and his observations will be cited often in this chapter.

First, I would mention that many of the harmonic expressions in Saint-Saëns's works, like certain of his rhythmic structures, have folk-music or exotic origins, which I will not investigate until the next chapter. The present discussion concerns only those works whose origins are not exotic or in folk music.

The harmonic structure of the nineteenth-century French solo concerto has two main features: (1) It is never independent, but merely complements and supports the solo part; and (2) as a rule, the melody tones are the uppermost tones of the respective harmony. Thus, modulations always follow the course of the melody. The harmonies of the solo passage are almost never determined by the orchestra. Moreover, the traditional principle of a tonal framework within the solo concerto is usually followed closely. That is, the second theme (of a sonata form movement) is in the dominant key in the exposition and resolves to the tonic in the recapitulation, and the minor mode is diverted to the major at the end (see Section 2.3).

Saint-Saëns was one of the first in France to break with this firmly established order. He never abandoned the basic tonal framework in the vertical structure of his concertante compositions, but here again he has a way of elevating the orchestra to equal-partner status with the solo. A clear symmetry can be seen even in his harmonic progressions. At the beginning of Op. 61, for example, the first four measures are split in half by the strings (m. 1 + 2) and the addition of the kettledrums (m. 3 + 4). The ensuing solo part adheres to the pedal-point style of the orchestra accompaniment for the first four measures, then harmonic development emerges in the last four (see Example 5.17). Through the contrary motion of the orchestra's ascending harmonies and the violin's descending scale, the composer creates strong harmonic tension.

Example 5.17. Saint-Saëns, Op. 61/1, m. 1ff.

The mirror technique, which we have already observed in the melodic-rhythmic context, is also found in the harmony. In Op. 22/3, the woodwinds and horns have a chord sequence that revolves around the G—the tonic—of the solo, as if on an axis. This mirroring is also seen in the rapid series of trills, whose main harmonic notes are shown in Example 5.18.

Example 5.18. Saint-Saëns, Op. 22/3, m. 122ff.

This excerpt from Op. 22 shows still another characteristic of Saint-Saëns's harmonies: Without heed to the laws of modulation, the composer changes the harmonies through parallel shifting. This procedure was later picked up again by Debussy, where it is correctly regarded as a novelty. The archaic effect found in Debussy's *La Cathédrale engloutie* (see Example 5.19) was anticipated by Saint-Saëns in Op. 22. Approximately half his concertante works are in a minor key.

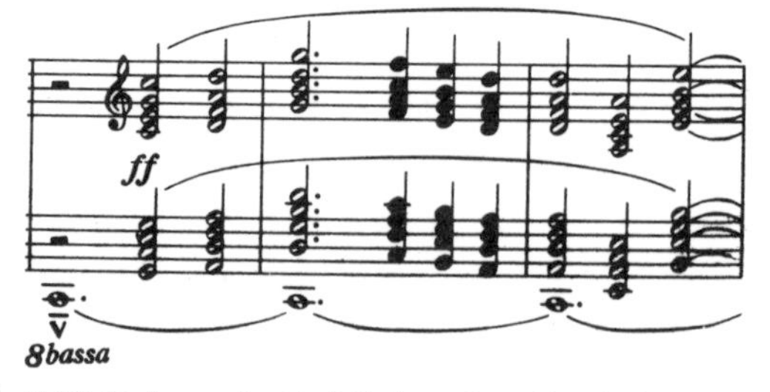

Example 5.19. Debussy, *La Cathédrale engloutie* (Préludes Ier livre), m. 28ff.

> Saint-Saëns has followed the general trend of the moderns in conceiving a great number of his motifs in minor keys. Even though the tonal nuances adapt themselves to the intimate voice of the melody, still the gloomy minor mode persists.[23]

Saint-Saëns was judged by his contemporaries as having a certain affinity to Wagnerian harmonies. It was often said in reproach that the Frenchman's music was clearly reminiscent of the "futuristic music" of the Bayreuth master. It is hard to understand how anyone could have thought to detect in Op. 44 any influence by Wagner,[24] but in Op. 29 there is in fact a bold harmonic progression. At the very beginning of the middle movement (Op. 29/2, m. 1ff.), which ends on the tritone, there are harmonic dissonances between the strings and the woodwinds. These dissonances find their resolution in a common tone B (m. 5), but fall into disharmony again through the insistent A minor of the solo (m. 6ff.) In effect, the orchestra's B major, which immediately follows, must have appeared to the Leipzig audience as a negation of the existing harmonic order, but in fact it issues logically from the chromatic nature of the passage.

> For the most part the modernisms in his chords are demanded by the phrase and serve to intensify it. . . . His changing moods, his violent passions, sometimes lead him to unintentionally strange harmonies that are all the more startling. There are dissonances similar to a vulture's cry, brutally savage—this, in his instrumental works, in his allegros, at the climax of a dizzying lyrical passage.[25]

How much more brutal the harmonies of Op. 29/1 must have seemed to the audience when heard in all clarity, due to the extremely slow tempo of the movement!

However, it was not typical of Saint-Saëns to leave the tonality open at the beginning of a movement.

> He likes to establish the tonality firmly at the outset in his works. They often begin with the tonic. He is in no hurry to modulate, but modulates to closely related keys, tones, and brings the motif back to the tonic almost immediately.[26]

In his harmonic progressions, Saint-Saëns usually retains the same tone color, as we have seen in the previous examples, and he likes to shift the tonality in chromatic increments.[27] But he always returns to the main key, and chromatic runs or cascades of diminished dominant seventh chords, especially in the fast movements, are to be regarded only as interjections.

Also significant is the harmonic function of the solo, which hovers above the accompaniment chords (see Example 5.20) and does not bring

Example 5.20. Saint-Saëns, Op. 27, m. 1ff.

out the customary tonic or dominant but rather the third. Here, as frequently in other places, the melody notes of the solo are isolated rather than doubled in the accompaniment (except in m. 4). This makes Saint-Saëns's scores highly transparent and, as Baumann points out, fundamentally distinguishes them from those of Beethoven or from the overly close harmonies of the "New Germans" and their French emulators.[28] As already shown in Example 5.17, the harmonic changes frequently move in opposite directions (see Example 5.21). In this way, irrespective of the tension of the harmonic progression, Saint-Saëns strikes a balance between solo and orchestra such as no French composer before him had achieved.

Normally the composer prefers complete triads, and the lack of the

Example 5.21. Saint-Saëns, Op. 43, m. 73ff.

Example 5.22. Saint-Saëns, Op. 22/3, m. 269ff.

third in Example 5.22, together with the piercing chords of the oboes and clarinets, has a strange effect.

Saint-Saëns's Classic orientation finds expression not only in the formal layouts of his works and their intrinsic structures, but also in the openness of the harmonic framework. Moreover, he rarely used keys with abundant sharps or flats, as many late Romantic composers did. With the influence of Wagner and the "New German" school, a clear shift can be seen in French music. Composers like Ernest Chausson and Vincent d'Indy strove for rich, often overly dense harmonic textures in which traditional modulation was replaced by chromatic shifts. Saint-Saëns distanced himself from this movement very early and spoke out in particular against the monumental *Cours de composition musicale* (1897–1907) of Franck's pupil, d'Indy. In his essay "Les idées de Monsieur Vincent d'Indy," published in 1919—the most comprehensive of Saint-Saëns's musical treatises, which indicates how important this theme was to him—he says:

The dissonance of yesterday, we are also told, will be the con-

> sonance of tomorrow; one can grow accustomed to anything. Still, there are such things in life as bad habits, and those who get accustomed to crime, come to an evil end. . . .
>
> It is impossible for me to regard the scorn of all rules as being equivalent to progressive, by which word we generally mean improvement. The true meaning of the word *progressus* is a going forward, but the end or object is not stated. There is such a thing as the progress of a disease, and this is anything but improvement.[29]

Such a profession of faith in the past, written a year after the death of Debussy, could no more be expected to find understanding or support than Saint-Saëns could be expected to appreciate Debussy's music.

> I suggest you take a look at *Noir et Blanc,* the piece for two pianos that Mr. Debussy has just published. It is *incredible* [underscored by Saint-Saëns], and a man capable of such atrocities must be barred from admission to the Institute at all costs. The piece belongs with the cubist paintings.[30]

Like the battle in Germany in the second half of the nineteenth century between the modernists, who rallied around Liszt and Wagner, and the followers of Schumann, a rift developed at the same time in France between the "wagnériens" of the Franck school and the classicists, who saw the future of music in Saint-Saëns and Fauré. Fauré more or less assumed the role of Brahms—which the French still ascribe to him today in the epithet "le Brahms français." He was one of the foremost defenders of the classic tradition and a presager of the interest in ancient mythology that flowered at the beginning of the twentieth century. As Saint-Saëns's pupil, Fauré must be regarded as his direct successor. It was Fauré who progressed logically from the harmonic language of his teacher to the close harmonies of the late Romantic period, which abound in enharmonics, yet are firmly based on tonality.

6

Folk and Oriental Elements

Nowhere was the influence of non-European cultures as strong as in France, where it can be traced back to Montesquieu's *Lettres persanes,* thought to have been written between 1717 and 1720, and the "chinoiseries" in eighteenth-century art.[1] In the nineteenth century, exoticisms were picked up by Eugène Delacroix, whose paintings inspired Baudelaire, in turn, and Victor Hugo, whose cycle of poems *Les Orientales* (1825–1828) was a great success.

In music, it was Félicien-César David who introduced Oriental elements with his 1844 symphonic ode *Le Désert* and employed them in most of his other works as well.[2] His comic opera *Lalla Roukh,* written in 1862, is an especially interesting example, since Robert Schumann had based his oratorio *Das Paradies und die Peri,* Op. 50 (1843), on the same text.

After David, musical exoticism was continued by Bizet with *Pêcheurs de Perles* (1863) and by Meyerbeer with *L'Africaine* (1864). Under Wagner's influence, the tradition became a blend of exoticism and symbolic mysticism, as manifested in Gustave Moreau's paintings and Ernest Reyer's *Salammbô,* which premiered in 1890.

French music received significant new impulses from the 1889 World Exposition, which left traces, especially in the works of Debussy and Ravel. The Hungarian gypsy bands and the Gamelan Orchestra of Java made a lasting impression on the young generation of composers. Musical exoticism in France finally came to an end with Albert Roussel and his opera *Padmâvatî* (1923), crowded out by a new trend that found expression in the "Groupe de Six" and Jean Cocteau. I might add that most of the composers mentioned here had come by exotic elements secondhand; they had never been in the countries whose sonorities they were trying to recreate.

Saint-Saëns lived through the entire development, from David right down to the decline of exoticism. Even in the pre-Romantic era he could have found enough to stimulate him if, for example, all he had cared about in Mozart's *Abduction from the Seraglio* was non-European sound.[3]

For Saint-Saëns, the music of the Orient was never just a device with which to fascinate audiences or else he would not have chosen a Far Eastern theme for *La Princesse jaune,* thus jeopardizing his attempt to gain a foothold in musical theater (see related discussion in Chapter 1). Rather, Oriental elements were essential to the form and content of his music. It would require exhaustive research, however, to substantiate and promote this idea, so it must be left for another time. The magnitude of the task is evidenced by a modern-day comment, which casts a totally false light on Saint-Saëns's Oriental elements: "It is not at all a matter of real assimilation of an art that was completely foreign to his way of thinking, but it is a superficial intellectual game."[4]

In addition to numerous vocal compositions—I will only mention *Samson et Dalila* and the song "Désir de l'Orient," which both date from the 1870s—several of Saint-Saëns's instrumental works contain Oriental elements (see Table 6.1). These works are all the more interesting in that the music came into existence without textual or contextual stimuli.

Table 6.1. Instrumental works by Saint-Saëns that contain Oriental elements.

Title of work	Date	Instruments
Orient et Occident, Op. 25	1896	Military band
Suite Algérienne, Op. 60	1880	Orchestra
Valse Canariote, Op. 88	1890	Piano
Africa, Op. 89	1891	Piano & orchestra
Caprice Arabe, Op. 96	1894	2 Pianos
Souvenir d'Ismaïlia, Op. 100	1895	Piano
Egyptien, Concerto No. V, Op. 103	1896	Piano & orchestra
Sur les bords du Nil, Op. 125	1908	Military band
Vision congolaise, second movement of the "Triptyque," Op. 136	1912	Violin & piano

In addition, we must take into account the instrumental works inspired by Iberian folk music, which Saint-Saëns came to know through Pablo de Sarasate (Table 6.2). Of course, this listing does not include influences that show up in works such as Op. 28 and 61/3.

Table 6.2. Instrumental works by Saint-Saëns inspired by Iberian folk music.

Title of work	Date	Instruments
Une Nuit à Lisbonne, Op. 63	1880	Orchestra
Jota Aragonese, Op. 64	1880	Orchestra
Havanaise, Op. 83	1887	Violin & orchestra
Caprice andalous, Op. 122	1904	Violin & orchestra

Forms such as the polonaise (Op. 77 for two pianos, 1886), the mazurka (Op. 21, 24, and 66 for piano, 1862, 1871, and 1882) and the tarantella (Op. 6, 1857 and Op. 22/3, 1868) were already firmly established in the art music of Saint-Saëns's day and were no longer characterized as foreign.

I should also mention a short composition for flute, oboe, clarinet, and piano, *Caprice sur des airs danois et russes* (Op. 79, 1887), although it is more like an occasional composition.

The distinctive feature of Oriental music is its linearity; harmony is disregarded as unimportant.[5] Therefore, a European analysis of this music is primarily concerned with rhythm and melody, and perhaps also with the choice of instruments. Since neither rhythm nor melody fit into European musical systems, the composer must either override them, perhaps with metric changes or accent shifts, or replace them with new tonal systems.

Several methods are found in Saint-Saëns's works. He almost always starts from the scale shown in Figure 6.1. This tonal system is different from that of the Javanese Gamelan music (see Figure 6.2), on which Ravel based later works, such as the suite *Ma mère l'oye* (III: "Laideronette, impératrice des pagodes") of 1908.[6]

Figure 6.1. Saint-Saëns's starting scale.

Figure 6.2. Javanese Gamelan scale.

At this point, let me interject a few general remarks about the phenomenon of exoticism in European—and in particular in French—art music of the late nineteenth and early twentieth centuries. Other than Félicien David, Camille Saint-Saëns was probably the only French composer of the Romantic period who could refer to authentic sources for the Oriental elements in his work. During his travels, especially to Algeria and Egypt, the composer devoted himself intensively to the study of North African folk music. He wrote down characteristic melodies and rhythms on the spot, as for instance in the sketch sheet to Op. 89 preserved in the Bibliothèque Nationale (MS. 916[10]). He also had friends send to him in Paris other material which they had heard in Algerian coffee houses.[7] In addition, he immersed himself in nature and the landscape. In Egypt he sketched out the "cri de la sauterelle (the chirping of the crickets)," which he used in Op. 103—a remarkable anticipation of the simulated bird calls in the music of Olivier Messiaen.[8]

Saint-Saëns was undoubtedly aware that in transposing original melodies into the Western music system—where notes must be confined to the diatonic scale, irregular rhythms rearranged as periodic rhythms, and finally the timbre changed to that of a traditional array of European instruments—he would compromise the authenticity significantly. The accusation that the character of this music had been distorted and estranged was never leveled against him, as it was later leveled by Albéniz and Granados against Bizet's *Carmen* and Pablo de Sarasate's *Danses espagnoles.* While this may have been due to a lack of competent advocates, surely there was also a recognition that Saint-Saëns was less concerned with a literal translation of Oriental music than with a free rendering, in which general characteristics are preserved, to convey a mood in the impressionistic sense.

There is another point worthy of mention. The scale favored by Saint-Saëns (Figure 6.1) bears a striking resemblance to the seventh (Mixolydian) church mode, just as the scale shown in Figure 6.3 corresponds to the first (Dorian) mode. It is beyond the scope of this study to show the relationship between the church modes and those classified as Oriental.[9] At any rate, one thing is certain: Saint-Saëns was aware of the relationship and saw a special charm in it.[10] The scale he favored accommodates neither the dominant seventh chord nor the triad of the subdominant; the tones lack the logical interrelation of Western systems; cadences and modulations are impossible as is the step to the subdominant.

Saint-Saëns often proceeds from the natural minor scale and modifies it as needed by sharping the sixth degree and thus arriving at the harmonic minor scale (Figure 6.3).

Figure 6.3. Saint-Saëns's harmonic minor scale.

In another place the minor third is sharped. This, together with the lack of leading tone and minor sixth, results in a distinctive sound akin to that of the scale shown in Figure 6.1. In Example 6.1, an accent shift links D major to G minor via its dominant.

Example 6.1. Saint-Saëns, Op. 89, m. 338ff.

The same scale that emerges there shows up again in Op. 103/2 (Example 6.2). It constitutes the main tonality of Op. 103/2 and appears

Example 6.2. Saint-Saëns, Op. 103/2, m. 48.

alternately with and without a flatted third. I was unable to determine who gave the work the epithet "Egyptien." It is certain not to have come from Saint-Saëns and is applicable only to the middle movement. It is primarily here that the composer recognized echoes of his Egyptian travel experiences and probably had the G major melody (m. 68ff.) in mind.[11]

At any rate, the Oriental allusions in Op. 89 are clearer and—as already evident in the title—absolutely intentional. Whereas the numerous sketches of Op. 103 contain no thematic references to Oriental folk melodies, except the "cri de la sauterelle" mentioned earlier, the composer noted separately several elements of Op. 89 and, among other things, left a fragment entitled "Danse des Almées," which appears again in Op. 89 (Example 6.3).

Example 6.3. Saint-Saëns, Op. 89, m. 154ff.

In addition to the composer's sketch sheet, there is another point which confirms the authenticity of this theme. Musicologist Julien Tiersot visited the great Paris Exposition of 1889 as an expert observer and reported on its musical aspect in an informative book.[12] The chapter on Arabian music contains a musical example which is reminiscent of Saint-Saëns's "Danse des Almées," especially in its rhythmic structure but also in its melody.[13] The example is taken from the "Danse de l'épée," a dance performed by an Algerian woman to the accompaniment of raita and darbukkas. Tiersot also designated this dance as belonging to the group of "Danses des Almées" (Example 6.4).

Example 6.4. "Danse de l'épée."

"Almée" denotes a "female Egyptian dancer whose lascivious performances are mixed with songs, often improvisatory in nature."[14] Thus, it is closely related to the art of belly dancing still cultivated today.

Saint-Saëns, who reported on the World Exposition, though more on the instruments than on the works heard, wrote his melody a few months later in North Africa (see discussion in Chapter 1). This melody is dated one year earlier than the date Bonnerot gives for the origin of Op. 89, the spring of 1891.[15] It must be assumed that Saint-Saëns resumed work on older material, as he had done before. We have already established that this was the case with Op. 44,[16] and there is also abundant sketch material for the first movement of Op. 103 that is dated exactly.[17] This touches on another problem, which will be discussed later in Chapter 7. At any rate, the accompaniment figure of "Danse des Almées" is also styled after Oriental music in timbre (oboe) and shape (Example 6.5).

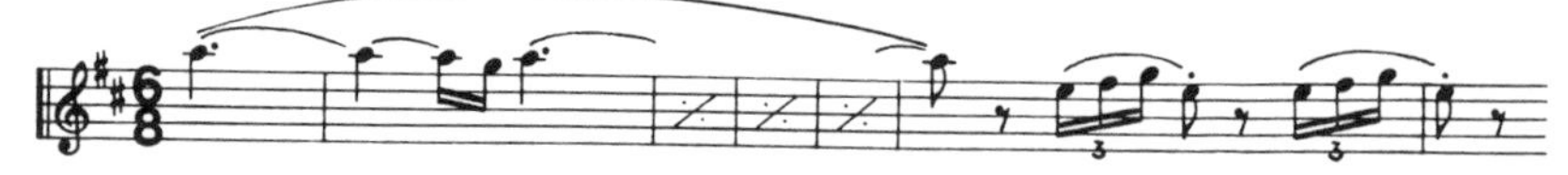

Example 6.5. Saint-Saëns, Op. 89, m. 157ff.

A distinguishing feature of Oriental rhythm is its nonperiodic sequence of stressed and unstressed beats—or at least it does not coincide with the periods of the melody. In the age of expressionism (Bartók, Stravinsky, Milhaud, etc.), it would have been no problem to change the time signature to fit the rhythmic structure, but toward the end of the nineteenth century, doing so would have made the performance of a work much more difficult. So Saint-Saëns fell back on the simple device of accent shifting, which does not break the basic meter (Example 6.6).

Example 6.6. Saint-Saëns, Op. 89, m. 2ff.

This device can be shown another way (see Example 6.7). In this example, accent shifting results in a sequence of 2 + 3 + 2 + 2 + 3 eighths, the whole of which forms a period and fits into a 6/8 meter. The effect is similar with the dotted quarters that accompany Example 6.3, which set 3/4 time opposite 6/8 time.

Example 6.7. Saint-Saëns, Op. 89, m. 2ff.

The following passage (Example 6.8) also gets a special rhythmic charm from timpani accents and pizzicato in the basses. Though this melody moves only in the range of an augmented fourth, the scale on which it is based gets its Oriental coloring from the flatted fifth, which causes the tonality to vacillate between B minor and D minor (Figure 6.4).

Example 6.8. Saint-Saëns, Op. 89, m. 444ff.

Figure 6.4. Scale used in Saint-Saëns, Op. 89, m. 444ff.

In summary it can be said that the composer had a clever way of working Oriental elements into European systems without changing the latter. The same goes for his choice of instruments. Though entirely traditional, it awakens an impression of the exotic.

> The hard and somber timbres of Arab instruments, the rumble of the tympani can be heard even through the sonorities of the piano. The descriptive intention prevails over lyricism.[18]

The composer may also have regarded the nasal sound of the oboe as an especially suitable timbre. The "Bacchanale" from *Samson et Dalila,* which actually begins with an elaborate solo cadenza, and Op. 89 both contain many solo oboe passages which do in fact convey an Oriental coloring. Saint-Saëns was certainly also familiar with the Arabian oboelike raita, one of the typical musical instruments of the Near East.[19]

Even more prevalent than the exoticisms were the Hispanic influences in the works of numerous composers in nineteenth-century France. Although Bizet's *Carmen* was still rejected by critics and audiences in 1875 because of its bold harmonies, audience tastes took a sudden turn with Pablo de Sarasate and found more and more appeal in Iberian folk music, which, of course, Sarasate knew just how to present in the appropriate "salon style."

The three most prominent Spanish composers at the turn of the century—Isaac Albéniz, Enrique Granados, and Manuel de Falla—were active in Paris for many years and brought a corresponding influence to bear on the music world there. The World Exposition of 1889 was an added factor. Albéniz must be regarded as the real founder of a Spanish national style and, understandably, he strongly opposed the Romantic salon pieces in which Spanish characteristics were distorted and misrepresented. Most often reproached for these "españoladas" were works by Glinka, Bizet, Rimsky-Korsakov, Chabrier, Sarasate, and Saint-Saëns.[20]

Then, in the first decade of the twentieth century, the French music world experienced a veritable glut of Spanish-style compositions. Leading the way was Debussy, with his *Estampes* (1903), whose middle movement is entitled "La soirée dans Grenade," and "Ibéria," the second part of his *Images* for orchestra (1907). Ravel followed suit with his *Rapsodie espagnole* (1908) and his first opera, *L'Heure espagnole* (1911). Massenet's *Don Quichotte* (1910) was a failed attempt to keep the Romantic "españoladas" alive in the new century.

Saint-Saëns, who witnessed this development, had already defended Bizet's *Carmen* against the critics' attacks, and he correctly attributed its failure to a general "crise théâtrale."[21] However, like Edouard Lalo, he would hardly have thought of enriching his own music with Spanish coloring, were it not for his acquaintance with Sarasate. One would think that the Moorish influence, with which Spanish culture is permeated, must have had a spontaneous appeal for him.[22]

The barcarole rhythm of Op. 63 obviously does not fit the title *Une Nuit à Lisbonne,* and the *Jota Aragonese,* Op. 64, composed around the same time, must be regarded merely as an orchestration of the famous theme—it is not an original composition like those of Glinka and Liszt. Both Saint-Saëns pieces owe their origin to the tour that he took through Spain and Portugal in the fall of 1880.[23]

As early as the late 1830s, Alkan, who was always receptive to extraordinary musical experiments, had written a "Zorcico" [zortziko] for piano, and in ignorance of its Basque origins, he called it "danse ibérienne." Later Albéniz (*Ibéria,* 1906) and Gabriel Pierné (piano quintet, 1919) fell back on this dance form, which was frequently confused with the habanera.[24] At any rate, Alkan must be regarded as the one who introduced the Iberian influence into French music.

Bizet was obviously not aware of the origin of the habanera when he labeled the famous scene in *Carmen* as "imitée d'une chanson espagnole." His referral was to the collection *Fleurs d'Espagne* by Sebastian de Yradier, composer of *La Paloma,* which had been published in Paris in 1864.

The Cuban dance, whose rhythmic pattern (Figure 6.5) is similar to

Figure 6.5. Rhythmic pattern in Cuban dance.

that of the South American tango, is also the basis for Saint-Saëns's Op. 83. It is worth noting that Tiersot discovered this rhythmic pattern in the Algerian music of the Aissaouas.[25] It is also interesting to compare the two basic elements of Op. 83, the rhythmic (Figure 6.6) and the

Figure 6.6. Rhythmic pattern in Op. 83.

melodic, the thematic nucleus (Figure 6.7) with the "Tango," the fourth movement of the song cycle *Lola,* Op. 116 (1900), in which almost the same structures turn up (Example 6.9).

Figure 6.7. Melodic pattern in Op. 83.

Example 6.9. Saint-Saëns, Op. 116/IV, m. 5ff.

No one is certain about the thematic-rhythmic sources for Op. 122. Contemporary critics also sensed that the work was not necessarily folkloric (see discussion in Chapter 1). The title may refer more to the general character of the piece than to specific adaptations.

There are also passages of Hispanic character in Op. 61 and Op. 28.

This is confirmed by the fact that the two works were written while the composer was in Spain and that both are dedicated to Sarasate and could contain "españoladas" as a sort of tribute to his friend's homeland.[26]

The allure of foreign lands somewhat inhibited interest in indigenous folk music in France, at a time when it was being fostered in Germany, for example, by Brahms. In addition to the "trois rapsodies sur des cantiques bretons" for organ, Op. 7 (1866), the fruits of a trip to Brittany, one of Saint-Saëns's most significant works is the *Rapsodie d'Auvergne,* Op. 73.[27] It is interesting that the composer chose the free form of the rhapsody for both works, just as Charles Bordes did later for his *Rhapsodie basque* (1900). Vincent d'Indy, who is often credited as the originator of an art music inspired by French folklore, did not commit himself to this trend until later (Op. 31, 1888, and Op. 25, 1895), after Wagner's influence on his music had faded.[28] His a capella choral arrangements of folk songs (Op. 82, 90, and 100), which are comparable to Brahms's efforts, and his editions of other folk songs (Op. 52 and an unnumbered opus) were generated beginning in the last decade of the nineteenth century and continuing into the 1930s.

Of course, it can hardly be assumed that Saint-Saëns conceived his Op. 73 with a view to music history or musicology. For him—and this can be said in summary about all folk and Oriental elements in his music—the source material was only the basis for a composition. We have already established that for Saint-Saëns a melody was only a cell in the broader development, not a musical entity in itself. Thus, his folk themes are also to be understood only as seeds of the resulting compositions.

7

Camille Saint-Saëns's Personality, Aesthetics, and Approach to Composition

Before delving further into Saint-Saëns's position and significance in nineteenth-century French music, I think it would be interesting, and perhaps necessary, to go beyond mere analysis of his concertante works to interpret them as an expression of his personality and aesthetic sense, and to describe the composer's creative process, insofar as it can be reconstructed. To this end, I have evaluated first the composer's letters preserved at the Bibliothèque Nationale in Paris and the Bibliothèque Municipale in Dieppe, as well as numerous documents from my private collection and that of Yves Gérard; next, the composer's journalistic, academic, and philosophical essays; and finally, to elucidate his approach to composition, the sketches of his concertos and concertante works, which are cited in Appendix A.

First, we recall the tragic deaths of his sons and the separation from his wife, which brought about a decided change in his nature (see Chapter 1). From earliest childhood, Saint-Saëns was reserved and wary of the outside world, probably in part because of his mother's warnings not to take compliments at their face value.[1] Friends his own age, such as

Georges Bizet and Alexis de Castillon, in whom he might have confided, died young. The only exception was Gabriel Fauré, with whom he enjoyed a warm, lifelong friendship. Saint-Saëns regarded his older friends—Hector Berlioz, Charles Gounod, and Gioacchino Rossini—more as patrons and kept a certain distance for the most part.

Following the events of 1878 [the deaths of his sons and the separation from his wife], the composer was even more reluctant to reveal his inner self. A comparison of his letters prior to 1878 with those of his last decades reveals an increased reticence, which he seldom let go, even with Fauré. Saint-Saëns saw the social obligations imposed on him by his position in the Paris music world as an ever-growing burden. When he finally broke up his household, he increasingly took refuge in foreign lands. If the composer had once hoped to find in his family life an escape from the numerous concert engagements and tours, his restlessness was now manifested in frequent changes of residence and countless foreign sojourns.

Several anecdotes furthered the impression that Saint-Saëns was an embittered, spiteful cynic, and his appearance in public tended to confirm this picture. "The audience . . . sees him . . . at the piano, his Assyrian profile fixed against the curtained backdrop; it also sees him at the moment of the applause, expressing his thanks almost mechanically."[2]

Actually, there was nothing the composer hated so much as the interest in him as a person. Once he opened himself to more intimate acquaintance, however, he revealed another side. He could be relaxed, amusing, and congenial. Yet through it all, a certain superficiality remained. Even Jean Bonnerot, the composer's private secretary for many years and later his biographer, confirms: "The work of the artist is all that counts. It explains and contains his whole life for that matter and seems to absorb him to the point that the one becomes commingled with the other."[3] However, none of Saint-Saëns's works can be considered an autobiographical document, as is the case of Hector Berlioz. The influence of external events is present only latently. Music serves not as a means for self-expression or self-mastery, but as a manifesto of aesthetic maxims that issue from the biographical field but do not place it in the forefront.

Naturally the change of 1878 also left musical traces. The second period, which in the sequence of his concertante compositions begins with Op. 61, differs from the preceding period in several fundamental points. Whereas the composer's first four piano concertos were written in less than two decades, between 1858 (Op. 17) and 1875 (Op. 44), nearly a quarter century lies between the fourth and fifth (Op. 103).

We know the chronological high points of certain genres for Mozart. Most of his violin concertos were written in 1775, his horn concertos between 1782 and 1786, and his great string quintets all in the last decade of his life. Similar periods of concentration can be established for Saint-Saëns. The three sonatas for winds (Op. 166–168) were written in the last year of his life. Then there is the proximity of the First Cello Sonata (Op. 32) to the First Concerto (Op. 33), which is repeated some 30 years later with the two second representatives of these genres (Op. 123 and 119).

The long time lapse between Op. 44 and Op. 103 is paralleled by a reduction in the virtuoso element, that necessary accessory to crowd-pleasing concertos. Op. 103 uses complexity of performance technique only marginally, for color, and not as an end in itself, as was sometimes the case in Saint-Saëns's earlier works. Virtuosity appears for the last time in abstracted form, so to speak, in his étude cycles, Op. 111 (1899) and 135 (1912). Also, the works with traces of Oriental or folk elements were almost all written after 1878.

The dualism of content and form was a lifelong problem and concern for Saint-Saëns. It found expression in his vacillation between imitative interpretation—that is, performance, and productive compositions—as well as in the corresponding change of balance between outward effect and inner substance. His striving for the ideal structure—one that has a strong influence on the musical material—is especially evident in his concertos. In the course of time, traditional form (Op. 58) had come to lack suitable content. As a composer, Saint-Saëns faced the task of either creating new forms appropriate for contemporary content—these include the Morceau de Concert and the two-part form consisting of introduction and main movement—or retaining the old form and giving it new meaning. He chose the second, decidedly more difficult way, which led modern critics to accuse him of epigonism.

Although Saint-Saëns always professed allegiance to traditional classic forms, his understanding of the term "form" was considerably broader.[4] For him there could be no other representation of musical thought than the one presented in a clearly defined formal framework. Curiously, he was in full agreement with his antipode Debussy in this regard. Especially in his later years, Debussy repeatedly advocated greater attention to musical form, which alone allowed freedom of musical development. Like Saint-Saëns, he only opposed

> blind acceptance of every art form. If after about 100 measures one no longer knows for sure what is going on, then the audience, or those who have it well in hand, are ready and willing to cheer the genius.[5]

Because a listener always "knew what was going on" with Saint-Saëns, the composer was accused of being a stuffy academic. The unconditional adherence to a framework, which determined nearly all his works, is certainly an eclectic position. For Saint-Saëns, form is synonymous with symmetry, and in this sense springs more from an ancient ideal than from a classic one. On the other hand, the idea of symmetry is consistent with his striving for balance or equilibrium. Of course, an impression of disproportion is certainly possible, as in the middle movement of Op. 17. Here the symmetry of the cadenza's 33 units is composed of 12 + 21 segments in one place and 2 + 31 segments in the other. It would be valid to question whether the symmetries shown in Sections 2.3 (which see) and 5.3 were actually intentional and planned, if their cumulative number did not prove that Saint-Saëns used them consciously.

If symmetry is understood as an aesthetic concept, then one cannot help but compare it to ancient architecture, which Saint-Saëns studied intensively. In his "Note sur les Décors de Théâtre dans l'Antiquité romaine," the composer refers to the apparent disproportionality of Pompeian pillars,

> these structures that seem to defy the laws of balance, these slender columns that are so far from the norm in their small diameter and excessive length and remind us of the small columns surrounding the pillars of our Gothic cathedrals.[6]

Saint-Saëns then presents a curious hypothesis that can easily be carried over to the structures of his concertos: Viewed individually, these pillars are indeed disproportional. However, as part of the overall architectural structure, and especially through the combined effect of load-bearing (vertical) and decorative, ornamental (horizontal) elements, they have a general symmetry that overrides the particular. To the beholder of Pompeian architecture as to the listener of one of Saint-Saëns's concertos, the basic structural principle can be conveyed only through the overall impression.

Saint-Saëns's intellect insisted on the form acknowledged as ideal, and he arranged the musical material within these limits. Again and again he tried to combine the two planes: The formal frame seldom corresponds to the arrangement of the substantial elements, so the result is a kind of counterpoint between content and form.

Most composers began with a clearly defined form and in the course of their artistic maturation arrived at a personal form that set new standards. Saint-Saëns did the reverse. He distilled the formal framework of his works to the point of eliminating all nonessentials, much as Brahms did in his Fourth Symphony. Thus, both were able to develop a specific musical idea grounded in absolute clarity of structure.

The question arises as to whether Saint-Saëns's aesthetic principles are classicistic in the emulative sense, or classic—that is, perfected ideas of an original nature. The answer is found in his views on ancient and humanistic principles, which he always presents in conjunction with contemporary theories. For him art is not a temporal phenomenon but a value transcending human development, which must continually be redefined. Analogies and overlaps seem to be the natural result of his persistent striving for perfection. Saint-Saëns saw himself as the preserver of a tradition that had produced valid works long before Mozart and that was not invented in the Classic period but merely defined.

Saint-Saëns's interpretation of the concertante concept, which he traces back to Bach and Handel, led him to a totally original redefinition based on three principles. First, solo and orchestra must be treated as equal and mutually complementary partners, with neither individual entity subordinate to the other. Second, in the course of the concertante work, dramatic tension in scope, structuring, and character must be created; it can be laid around the musical content as an ideal frame. Finally, the content in its basic form must always follow a consistent, clearly recognizable line, which is never obscured by ornamentation or superficial effects.

While the Romantic view of art gradually declined in importance, Saint-Saëns, with these requirements, bridged the way to a new century in which musical aesthetics realized and continued to develop this very clarity. His position in the nineteenth century is definitely Classic, and references to traditional ideas are only references, nothing more.

A few statements and their interpretations by Saint-Saëns's contemporaries have given rise to the assumption that the composer's compositions were mainly the fruit of spontaneous inspiration.[7] The often-quoted remark that he creates "as naturally as a tree produces apples" seems to confirm this assumption.[8] How little this is borne out in reality, however, is evident from his sketches. We must rely on these alone in describing his approach to composition, since personal statements from Saint-Saëns about his work are as rare as they are uninformative.

The fact that the composer often let long periods of time elapse between the initial idea and its ultimate realization is illustrated by MS. 909, the symphonic sketch to Op. 44, which has already been mentioned several times in the course of this study. Even works of a specific coloring, such as Op. 89 and 103, which seem to owe their origins to actual travel experiences in northern Africa, are the fruits of longer planning, independent of location, as evidenced in sketches recorded years before the two compositions were completed. Some of these sketches were only later dated by the composer and assigned to the corresponding works, which proves that their ultimate use had not yet been determined at the time they were written.

In this connection, it is interesting to note that Saint-Saëns often subjected his sketch material to major revisions. For instance, in the manuscript of the previously mentioned *Danse des Almées,* we find another sketch (Example 7.1), which was later used in Op. 89, but in a different key and new rhythmic form (Example 7.2).

Example 7.1. Saint-Saëns, MS. 916[10] (Bibliothèque Nationale, Paris)

Example 7.2. Saint-Saëns, Op. 89, m. 84ff.

Further, the often-mentioned allegation that Saint-Saëns borrowed from one of Fauré's works for the main theme of his Op. 22 was interpreted as a sign that he composed spontaneously.[9] Meanwhile, it has been determined that Op. 22 was not written in only two weeks, as was long thought. Granted, the actual notation only took Saint-Saëns 17 days, but he had already been planning the work for several months.[10]

In summary it can be said that Camille Saint-Saëns did not compose as effortlessly as many of his contemporaries claimed he did. Out of one or more thematic and, as such, secondary ideas, he developed basic musical material and assigned it to a formal concept. The latter represents an ideal, clearly proportioned frame for a development of content that is fundamentally determined by it. The composer's striving for this ideal form can be regarded as basic to his personality as an artist and as a human being. The form, in turn, represents not a personal aesthetic manifesto but one with general validity.

The French Solo Concerto in Saint-Saëns's Time

8

Historical Background

As stated in the Introduction, the preceding analysis is only meant to serve as a basis for the following examination of Saint-Saëns's position and significance in the history of the French solo concerto. The comparison of his concertante works with those of his French contemporaries is based on a thorough study of several hundred compositions, which are compiled in tabular form in Appendix B. To undertake this examination of Saint-Saëns's concertante works, we must first try briefly to visualize the development of the French solo concerto—or more accurately, the solo concerto in France—up to the middle of the nineteenth century.

The birthplace of the instrumental concerto was Italy, where it developed from the concerto grosso. The concertante works of Vivaldi and his predecessors and successors are the actual source of European concertante music. Joseph Bodin Sieur de Boismortier, in his *Six Concerts pour cinq Flûtes traversières sans basse,* Op. 15, also oriented himself to the Italian model[1]. This 1727 work is the earliest document of the French solo concerto which Jean Marie Leclair perfected and enriched in the virtuoso style of Locatelli and Tartini.[2] Thus, in French music, the soloist stood also in the limelight, whereas the Italian tradition in Germany, especially as it was continued by J. S. Bach, neglected the virtuoso element in favor of formal development. The form and character of concertante compositions changed around the middle of the eighteenth century. Sonata form emerged and was thereafter frequently chosen for the first movement of solo concertos as well.

There arose a new type of concerto, which "is created by an artist who wants to be the focal point of an aesthetically perceptive society."[3] This led to an especially rapid development in France, which can be clearly traced in the concertante violin style. The Paris-based Italian violinist and composer Jean-Pierre Guignon still followed the tradition of Tartini, combining lyric cantilenas with virtuoso passages. His successes were surpassed by those of Pierre Gaviniés. Composers such as Barthélémon, Emmanuel Guérin, Jean-Jacques Grasset, the Chevalier de Saint-Georges, and Simon le Duc l'aîné also represented the style coined in Italy.

Another Italian brought about the change: Paris- and London-based Giovanni Battista Viotti, in collaboration with Rodolphe Kreutzer and Pierre Rode, created a formal prototype that was valid far into the nineteenth century, and not only for the violin concerto. Even Johannes Brahms expressed his view:

> The A Minor Concerto by Viotti is my special passion. . . . It is a splendid specimen, strangely free in its invention. It sounds as though he is improvising, yet everything is masterfully conceived and wrought.[4]

While Louis Spohr and others were influenced in their violin concertos by Rode, the violin style of Niccolò Paganini, which was prominent in France, is directly traceable to Viotti. In the early decades of the nineteenth century, Paganini developed the technical capabilities of his instrument to an enormous extent, using the formal foundation of his predecessor.

Paganini's concertos already show clearly the conflict that was affecting the concerto form more and more. Whereas efforts to balance form and substance were still perceptible in Viotti's works, Paganini brought the solo part sharply to the fore, thus robbing the concertante idea of its true meaning, aside from the neglect of the orchestra mentioned earlier (see Section 3.1). There was no longer any relationship between the development of form and performance technique.

Pierre Baillot and Charles Auguste de Bériot continued Paganini's style but called for a return to the dualism of virtuosity and lyricism which Viotti had fostered. "It is the province of genius to create new effects, of taste to determine their use, and of time alone to sanction them."[5]

It was also de Bériot who taught the young Henri Vieuxtemps and helped the 10-year-old boy make his Paris debut. As a composition pupil of Simon Sechter and Anton Reicha, Vieuxtemps acquired a solid foundation for his own work, which audiences received enthusiastically beginning in 1836. When he went to St. Petersburg in 1846 as violin soloist at the court of Czar Nicholas I, he was considered the leader of the new French violin school. He became an instructor at the Brussels Conservatory in 1871 and together with Hubert Léonard, Lambert Joseph Massart, and Jehain Prume founded the Ecole Liégoise. The school's main feature was a lyricism whereby even technically complex solo passages sounded smooth and euphonious, because the theme was kept vocal throughout and therefore easy to grasp.

Léonard, one of the first "wagnériens" of the Belgian Romantic period, found a worthy successor in his pupil Eugène Ysaye. Like César Franck, Léonard was decisively influenced by German music; he was one of the first to play works by Brahms and Schumann in France, and Lalo and Saint-Saëns were also part of his repertoire. By no means do his own compositions represent mere "academic neoclassicism."[6] Rather, he broke away from the strictness of his predecessors, particularly in regard to form, albeit more unconsciously than intentionally. In an effort to give maximum prominence to the solo part, he adjusted the Classic proportions to favor the violin and consequently was forced to let the traditional form become more and more blurred.

The circle that formed around the Ecole Liégoise in Belgium also included the violin virtuosos and composers Snel, Servais, de Bellaire, Jacques Dupuis, Colyns, Leenders, and the Singelée brothers.[7] Delphin Alard and Charles Dancla in France were under their influence.[8] In their works they exhibited a "dramatic element fostered by grand opera."[9] Saint-Saëns, in his Op. 58, also oriented himself directly to the concerto model of the Franco-Belgian school, and until his acquaintance with Sarasate, he regarded it as binding.[10]

The development of concertos for keyboard instruments was definitively influenced by the sons of Bach, especially Johann Christian, Mozart's model. One of the earliest representatives of the Mozartean concerto style was Ignaz (Ignace) Pleyel, an Austrian. In addition to a Piano Concerto in C Major, he also wrote a violin concerto, two concertos for viola, and two for cello.[11] His son Camille and the latter's wife, Marie Félicité Denise, one of the best female pianists of her day, were part of the circle that formed around Chopin, Liszt, Kalkbrenner, Moscheles, and Herz in the middle of the nineteenth century. John Field, a composer highly esteemed by Robert Schumann, developed a new dramatically enriched and romantically styled concerto form, which was continued and perfected by Herz and Chopin.

Henri Litolff was one of the first to try expanding the Classic form. His symphonic concertos, all of which were in four movements, were especially influential on Franz Liszt. "In linking several movements thematically and drawing them together into one movement, Liszt arrived at a new concerto form."[12] His successors in France included Auguste Dupont, Edouard Lalo, Alphonse Duvernoy, Cécile Chaminade, Fernand de la Tombelle, Pierre Douillet, Léon Delafosse, Léon Moreau, and Raoul Pugno.[13] These composers certainly did not just write concertos that pandered to "salon tastes."[14] The most important composer in the Liszt tradition is unquestionably Saint-Saëns.

Before we deal in more detail with conditions in Paris around the middle of the nineteenth century, I should point out something unusual about the development just described. The French solo concerto was molded primarily by foreign composers; only later did it find emulators at home. It was not only in the instrumental realm that French music underwent a long struggle for national autonomy. Not until the turn of the century were the influences of the Italian composers and later Richard Wagner and the Russian school finally overcome.

To understand conditions and opportunities particular to the French music world, one must bear in mind that from about the time of the great revolution all cultural activity was concentrated in the capital city. "From its central position in the world of art, Paris provided French music with all its developmental impetus. In the course of the nineteenth century, centralization spread to all areas, to theater, concerts, music education, and the dissemination of music."[15] The Napoleonic era brought a flowering of the city itself, so that Paris became not only an intellectual center, but also an architectural and business center for Europe.

The prerevolutionary rift between the nobility and the middle class, which had largely disappeared in the last decade of the eighteenth century, was now showing up again, though not nearly as sharply as before. This situation is significant in that it remained even after the fall of Napoleon and lasted through the subsequent transition from the

Republic to the Third Empire. To be sure, there were no more hereditary rights, and impoverished nobles were just as numerous as the middle-class families who had worked their way into the upper social stratum. But in the artistic realm, a different kind of split was taking place. On one hand, the "Bohemian" artistic circles came to be the stronghold of an avant-garde trend in literature, music, and the fine arts. In contrast, a more elitist art style was cultivated in the salons. Of course the middle class, to whom the salon was inaccessible and the Bohème suspicious, was looking for a field of art that was accessible, comprehensible, and attractive. Fortunately Italian opera had secured a firm foothold in Paris. With its catchy melodies and romantic subjects, it became the ideal object of cultural interest for the middle class.

While the Italians—Bellini, Donizetti, and Rossini, to name only the most prominent—reigned in music theater, countless other foreign musicians, especially those with a virtuoso bent, found appreciative audiences in the salons and concert halls. Their activities were fully oriented to popular taste, as evidenced by the enormous number of paraphrases, potpourris, and fantasias on "airs favoris" of the operas that were in vogue in Paris.

The public, for whom the music of the eighteenth century already lay in the remote past, counted anything indigenous to Paris as a cultural asset of the nation. Since there had been no "Classic period" in France such as that in Austria or Germany, the French public perceived the operas of the Italian masters as Classic and even saw French music in the epigones of the lyric bel canto style such as Halévy. Then Giacomo Meyerbeer, whom they proudly called "notre Meyerbeer," established the grand opera in the 1830s, with his *Crociato* and *Robert le Diable*. It soon reached an absolute low with Ambroise Thomas.[16] Meyerbeer's recipe for success was a conglomeration of styles, "and never was music made in France any worse or more un-French than during his time."[17] Saint-Saëns began his artistic career during these years, before Charles Gounod had created an original French form with the drame lyrique, and set Meyerbeer's throne tottering.

Two musical genres were virtually forgotten in France at that time, since they had not proven successful in the concert hall, in the salon, or at the opera. Chamber music was certainly "a genre to which French musicians have paid little attention thus far."[18] Even Franck had to identify his three piano trios, Op. 1, as "Trios concertants" or "Trios de

Salon," in order to establish a foothold with them in Paris.[19] Virtuosity was not appropriate for chamber music but was accepted as soon as someone took themes from popular operas and paraphrased them, as Chopin did in the *Grand Duo concertant sur des thèmes de* "Robert le Diable," which he composed in collaboration with cellist Albert Franchomme.

Like chamber music, the concertos and concertante works of the French Romantic period were largely neglected insofar as they did not promise success to famous soloists as virtuoso showpieces. All the more admirable are the efforts of Litolff, who was the first to strive for a combination of virtuosity and strict form. Other less fortunate composers paid the price of their fight for musical substance by forfeiting fame and success. An extreme case was Alkan, who had grown weary of the contemporary music world and withdrew from everything and everyone for the rest of his life to work in the enclave of his own four walls.

Thus, it is understandable that Camille Saint-Saëns, with his 29 concertos and concertante works, did not have an easy time of it. Though he was the genre's first master of international standing to come out of France, his significance for the French solo concerto is underestimated to this day.[20] This is largely because of all his works, those that tended to reflect contemporary taste—Op. 28, 22, 61, and 83—still are audience favorites. On the other hand Op. 44 and 33 appear less often in contemporary concert programs, even in France. This lopsided picture will soon be corrected by the renaissance that is now underway; recordings of nearly all his concertante works (Op. 27 and 162 excepted) are already on the market.

9

The French Solo Concerto from 1850 to 1873 (from Op. 6 to Op. 33)

> Concessions to the general public's taste, which we encountered several times in Saint-Saëns's operas, are not an issue in the field of concert and chamber music. It is here that he reveals himself most eminently, most naturally and most nobly.[1]

First of all, this was all the easier when "concert music" per se did not reflect popular taste. If we look at the concertante compositions of the period from 1850 to 1856—that is, before Saint-Saëns's Op. 6—we are immediately struck by the predominance of the Ecole Liégoise and its followers.[2]

Certainly Litolff was represented, with his Fourth Concerto symphonique in D Minor, Op. 102, whose scherzo became more famous than all his other works. However, his heyday had long since passed. His last Concerto symphonique in E-flat Major, Op. 45, in which he used the Dutch national melody, "Wien Neerlands bloed door d'aderen vloeit," was written many years earlier. Liszt, once inspired by Litolff, had far surpassed him in success.[3] Yet this very Op. 102 was highly praised by Berlioz, and even Saint-Saëns must "have known [it] very well, for the entire piano layout and melodic format is very close to the work [reference is probably to Op. 44] of the later French composer."[4]

Léon Gastinel, on the other hand, had appeared in public primarily as author of dramatic theatrical and choral works. Nearly all his instrumental works, including the double concerto for two violins, remained unpublished. This work, like the others, is also of no importance; in form and style it is more like a late-Classic sinfonia concertante than a concerto. Offenbach's cello concertino is a virtuoso lyrical salon piece at best. The fact that Schumann's last two concertos were written during the same period says enough about the concertante music of France at that time.

Far from having found a personal style with his Op. 6, the 22-year-old Saint-Saëns was still very much under the influence of Rossini. This is evident not only in the form of the tarantella, but also in the history of the premiere performance of the piece.[5] Charles Henri Valentin Alkan's Concerto for Piano without Orchestra was written in the same year, 1857, as part of the monumental cycle Op. 39 *Douze études dans les tons mineurs.* It is not only far more interesting, but in its eccentric style is probably the most fascinating French solo concerto of its day—insofar as this genre label is at all appropriate here.

Delphin Alard (spelled Allard in other sources), a link between Paganini and Vieuxtemps, shows a tendency similar to Gastinel's in his symphonies concertantes. Here the Baroque technique of concertino and ritornello is taken up again, but the solo parts are rather unoriginal. Played in ensemble, they exhibit mainly figuration; there are no cadenzas of virtuoso caliber.

Just how strong an influence the Ecole Liégoise was at that time can be seen in Saint-Saëns's Op. 58. The "goût italien alors persistant" that characterized the work was being successfully proclaimed by Vieuxtemps and his circle. This style was the most obvious model for a young composer who wanted to try his hand at the violin concerto form.[6]

Unfortunately, neither Saint-Saëns's letters and sketches nor his biographers offer any clue as to the occasion for the composition. The fact that Op. 58 bears no dedication, an extremely rare circumstance for the composer, suggests that he himself regarded it more as a study than as a serious composition intended for the public.[7] Saint-Saëns was far from becoming addicted to the "vanity and thirst for glory of the composer-virtuosos" of his time.[8] It is a sign of his sense of artistic responsibility and healthy self-image that he withheld this work from publication for more than 20 years.

In 1858 Henri Herz also belonged to a bygone age. His gigantic Fourth Concerto for Piano, Choir, and Orchestra, Op. 192, in which the influence of Beethoven (Op. 80) shows up markedly, and whose scoring is an amazing anticipation of Busoni's 1906 piano concerto, passed by the public of his day almost unnoticed. Herz and Kalkbrenner had been the two most celebrated pianists in Paris before the days of Chopin and Liszt. When his star began to wane, Herz decided to move to the United States in 1846, where he became renowned in the salons just as he had been in Paris.[9]

Herz's Op. 192 is a tragic attempt to repeat successes of the distant past. It was bound to fail, if only for its extravagant demands. The composer calls for an enormous array of brass players but does not know how to employ them skillfully. The result is countless doublings which contribute to the volume but not the color of the work. Furthermore, the pianist is forced to let the orchestra have acoustic predominance for long stretches, especially in the finale, since it is virtually impossible for a soloist to hold his or her own against the orchestra.

Audiences since the first decades of the nineteenth century had also changed.

> Given the basic assumption that a concert involves both performers and an (often not well-educated) audience, the superficiality of musical taste can easily be accounted for, even among the composers, who, unlike in the days of royal patronage, now feel compelled by hard economic necessity to produce music for popular taste."[10]

Brahms, who wrote his first piano concerto around this same time, would surely have agreed with his mentor Schumann's opinion of Herz: "What does he want but to entertain and get rich in the bargain?[11]

Baumann sees a direct line of development for the concertante form from Mozart and Beethoven, through Mendelssohn, Schumann, Liszt, and Rubinstein, to Saint-Saëns.[12] Of course, there is one factor not mentioned in this list which may have influenced Saint-Saëns more than any others. Without Berlioz's *Treatise on Instrumentation,* he would hardly have attained that mastery and facility with the orchestra that distinguish his concertos. He also had Berlioz to thank for acquainting him with Gluck, which influenced his Classic thought and perception considerably.[13]

Several experiences converge in Saint-Saëns's Op. 17: on the one hand, the composer's own previous symphonies (see discussion in Section 2.1), and on the other, Litolff's concept of the symphonic concerto and Liszt's continuation of it. The result was not entirely successful, possibly because a third influence was present that could not be reconciled with the others: that of Beethoven. Here again, Saint-Saëns showed farsightedness in withholding Op. 17 until 1875.[14]

One of the earliest examples of the slow introduction to a solo concerto is the eight-measure maestoso deciso of the Oboe Concerto in E-flat Major by Vincenzo Bellini. Since it was not published until 1961, it is unlikely that Saint-Saëns even knew of this work, much less that he was influenced by it.[15]

Georges Pfeiffer, with his First Piano Concerto, Op. 11, is still very much in the tradition of the great virtuosos, from which he was never able to free himself completely.[16] He collaborated closely with the firm Pleyel-Wolff.[17] Like Litolff and Herz, he belonged to a school of the past, although he was only 24 years old when he wrote his Op. 11. Without being developed, the thematic material of this work appears in ever new and brilliant form. His other concertos from the period up to 1863 are also still influenced by the style of the Ecole Liégoise.

Adrien-François Servais, successful as a cellist and composer, was associated with Saint-Saëns through his [Belgian] compatriot Auguste Tolbecque.[18] It was Tolbecque who gave the premiere performance of Saint-Saëns's Op. 33, which was dedicated to Servais. The *Concerto militaire,* Op. 19—a First Cello Concerto, Op. 5, had been written a few years earlier—illustrates Servais's tendency toward a dramatic-programmatic style, as championed by Liszt and the new German school.

It is quite possible, however, that Servais was also influenced by the *Concerto militaire* in C Major for flute and orchestra by the Paris-based Italian Luigi Gianella. The highly virtuosic solo part of his two-movement concerto has its counterpart in Servais's breakneck cello passages. Servais's *Grande fantaisie,* Op. 20, whose subtitle *Souvenir de Bade* seems to refer to a concert tour, is little more than clever background for a tour de force of performance technique; almost without exception, the orchestra clings to repeated stereotypical accompaniment figures. As a virtuoso, Servais must have been astounding, and Berlioz may have meant his composition as well when he pronounced him the "Paganini du violoncelle."[19] At any rate, in both Op. 18 and Op. 20 Paganini's influence can also be recognized in the orchestration.

The Spanish violin virtuoso Pablo de Sarasate was 12 years old when he entered Delphin Alard's class at the Paris Conservatory in 1856. No other violinist influenced French music as profoundly as Sarasate. Not only were Bizet, Lalo, and Saint-Saëns inspired by Sarasate's playing, but composers such as Max Bruch and Karl Goldmark also created works for him.

Sarasate developed a very personal violin style, which stood out for its transparency opposite the rich sonority of the Ecole Liégoise. Without having a large tone, he captivated audiences with an astounding clarity of intonation.[20] Shaw compared Sarasate's playing to that of Ysaye, the last representative of the Liège School.[21] He judged the Spaniard thus:

> He never interprets anything: he plays it beautifully, and that is all. He is always alert, swift, clear, refined, certain, scrupulously attentive, and quite unaffected. This last adjective will surprise people who see him as a black-haired romantic young Spaniard, full of fascinating tricks and mannerisms. . . . There is no trace of affectation about him: the picturesqueness of the pluck of the string and stroke of the bow that never fails to bring down the house is the natural effect of an action performed with perfect accuracy in an extraordinarily short time and strict measure.[22]

Saint-Saëns had already written his Op. 20 at Sarasate's prompting. Another work, Op. 28, followed in 1863, this time revealing the influence of the Spaniard in its very nature.[23] It is probable that Sarasate also appeared as a quartet player at the soirees that the composer held regularly on Mondays. Since the beginning of the 1860s Sarasate had been part of a string quartet in Paris, which also included Alfred Turban (to whom Saint-Saëns dedicated his Op. 48) as second violinist and Jules Delsart (to whom the *Chant saphique,* Op. 91, is dedicated) in the cellist's seat.[24]

The two symphonic poems by Flemish composer Peter Benoit—who, incidentally, directed the orchestra of the Thèatre des Bouffes Parisiens founded in Paris by Offenbach—are concertante compositions only in the broadest sense. They can best be compared with

Franck's *Les Djinns.* In both works Benoit shows "natural talent for descriptive music" and remained uninfluenced by Liszt's school.[25]

> Richness of combinations, strength of imagination and thought, robust and solid substance, profusion and verve, spontaneity, the vigor of popular inspiration, such are characteristics of these truly brilliant sketches.[26]

Pfeiffer's Second Piano Concerto in E-flat Major, Op. 21, differs very little from its predecessor of 1859. Like Op. 11, it is in three movements—the first in sonata form, the second in three-part song form, and the third, a rondo—and is overladen with virtuosity. It is of little interest, since we are already familiar with such runs, cascades, and chord sequences from the works of Liszt, where they are applied more sensibly.

Compared with Pfeiffer, Michel Bergson's Concerto symphonique, Op. 62, is much more charming. Bergson, who deliberately dissociated himself from the new German school and is considered part of the Brahms circle, was quite popular in Paris in his day. His concerto could certainly have claimed a place on concert programs, were it not for the fact that the solo part is far too scanty.[27] In general, Bergson tends to express the symphonic idea not so much through the sequence and form of the movements—Op. 62 is in three movements, thoroughly conventional in format, and thus not an extension of Litolff's and Liszt's ideas—but through the predominance of the orchestra, which carries all the thematic material; the piano is at best an echo or figuration of the orchestra.

> Fétis is offering insults both to Beethoven and good sense. His corrections are crimes. . . . Your professor shall soon be treated as he deserves by those who respect genius and distrust pretentious mediocrity.[28]

Unfortunately, François-Joseph Fétis, whose famous *Bibliographie universelle des musiciens et bibliographie générale de la musique* is still recognized today as one of the standard works on French music, was actually "behind the times" as a composer.[29] Fétis was well deserving of Berlioz's hostility in light of his "corrections" of Beethoven's works, where dissonances were culled out as "obvious errors." His Fantasia for Orchestra and Organ already reveals in its title the thankless role assigned to the solo. The work is at best showy, fully adhering to the style of the admired Classic composers, yet glossed over with "a discrete, somewhat Mendelssohnian romanticism."[30]

The year 1886 can claim the dubious honor of having produced not only Fétis's late work, but also the worst French solo concerto ever, which, for this very reason, merits special examination. Félix Ludger Rossignol, who became one of the most prolific composers of his day in Paris under the pseudonym Victorin de Joncières, was one of Wagner's first advocates in France.[31] Thus, his inclinations soon turned in the direction of musical theater, where he was fairly successful with his smooth and pleasant style. He was praised by critics especially for his sensitive orchestra settings and melodic creativity. His scores would captivate audiences with their "orchestration sonore et brillante."[32] But de Joncières's works for musical theater, a conglomeration of Italianisms and styles borrowed from Meyerbeer and Wagner, faded into oblivion soon after his death in 1903.

Joncières's violin concerto in D minor of 1866 was premiered 12 December 1869, in a concert at the Paris Conservatory.[33] In looking through the score we are first struck by the composer's overuse of string tremolos in the first movement (Allegro in D Minor, 4/4) and the last (Rondo. Allegretto in D Minor, 6/8), which are used almost continuously as an accompaniment figure. These two movements—like the middle movement (Adagio in F Major, 2/4), which is connected attacca to the first—are entirely conventional in form.

The traditional contrast between first and second theme is also preserved in the first movement of de Joncières's concerto. Whereas the first theme (Example 9.1) is rhythmically accentuated, the second (Example 9.2) is more lyrical, almost in the style of the Ecole Liégoise.

Example 9.1. de Joncières, Concerto ré mineur (1).

Example 9.2. de Joncières, Concerto ré mineur (1).

Indeed, both themes document "une inspiration parfois peu originale [an inspiration occasionally lacking in originality]," as a contemporary critique puts it.[34]

The development section of the first movement is a dull string of identical figurations, and the abridged recapitulation is followed by a written-out cadenza, which proves, despite its virtuosity, that the composer himself had not mastered the violin. The few contrapuntal interjections by the woodwinds are hardly enough to add color to the score.

The absence of the tiresome string tremolos alone makes the middle movement stand out positively from the two outer ones. Although its main theme (Example 9.3) is also rather unoriginal, the composer does

Example 9.3. de Joncières, Concerto ré mineur (2).

try to give more importance to the solo. One passage, in which the violin carries on a dialogue with the solo clarinet against a background of subdued string chords, comes across especially well. A similar passage is found in the middle movement of Saint-Saëns's Op. 61 (see Section 3.1). It is highly unlikely that Saint-Saëns had any knowledge of de Joncières's concerto, since he never mentioned the work in his correspondence and did not own the score.[35]

The final rondo of the concerto quickly spoils the good impression of the Adagio, because its theme (Example 9.4)—accompanied by the inevitable string tremolos—is altogether too simple for a concertante finale.

Example 9.4. de Joncières, Concerto ré mineur (3).

Completely forgotten and rarely mentioned in contemporary sources are the works of Emile Wrobleski. His *Grand concerto symphonique* continues the tradition of the four-movement concerto, following in Litolff's footsteps, without adding anything new of consequence. Saint-Saëns's Op. 22, which also was written in 1868, is far more interesting, and soon after its premiere was justifiably hailed as the most important representative of the French piano concerto.[36]

The uproar in Leipzig over Saint-Saens's Op. 29, composed the following year (see Chapter 1), seems almost incomprehensible today. The modulation from E major to E-flat minor at the beginning of the slow movement, which constituted an "infraction of the rules" (see Section 5.3), was indeed "modern" for a solo concerto of that time. Yet Op. 29 is perhaps the weakest of Saint-Saëns's piano concertos. This may be due mainly to the "rather obtrusive passage work," although the cadenzas before and after the development of the first movement (i.e., in unusual positions) lend formal charm to the work.[37]

Alexis Vicomte de Castillon, "précurseur de la musique de chambre sérieuse en France [precursor of serious chamber music in France],"[38] would certainly have had a great career, if the war of 1870–71 had not so sapped his strength that he died in 1873 at only 35 years of age.[39] Under the influence of his teacher, César Franck, he produced numerous chamber music works—a piano quintet Op. 1, a string quartet Op. 3, a piano trio Op. 4, a violin sonata Op. 6, and a piano quartet Op. 7. These were among the best to emerge from French nineteenth-century music. Like Franck, de Castillon had strong leanings toward German Romanticism, so the claim of his publisher, Georges Hartman, is certainly justified: "S'il eût vécu, il eût été une sorte de Beethoven moderne [Had he lived, he would have been a modern Beethoven]."[40]

While the general public showed little appreciation for de Castillon's music, considered him long-winded and dilettantish, and protested his bold style, the French music world recognized him as one of its greatest talents.[41] At his funeral in the Eglise Saint-Pierre-de-Chaillot, Saint-Saëns improvised on the second theme of his piano concerto Op. 12.[42] This was the concerto that had been booed by the audience at its premiere performance on 10 March 1872:[43]

> Not since the premiere of the *Meistersinger* overture had there been a more indescribable commotion in the theater. For three

> quarters of an hour Mr. Saint-Saëns, who played the piano part, stood up to the audience with magnificent courage. He was truly beautiful that day, uncompromising and impassioned amid the iniquitous booing, testifying to the strength of his convictions.[44]

Incidentally, de Castillon was also a founding member, possibly even *the* actual initiator, of the Société Nationale. His Symphony in F Major (1865)—the composer left a second one uncompleted—would be just as worthy of being revived as his other works.

Although the Belgian cellist and composer Jules de Swert (Deswert) was active mainly in German territory, including Düsseldorf, Weimar, Berlin, Leipzig, and Wiesbaden, it is safe to assume that his works were played often in Paris as well, since he taught at the conservatories of Ghent and Bruges until his death.[45] His Fantaisie Op. 25 is a virtuoso work similar to the pieces by Servais mentioned earlier and is somewhat reminiscent of Mendelssohn.

> As for schools, Mr. Widor has covered the entire range; his field of activity extends from Bach to Richard Wagner. Erudite like Gevaert, a pianist like Saint-Saëns, he has the curious and patient intensiveness of the modern artist who is determined to leave nothing unexplored.[46]

Widor's Cello Concerto in E Minor, Op. 42, is conventional in concept, but the composer is able to create balance by cleverly splitting the melody line between solo and orchestra. The wealth of counterpoint in the score and the instrumental combinations, which are adapted from the organ registration characteristic of the French Romantic period, call to mind the eight organ symphonies for which Widor is still famous today.

The organist Marcel Dupré witnessed an encounter between Saint-Saëns and Widor that merits mention. It concerns Debussy, whose acceptance in the Académie des Beaux-Arts was then being negotiated.

> One day Saint-Saëns visited Widor, the illustrious permanent secretary of the Académie des Beaux-Arts, who drew him to the piano, and said, "Come, turn the pages for me." He had a roll of music under his arm and played as only a virtuoso can. From time to time he gave Widor a nudge: "Hey, do you like that?" and when he had finished: "Will you vote for him?" Widor's

superb response was: "You played them in such a way that you have made me love them!" They were Debussy's Etudes.[47]

In spite of the opposing stand that Widor took as pupil of Fétis and successor of Franck at the Paris Conservatory, he always defended Saint-Saëns's music and paid tribute to his life and works in an interesting study.[48]

Jules Garcin's Violin Concerto in D Minor, Op. 14, was written in the same year as Saint-Saëns's Op. 33. Except for Garcin's participation in the founding of the Société Nationale and his birth and death dates (11 July 1830–30 October 1896), I was able learn little about him. According to a note on the piano score of the work, he was solo violinist in the orchestra of the Paris Opéra.[49] He reveals great virtuosity in his concerto, which he created presumably for his own repertoire. It is regrettable that Garcin's Op. 14, which is better and more interesting than most other French violin concertos of that era, is completely forgotten today. Despite intensive research, I was unable to turn up a score of the work, and therefore the matter of instrumentation must remain unconsidered. Nevertheless, I feel justified in examining Garcin's concerto more closely, since it comes close to Saint-Saëns stylistically.

After a 22-measure orchestra introduction (Andantino con moto in D minor, 6/8), which states the theme of the main movement and also has an unusual harmonic density, the violin enters in m. 23 with a 16-measure cadenza, written out and set off from the introduction and main movement by a change in meter (4/4). Solo entrances of similar structure are found in Beethoven's Fifth Piano Concerto in E-flat Major, Op. 73; Mendelssohn's Second Piano Concerto in D Minor, Op. 40; Moszkowski's Piano Concerto in E Major, Op. 59; and Bruch's First Violin Concerto in G Minor, Op. 26.[50] However, none of the works mentioned have more than a brief introductory cadenza, comparable to recitative.

The main movement of Garcin's concerto (Allegretto tranquillo in D minor, 6/8) begins immediately with the theme (Example 9.5) from the introduction. It is played by the violin and swirled about in virtuoso style as the movement progresses, without the musical substance of the work being sacrificed to a superficial show of technique. Garcin manages to give the accompaniment an independent and equal role without obscuring the solo part. Especially in the harmonic substruc-

Example 9.5. Garcin, Concerto Op. 14/1, m. 39ff.

ture, he skillfully avoids the stereotyped use of the melody notes of the violin as top notes in the tonic function, as was the case with de Joncières.

The second theme (Example 9.6) derives from the first, but whereas the first was more like a wide-ranging cantilena, Garcin now emphasizes the rhythmic structure, accentuating it by chords in the orchestra that accompany it.

Example 9.6. Garcin, Concerto Op. 14/1, m. 121ff.

The thematic material of the movement is featured again in a brilliant coda (Allegro molto in D minor, 6/8). Because of the faster tempo, the first theme, which is now dominant, becomes more triumphal than lyrical in character.

Aside from the orchestra introduction, the violin has very few rests in the 234 measures of this movement, yet the work does not give the impression of superficial virtuosity. This attests to the earnestness of a composer who never let form or effect take precedence over musical ideas.

The soloist also is busy, almost continually, in the middle movement (Andante sostenuto in B-flat major, 9/8), which is joined attacca to the first, after a 10-measure introduction. The basic rhythmic pattern of the first movement (Figure 9.1) is essentially retained in the melody

Figure 9.1. Rhythmic pattern in Garcin, Concerto Op. 14/1.

Example 9.7. Garcin, Concerto Op. 14/2, m. 11ff.

(Example 9.7) until m. 41 (un peu plus animé). Here Garcin gradually shifts to a 16th-note motion, which becomes more and more compressed and leads in ascending octaves to the climax of the movement (m. 61). There is a striking similarity here to a passage in the middle movement of Saint-Saëns's Op. 58 (m. 122ff.). In both movements, the similar octave progressions are in an exposed position directly before the climax; with Garcin, they lead into a 16th-note passage and with Saint-Saëns, a 32d-note passage. It is quite possible that Garcin was familiar with the work written in 1858, even though it was not published until 1879. The 16th notes, which call for extreme certainty of intonation on the part of the soloist, are featured in the second part of the movement as well. Noteworthy is the fact that Garcin forgoes a repetition of the first section, thus leaving the middle movement of his concerto in two-part form.

The finale (Allegro con spirito in D minor/D major, 2/4) first picks up the 16th-note motion of the middle movement (Example 9.8) and then introduces a melody (Example 9.9), which bears a certain

Example 9.8. Garcin, Concerto Op. 14/3, m. 12ff.

Example 9.9. Garcin, Concerto Op. 14/3. m. 95ff.

resemblance to the second theme of the finale of Saint-Saëns's Op. 61 (Example 9.10). From this, a third theme is derived (Example 9.11).

Example 9.10. Saint-Saëns, Op. 61/3, m. 88ff.

Example 9.11. Garcin, Concerto Op. 14/3, m. 112ff.

Figure 9.2 illustrates the great rhythmic unity of Garcin's concerto.

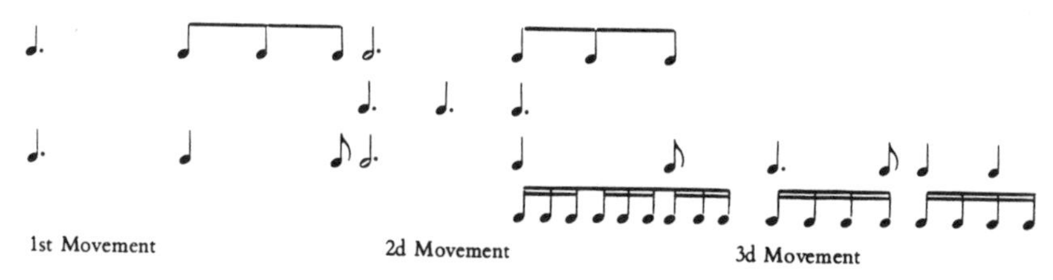

Figure 9.2. Rhythmic unity of Garcin's Concerto pour violin en ré mineur, Op. 14.

The main impetus for Edouard Lalo's development as a composer came from his membership as violinist in the Quatuor Armingaud-Jacquard, whose repertoire consisted mainly of works by Schubert, Schumann, and Mendelssohn. Thus, a strong German Romantic influence can be detected in Lalo's music beginning about 1855.[51] Along with Alexis de Castillon, César Franck, and Saint-Saëns, Lalo is one of the most important representatives of the new French school. "He added grace, refinement, ease, and clarity, combined with a rhythmic ardor and a tonal brilliance that, despite the sometimes long-winded developments, lend a special flavor to his style."[52] Nevertheless, the only work to win him greater acclaim was his opera *Le Roi d'Ys* (1875–1886).

Like Saint-Saëns, Lalo was strongly influenced by Sarasate in his violin compositions. His *Symphonie espagnole,* which "combines the characteristics of the symphony, the concerto, and the suite," was premiered by Sarasate on 7 February 1875, in one of the Paris Concerts populaires.[53] The wording of the title *pour violon principale* suggests a concertante idea in which special importance is attached to the equality of solo and orchestra.[54] This equality becomes clear even in the opening measures of the first movement (Allegro non troppo D minor, 2/2), which are structured symmetrically, like many of Saint-Saëns's concerto introductions (see Figure 9.3). Twenty-two measures of orchestra follow, of which the last two are complemented with runs on the violin before it states the actual main theme (Example 9.12).

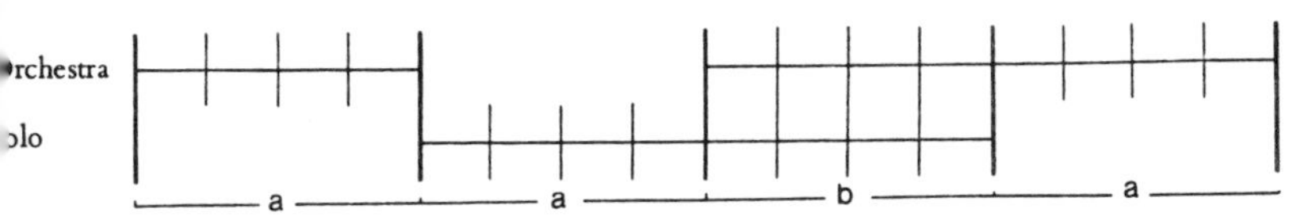

(Cf. Mies, *Das Konzert,* 72.)

Figure 9.3. Structure of opening measures of Lalo's *Symphonie espagnole,* Op. 21/1.

Example 9.12. Lalo, *Symphonie espagnole,* Op. 21/1.

Lalo's Spanish ancestral heritage found expression in the *Symphonie espagnole.*

> One could quibble over the quality of its "Hispanicisms" and declare them more or less authentic, as was done in Bizet's case the same year. Nevertheless, Lalo was the first to transform a series of folk melodies, brought to him from beyond the mountains by Sarasate, into a magnificent orchestral suite.[55]

A scherzo as second and an intermezzo as third movement expand the work into an unusual five-movement format. Incidentally, Pierre Lalo, music reviewer for the *Journal des Débats* and other renowned newspapers, who has been mentioned several times in this work, was the composer's son.[56]

In 1873 Saint-Saëns was finally able to realize a plan he had been contemplating for a long time. With the founding of the Société Nationale de la musique, he created the most important prerequisite for a French national style. If we look at the background of the French solo concerto over the past quarter-century, we find, all in all, a downright sorry state of affairs.

Consider Adolphe Boschot's judgment of this period, the prime years of Napoléon III's Second Empire, which came to a bloody end in the war of 1870–71:

> I would like to describe the musical taste of this epoch—which kinds of music were successful, whether at the Opéra or at the Théâtre des Italiens; which musicians and which theatrical works between 1848 and 1870 were favored by fashion; and which other composers, in contrast, were ignored and disdained because their genius was not currently in vogue.
>
> In the domain of musical theater, fashion is all-powerful. Its rule is steadfast, capricious in its effects, but unfailingly applied, whatever the political or social order. Governments come and go; women change the style of their dresses or hats while men change the style of the government; barricades are erected in 1830 and rebuilt in 1848; Charles X, Louis-Philippe, and Napoléon III are overthrown; in the theater, Rossini, Auber or Adolphe Adam, Bellini or Donizetti, Meyerbeer, Verdi or Gounod are applauded in turn; Wagner is hissed, Berlioz scorned; but in this world full of surprises, the successes of the lyric theatre, even when the composers are extremely gifted, are always determined by one inescapable force: fashion.[57]

While the surest way to success in Paris led across the stage of the Palais Garnier, the Opéra-Comique, or the Théâtre des Italiens, the solo concerto was in the throes of death. De Castillon's concerto was booed. He died too early to win audience favor, and today he is just as forgotten as Garcin. Lalo's instrumental works foundered because of the predominance of the opera. Saint-Saëns managed to survive thanks only to his versatility. It is truly ironic that he, of all people, strove all his life for success in the realm of musical theater. He once said to Bizet, not without resignation, "Puisqu'on ne veut pas de nous au théâtre, réfugions-nous au concert [Since they don't want us at the theater, let us take refuge at the concert]!"[58]

The heyday of the instrumental virtuosos who had flooded the French capital in the first half of the last century was over. The new generation—Diémer, Sarasate, and Hollman—had not yet emerged. The Ecole Liégoise, with its lyrical Italian operatic style, fell victim to the drame lyrique of Gounod, who was able to oust Meyerbeer, but in turn had to capitulate in the face of Wagner's success in Paris.

The premiere of Wagner's *Tannhäuser* had unleashed a storm in the French music world, and soon opponents and defenders of the Bayreuth master were split into two opposing camps.[59] It was especially disastrous

> that there are countless Wagnerian critics so unenlightened that they will have no other music than that of Richard Wagner. They despise all the rest and, for lack of anything to compare it with, indulge in bizarre appraisals, go into ecstasy over trivialities, and marvel over the most commonplace things.[60]

Although Saint-Saëns took a neutral position in the fanatical fight for and against Wagner,[61] his reports on the Bayreuth premiere of the *Ring*[62] were interpreted as a profession of "wagnérisme," especially by the opponents of the new music drama.[63] Saint-Saëns, who later did not turn against Wagner's music but condemned the political misuse of it during World War I, was one of the first to recognize that the potential for a French national style could be nipped in the bud by Wagner's influence.[64] Even the "wagnéristes"—the painter Fantin-Latour immortalized them on canvas in 1885: Adolphe Jullien, A. Boisseau, Camille Benoit, Antoine Lascoux, Vincent d'Indy, Emmanuel Chabrier, Edmond Maître, and Amédée Pigeon[65]—admitted that their enthusiasm for Wagner's *Gesamtkunstwerk* jeopardized their own momentum.[66]

A few composers tried to capitalize on their successes in musical theater to gain recognition for their instrumental works. This was probably the only way de Joncières could get his violin concerto before the public. Several decades later Massenet's piano concerto underwent a similar experience. The war of 1870–71 had awakened a national consciousness in the French cultural scene, the early results of which were visible. After the crisis of the last few decades, the solo concerto managed to recover a little; Saint-Saëns proved with his concertos and concertante works that French instrumental music did not have to linger behind that of the rest of Europe.

10

The French Solo Concerto from 1874 to 1890 (from Op. 36 to Op. 94)

> Young musicians of today would find it hard to imagine the French music world at the moment Gounod appeared. . . . It revered and idolized melody—or more specifically, the motif which implanted itself in the memory with no effort, which was easily grasped the first time around.[1]

With the success of Gounod's drame lyrique, France saw a new flowering of the instrumental romance, the performance-practice of which traces back to Sperontes's *Singende Muse an der Pleisse.*[2] Just as the cantabile lyricism of Italian opera had influenced the style of the Ecole Liégoise, composers now preferred melodies of a simpler nature, "whereby violin, violoncello, and piano proved to be especially suitable for conveying the lyricism of the romance."[3]

Saint-Saëns, with his Op. 27, originally written as chamber music, had already contributed to the genre that was back in vogue. Now in 1871 and 1874 he followed with Op. 36, 37, and 48. All four works are occasional compositions, first written for piano accompaniment and later orchestrated.

While de Swert's Op. 25 was still more of a pleasant virtuoso piece, in his Cello Concerto in D Minor, Op. 32, the composer shows the influence of German musical tradition to an increased extent. The work calls for lavish instrumentation, which must certainly have stood in the way of its success in Paris. Melodies are rhythmically concise and well-adapted to the technical capabilities of the cello, but at the same time they are rather dry. The composer's predilection toward a chordal style could indicate an orientation to Schumann's Op. 129.

"Allow me to say that in the complete works of Berlioz . . . and . . . the works of Madame de Grandval . . . , we have a French repertoire that should not be looked down upon."[4] Whether this judgment by Saint-Saëns is very objective remains an open question. But one thing is certain: the composer esteemed the Vicomtesse de Grandval—as Marie Reiset, she had been a pupil of Friedrich von Flotow—not only as a pupil, but as a woman.[5]

> As the new Vicomtesse de Grandval, Miss Reiset did not stop cultivating her musical talents; and in order to obtain solid instruction, she became a pupil of Saint-Saëns. She studied thus for several years, until she had achieved the desired result.[6]

The Vicomtesse, who as author of several novellas hid behind countless pseudonyms and anagrams such as de Valgrand, was successful primarily as a composer of works for musical theater.[7] Especially appreciated in her day were the three-act opera *Piccolino,* premiered in 1869 in the Théâtre des Italiens, and her late work *Mazeppa,* which was first heard in 1892 in Bordeaux. As far as I have been able to determine, the only concertante composition by the Vicomtesse is a Concertino in D Major for Violin, written presumably in 1873 or 1874.[8] In this case, as with Garcin's Op. 14, I only had access to a piano score. Therefore, I must forgo comment on the orchestra treatment in the following discussion of this piece that was greatly influenced by Saint-Saëns.

After a six-measure orchestra introduction, the main theme of the first movement (Andante con moto, D major, 4/4) (Example 10.1) is

Example 10.1. de Grandval, Concertino pour violon 1, m. 7ff.

stated by the solo violin over arpeggiated chords, possibly by harp(s). It appears again in octaves in m. 33, after a short solo cadenza.

In the development of the almost monothematic movement, the composer strives for balance between violin and orchestra, having learned her lessons well as Saint-Saëns's pupil. Unfortunately, she errs in the opposite direction, neglecting the solo part to a great extent; it merely echoes the orchestra, which determines the course of the work. The possible relationship between this compositional style and the title will be discussed later.

The scherzolike middle movement (Allegro con moto—allegro moderato molto, F-sharp minor, 2/4), after 14 introductory measures, has the violin speak with the dancelike theme (Example 10.2). Although

Example 10.2. de Grandval, Concertino pour violon 2, m. 15ff.

the composer shows great talent here as a rhythmist, the subordinate role of the solo is again regrettable; rather than lead, it merely offers commentary and never blends with the orchestra to form an integrated whole. There is almost no counterpoint, as far as the melody is concerned, but the Vicomtesse had a knack for working in very clever rhythmic overlays.

The finale (Allegro, D major, 4/4), in spite of its faster tempo, returns to the mood of the first movement. The opening theme (Example 10.3) offers respite again and again from the complex combination of independent elements of the movement, which has a vague rondo structure.

Example 10.3. de Grandval, Concertino pour violon 3.

The term "concertino" is striking in that its use here was quite unusual for the nineteenth century. The term originally denoted "the smaller group of solo instruments in the concerto grosso after 1650, as opposed to the ripieno, the tutti of the full orchestra."[9] Either the Vicomtesse intended to indicate the subordinate role of the solo in the title of her work and thus have it understood more as a continuation of the concerto-grosso tradition than as a solo concerto; or—and this seems more likely to me—she understood concertino as a diminutive form of the word "concerto."

No less unusual is the sequence of movements, slow—fast—very fast, which was not at all in keeping with the prevailing norms for the solo concerto. It is not inconceivable that the composer was influenced in this regard by Saint-Saëns's Op. 22, which has certain structural parallels (see Section 2.1).

It was also in 1874 that Lalo wrote his Concerto in F Major, Op. 20, for violin, dedicated to Sarasate once again.

> The concerto is conceived in the image of its dedicatee: it seduces and sings. We have not heard a "singing" concerto since Mendelssohn. The romance of the andantino, admirably phrased by the great Pablo [de Sarasate], captivated the listeners in the Châtelet, as did the energy of the allegro con fuoco, which one can easily imagine under the winged bow of the marvelous virtuoso.[10]

Pitrou's opinion is euphemistic. The success of the work, which was premiered and published before the *Symphonie espagnole,* was limited to the middle movement; in reality the public rejected Lalo's dull concerto, and it disappeared from concert programs forever. Its motivic detail, which only rarely was able to rise to great melodic contours, is occasionally reminiscent of the posthumously published violin concerto of Robert Schumann.

Although "as an eclectic and neoclassicist . . . [he] represented the traditional French school," Théodore Dubois was one of the most prolific composers of concertante music in France.[11] In 1877 he succeeded Saint-Saëns as organist at the Madeleine. He held that post until 1896, when he took over the directorship of the Paris Conservatory, where he had taught since 1871, as the successor of his instructor, Ambroise Thomas. However, his dry academism made him despised by his pupils, among them Albéric Magnard and Paul Dukas. Thus, when he passed his position on to Gabriel Fauré in 1905, the news was received with widespread satisfaction.[12] The main reason for his dismissal, incidentally, was the repeated failure of Ravel to win the Prix de Rome.[13]

Dubois's *Concerto-Capriccio* for piano is a one-movement concertino.[14]

> The piano begins in a recitative mode, using the baritone recitative from Beethoven's Ninth Symphony; the subsequent allegro movement brings in familiar thematic phrases and includes a slow section.[15]

Already we see here a characteristic of Dubois's concertante works that will last until his *Fantasie-Stück* of 1912: his great liking for sequences. The composer always makes a great effort to avoid superficial virtuosity, and he is especially successful in the free forms. Saint-Saëns held him in high esteem and in 1873 appointed him as co-founder of the Société Nationale.

After studying violin under Richard Hammer and Henri Vieuxtemps, 14-year-old Benjamin Godard entered the composition class of Henri Reber at the Paris Conservatory, and the music world predicted a bright future for him. His failure to fulfill these hopes, however, is documented by his *Concerto romantique* in A minor, which "held the musicians' attention," as Lavignac remarked laconically.[16]

> Unfortunately, composition came all too easily for him, and he wasted the talent he undoubtedly possessed by cranking out salon pieces in large quantities. He had ideas and experience, but he did not perfect his ideas, and furthermore, his music was pretentious.[17]

His *Concerto romantique* is a smooth three-movement concerto of traditional cut, whose gushing lyricism is in the style of Vieuxtemps.

De Swert's Second Cello Concerto, Op. 38, differs very little from his work in D minor, Op. 32, while Vieuxtemps's attempt to adapt the lyric violin style to the lower string instrument in his Cello Concerto in A Minor Op. 46 resulted in a pleasant, though not very successful work. The disdain that cellists have accorded it is actually undeserved.

Brahms and Tchaikovsky created two of the most significant violin concertos of the nineteenth century in 1878. The same year also marks the origin of Sarasate's *Zigeunerweisen* [Gypsy Airs], Op. 20, for which the virtuoso is still well-known today. This work is testimony to the increased interest of the late Romantic period in the folk music of foreign lands, whose melodies were the raw material for the works of the national schools.

Evidence that Sarasate's Op. 20 was by no means completely original is found in the parallels to Liszt's Thirteenth Hungarian Rhapsody, published in 1854. The theme of the vivace section in Liszt's work (Example 10.4) is identical to that of the second part of Sarasate's *Zigeunerweisen.* Of course, it could be a matter of coincidence, since the themes Liszt used were also taken from Hungarian folk music.

Example 10.4. Liszt, Thirteenth Hungarian Rhapsody, m. 101ff.

It was probably also Sarasate who prompted Fauré to compose a violin concerto. However, only the first two movements of Fauré's A-major work, Op. 14, were completed, and these clearly reveal the influence of Saint-Saëns. The romance, intended as the middle movement, is definitely the better of the two. Why Fauré did not complete the work is uncertain. It is a delightful composition, especially in its transparent instrumentation which features the harp. It offers a preview of the composer's later style.

Godard's Piano Concerto in A Minor, Op. 31, is superior to his violin concerto in every respect. In its four-movement format and the structure of the movements, it is similar to works by Saint-Saëns. Like him, Godard

> precedes the first allegro movement with a slow introduction, which already contains the first theme. Second is the scherzo movement, largely in dialogue form; the most significant movement is the third, which resembles a funeral march.[18]

The work, which enjoyed several successful performances, projects Godard's piano style at its best—a style still in effect in the early works of Debussy.[19]

The two violin compositions by Dancla, as late works, represent the last fading echoes of the Ecole Liégoise. Little is known about the third *Grand Concerto* in D Minor, Op. 46, by Jacques Franco-Mendès, an extremely difficult virtuoso piece that sends the soloist to the highest registers of the violin.

Lalo's Cello Concerto in D Minor, written in 1876 and published the following year, is probably the most eminent French cello concerto after those of Saint-Saëns. It approaches the symphonic form in its overall structure, although it holds to the traditional three movements.

The first movement (Prélude in D minor, 12/8) begins with an eight-measure introduction (Lento) before the actual main part (Allegro maestoso). The juxtaposition of motifs and chords in the introduction, which divides into tutti and solo phrases, gives it a recitative character.[20] The first two orchestra measures (Example 10.5) are followed by an ad-libitum statement from the cello (Example 10.6), which occurs again in modified form in the main movement. The middle movement

Example 10.5. Lalo, Concerto pour violoncelle 1, m. 1f.

Example 10.6. Lalo, Concerto pour violoncelle 1, m. 3f.

(Intermezzo, Andante con moto) is transitional as a whole. The final rondo (Allegro vivace) is also preceded by a slow introduction (Andante), which continues with the thematic material of the intermezzo.

The three-movement *Fantaisie norvégienne* for violin and orchestra[21] was again written for Sarasate, "who, during a Scandinavian tour, had collected folk melodies that delighted Lalo."[22] The premiere took place on 27 October 1879, but the work was not published until the following year. "The three movements, from which the composer has deleted most of the purely virtuoso passages, are most impressive in the quality of their orchestration."[23] The composer later rewrote the piece as a two-movement *Rhapsodie norvégienne* for orchestra, whose first movement is identical to that of the concertante work. "The *Rhapsodie norvégienne* has given its composer that magic touch of fame that the *Danse macabre* brought to Camille Saint-Saëns."[24]

Like many other composers, Auguste Dupont has now faded into oblivion. Even the Bibliothèque Nationale in Paris has very few of his scores, and numerous titles are known only through their mention in contemporary newspaper articles.[25] Dupont, who must have been an outstanding pianist, first become famous as the accompanist for Alexandre Batta, Léonard, and Wieniawski; from about 1845, he also came to the fore as a composer. In addition to numerous concert études composed for his own use, he wrote three piano concertos and a very commendable *Symphonie-Concerto,* which, despite its three-movement form, is in the tradition of Litolff and Liszt.

In general Dupont, as a composer, must be regarded as Liszt's successor in France, even though at first the Parisians contented themselves "with the simple thematic linking of movements and retention of the multi-movement form, which is known to go back to Berlioz."[26] In this respect Saint-Saëns is an exception (Op. 44 and 119), like Dupont with his two-movement Morceau de concert in C Minor, Op. 42,

> in which the (fast) first movement ('Ballade') includes a slow section; the second movement (Minuetto-Scherzo) picks up the rhythms of the first movement at the beginning and is then carried by two alternating themes.[27]

Dupont's Op. 42 is certain to have been influenced by Saint-Saëns's Op. 44. Not only does it correspond to the Fourth Piano Concerto in its four-part two-movement structure and in the sequence of sections, but the orchestra scoring and the key are also identical. Furthermore, the solo figurations in the two works are very similar.

Saint-Saëns wrote his Third Violin Concerto and the Morceau de concert, Op. 62, for violin in 1880, the same year in which Dvorák wrote his Violin Concerto in A Minor, Op. 53, and Tchaikovsky his Second Piano Concerto in G Major, Op. 44. The years between 1871 and World War I brought a new flowering of concertante music all over Europe. The virtuosity of the first half of the nineteenth century had largely been cast aside, and new momentum developed with the spread of the national schools.

In France it was acknowledged that a national musical style, if it was to gain international recognition, had to concentrate more on the great forms of "serious" music—the symphony, the concerto, and chamber music—and move away from the supremacy of musical theater. Thus Italian opera, once the *non plus ultra* of the French music world, was nearly forgotten by the turn of the century. Even theoreticians regarded it with contempt.

> If you read the very latest French studies on musical aesthetics, you will be astonished at how little these are based on French composers. . . . Most space is taken up by the great Germans, Beethoven and Wagner, . . . and you can search almost in vain for examples from Italian composers.[28]

In 1881, Charles-Wilfrid de Bériot, the second son of Henri Vieuxtemps's famous teacher, made his public debut with four piano concertos. Of course, we can assume that the works had already been written in his earlier years. Unfortunately, I was unable to locate any of the concertos. Even a direct inquiry to Editions Hamelle, which had published them during his lifetime, was unsuccessful, since the major part of their archives has not yet been recorded and catalogued. Nor did a search for reports on contemporary performances bring any material to light. Thus, I must limit myself to the following quotation:

> Another somewhat old-fashioned composer is Charles W. de Bériot (1833–1914), whose two concertos belong here [referring to the so-called new German Weimar school]—Op. 40 in D minor (1882; *Hommage à Franz Liszt*) and Op. 46 in C minor. To some extent his pianistic style is based on [Liszt's] Concerto in A Major.[29]

Godard's *Introduction et Allegro* Op. 49, a virtuoso bravura piece, is uninteresting, but the Ballade in F-sharp Minor Op. 19 by Gabriel Fauré merits special attention. The composer had attended the Munich performance of Wagner's *Ring* in 1879 and later commented to Alfred Cortot that the Ballade was an "impression of nature analogous to the one that inspired Richard Wagner's musical evocation of the 'Waldweben' [Forest Murmurs]."[30] When Fauré traveled to Zurich with Saint-Saëns in July 1882, he met with Liszt and showed the aged composer his Op. 19 in its original arrangement for solo piano. At the same time he declared that he considered the work too heavy and too long.[31] Liszt reassured him: "Too long, young man, that makes no sense. One writes as one conceives it."[32]

The most remarkable aspect of the Ballade is its formal conception; the basic three-part format puts a fast section between two slow ones, and the three main themes overlap as *AB—C'B'—C*. The first

Example 10.7. Fauré, Ballade, Op. 19, m. 2ff.

theme (Example 10.7) is the only one to appear just once. To his friend Marie Clerc, the composer wrote: "I have found a way to develop the second theme in a kind of intermezzo" (Example 10.8) "and to prepare the way for the third theme" (Example 10.9) "so that the three pieces blend into one. The result is a fantasia that is a little different from the traditional one."[33]

Example 10.8. Fauré, Ballade, Op. 19, m. 37f.

Example 10.9. Fauré, Ballade, Op. 19, m. 86f.

In the same year in which the concertante works of Bériot, Godard, and Fauré were written, Johannes Brahms composed his Second Piano Concerto in B-flat Major, Op. 83; and in Munich, 17-year-old Richard Strauss was working on his Violin Concerto in D Minor, Op. 8.

Louis Diémer is known today mainly as a superb educator. Among his pupils at the Paris Conservatory, where he succeeded Marmontel in 1887, were Edouard Risler, Alfred Cortot, Robert Casadesus, and Marcel Dupré. While Hanslick praised him as a delicate and graceful artist, others called him a "dry-as-dust player with a hard, rattling tone."[34] He was one of the first pianists also to master the harpsichord. He repeatedly presented (and surprised) his audiences with early music, edited the works of harpsichord composers, and founded the Société des instruments anciens,[35] of which Saint-Saëns was also a member.[36] Saint-Saëns dedicated Op. 73 and 103 to Diémer, and several of Fauré's works are also dedicated to him. Diémer shone brilliantly as soloist for the premiere of Franck's *Variations symphoniques,* as in his performances of countless other contemporary piano works. He made successful tours through France as Sarasate's accompanist, but with his own works, he chalked up only fleeting successes. The Morceau de concert Op. 31 and his only piano concerto, Op. 32 in C minor, testify to their composer's virtuosity, "which is based on both elegance and impeccable precision in playing."[37] The Morceau de concert for violin, Op. 33, presumably owes its origin to his friendship with Sarasate.

Lalo's *Concerto russe,* whose date of origin is somewhat uncertain, was probably also inspired by Sarasate.[38] The premiere performance on 30 January 1881 in the Pasdeloup concerts was played by violinist Pierre Marsick. Though it is no match for Lalo's earlier concertante violin works, this opus is also "very melodious, especially in the slow movement and in the final vivace, where the mystic accents of Slavic folk tunes prevail."[39] According to Stengel, "another one-sided virtuoso composer was Georges Pfeiffer, as illustrated in his Third Concerto in B Major, Op. 86."[40] A look through the score fully confirms this judgment. The concerto's disproportionate passage work entwines itself around scanty thematic material, which is essentially based on a simple triadic melody.

The increased consciousness of a need to emulate the works of Classic composers sometimes led to strange results, even in the concertante realm. For instance, Louis Brassin draws upon Beethoven when he entitles the movements of his programmatic *Concerto pastorale* "Ländliche Eindrücke" (Mässig bewegt) [Rural Impressions (Moderately fast)], "Bei Bauern" (Im Zeitmass des Menuetts) [Among Farmers (At a minuet tempo)], and "Aufschwung" [Upsurge] (Allegro con fuoco). The sequence of sonata form in the first movement, scherzo in the second, and rondo in the third resembles Saint-Saëns's Op. 22 and the Vicomtesse de Grandval's Concertino. Brassin falls back on Beethoven in the orchestra as well: Bird calls by the flutes and a shepherd melody by the oboe had already depicted the rural landscape in the *Pastorale* symphony. However, [Brassin's] "piano composition is not always elegant; too often the piano falls into worn-out figures."[41]

In 1849, 12-year-old Ernest Guiraud, whose father had emigrated to New Orleans in the thirties, returned to Paris. There, as a composition pupil of Halévy, he soon became famous. Beginning in 1880, he taught at the Paris Conservatory, and among his students were Debussy and Dukas. He had little success with his works, and faded into oblivion soon after his sudden death in 1892. Shortly before his death, Guiraud had finished orchestrating Offenbach's *Tales of Hoffmann;* now he left his own opera sketch "Frédégonde," which Dukas and Saint-Saëns completed and staged fairly successfully in December 1895. Guiraud's Caprice for Violin is a colorfully orchestrated virtuoso piece with a tendency toward a chromatic style.

Emile Sauret, a pupil of Bériot and presumably also of Vieuxtemps, continued the tradition of the Ecole Liégoise, both as a violinist and in his numerous compositions. "He differed from Sarasate in his passionate, often stormy delivery, which, in his varied programs, was also useful for contemporary works, such as the concertos of Busoni, Dvorák, and Moszkowski."[42]

Even in its title, D'Indy's *Lied* for violoncello, Op. 19 (1884), reveals the strong influence that German Romanticism had on the composer at the time. The piece in three-part song form, which takes a scant 10 minutes to play, essentially consists of two contrasting themes—one in B-flat major and one in G minor. The periodic symmetry of the melody testifies to the distinct form-consciousness of the composer, who had been schooled in the Classic style.

It was also in 1884 that César Franck wrote his poème symphonique *Les Djinns,* based on Victor Hugo's poem by the same name. This work presents a special interpretation of the concertante idea, designating the piano as "un des exécutants."[43] Originally written for two pianos, the work was not performed until 1885, and then in an orchestral arrangement.[44]

Without making clear programmatic references to Hugo's poetry, Franck manages to create the ghostly mood of his textual model in a musically effective way, through swelling and fading dynamics and through the ostinato rhythmic motif (Figure 10.1). The basic key of F-sharp minor undergoes copious modulation. The formal pattern *ABAB'* allows the lyric cantilena to triumph over the ominous ostinato.

♩. ♪♩. ♪♩ ♩

Figure 10.1. Rhythmic motif in Franck's *Les Djinns.*

Diémer had performed *Les Djinns* very successfully in the Châtelet the same year it was written, and Franck showed his gratitude to his interpreter by dedicating the *Variations symphoniques* to him. His Violin Sonata (1886), *Prélude, Choral et Fugue* (1884), and *Prélude, Aria et Final*

(1886–87) show how heavily his composing in general was concentrated on the piano in the decade of the eighties.

In his variation work, Franck follows one of the basic symphonic principles, thematic dualism, as expressed in the two themes of the sonata movement. Both the first theme (Example 10.10) and the second (Example 10.11) are varied in the course of the work. The composer strives for a much stronger link between the two themes—no doubt due to the concentrated form—than Saint-Saëns did in his Op. 44, where the variations are also based on two themes.

Example 10.10. Franck, *Variations symphoniques,* m. 5ff.

Example 10.11. Franck, *Variations symphoniques,* m. 99ff.

The title of the work is a conscious attempt to get away from the traditional concertante idea. The piano breaks away from the orchestra and appears solo only three times, each time for a period of seven measures. As in *Les Djinns,* Franck thought of the piano as a part of the orchestra, so the danger of superficial virtuosity was ruled out from the outset.

The *Variations symphoniques* reveals a vague three-part structure. After a clearly defined four-measure orchestra introduction, the first section (Poco allegro, F-sharp minor, 4/4) presents the first theme. The second part begins with the introduction of the new theme in m. 92 (Allegretto quasi adagio in F-sharp minor, 3/4), which is subsequently presented in six variations. The last section, beginning in m. 285 (Allegro non troppo, F-sharp major, 2/2), consists of a brilliant rondo in which the first theme predominates. The rondo is certainly the most concertante section of the entire work.

The variation form is one of the oldest forms in Western music.[45] As a component of concertante works, it can be traced back to Johann Christian Bach. Mozart also used it several times (e.g., in the finale of his 24th Piano Concerto in C Minor, K. 491, and as the final movement of his Sinfonia concertante for four wind instruments in E-flat Major, K. 297b, Appendix 9). But not until Liszt's *Totentanz* (1849–55), a paraphrase on the *Dies irae* of the Gregorian Requiem, does it appear as the basis for an entire work. It is interesting to note that the first performance of this work with orchestra did not take place until 1881, in a concert in Antwerp under the direction of Peter Benoit, with Julius Zarembski as soloist.[46] Thus, it is quite possible that Franck was under the influence of the *Totentanz* when he created his *Variations symphoniques*. On the other hand, Saint-Saëns's Op. 44, which had already been written in 1875, could not have been influenced.

Although "one of his most remarkable works, modern in style and of utmost elegance"[47] in the opinion of the contemporary press, Lalo's *Fantaisie-Ballet* for violin was no more successful than his concerto Op. 20 or the *Concerto russe*. Presumably this work was also written for Sarasate. Only a brief note could be found concerning the Belgian H. Balthasar Florence, who later became a piano and harmonium manufacturer: "His theater works are forgotten. His mass, his violin concerto, and his meritorious Sanctus for male chorus are still performed."[48] Florence's Violin Concerto in A Minor is a distinctly lyrical single-movement work, for which the designation "concertino" is more apt than for Saint-Saëns's Op. 20. The format, an animated middle section framed by two slow sections, corresponds more to song form than to three-movement concerto form.

Emile Bernard, organist at the Eglise Notre-Dame-des-Champs, began his career as a piano virtuoso.[49] While his Romance Op. 33 for flute embraces a pleasant salon style, his two-movement *Concerto Fantaisie* of 1886 exhibits "unabashed virtuosity."[50] The only interesting aspect, at best, is the structure: two fast movements, both in rondo form.

After his enormous triumphs as an opera composer, Charles Gounod, in the last decade of his life, turned to instrumental music and wrote three works. His Fantasia on the Russian National Anthem, a work with variations, was followed by the waltz series *Le Rendez-vous* and a Suite concertante.[51] All three were for pedal piano, the instrument to which Schumann devoted his three cycles, Op. 56, 58, and 60, and for which Saint-Saëns conceived his Op. 22. All three works are nothing more than occasional compositions. The piano part is undemanding and, especially in the Fantasia, is often obscured by an excessively heavy orchestra part.

The cellist Joseph Hollmann, dedicatee and superb interpreter of Saint-Saëns's Op. 119, who later gave the premiere performance of Op. 132 with Eugène Ysaye, also tried his hand at composing. Although his Second Concerto in A Minor has a wealth of melodic ideas and a well-thought-out format, the cellists of his day were frightened off by the enormous complexities of the solo part, so that with the death of its composer the work lost its only interpreter as well. At any rate, Hollmann always uses virtuoso passages in an intentional way, well-adapted to the development of the music.

Gabriel Pierné, an organ pupil of Franck and his successor at the Eglise Sainte-Clotilde, received his composition training under Jules Massenet. Although his wide-ranging works are among the best that French music of the late nineteenth and early twentieth centuries had to offer, his real significance lies in his work as director of the Colonne concerts and as an educator:

> Mr. Gabriel Pierné's talent, as Charles Malherbe has defined it, is founded on elegance and charm. Yet he also has no difficulty in rising to the level of the subject with which he is dealing, so that he becomes almost Classic in his works for harp and his piano concerto.[52]

His first concertante work, the *Fantaisie-Ballet* Op. 6 for piano, is a kind of concertante suite, whose movements are connected.[53] The piano part, with its alternating chordal and linear work, is especially well-considered.

Pierné's Piano Concerto in C Minor, written the following year, already shows great maturity.[54] "It ought to number among the most worthy works of its genre, but unfortunately it did not receive the necessary attention, even in France."[55] Especially remarkable here is the unconventional movement sequence, which is strongly reminiscent of Saint-Saëns's Op. 22. The first movement, an Allegro in sonata form, is preceded by a slow introduction. Here the piano predominates with a motif that appears again and again throughout the work, giving it an almost cyclic character. The soloist's prelude leads to the first prominent theme in double octaves. Here Saint-Saëns's Op. 29 could also have been an influential force.

As in Op. 22, Pierné uses a three-part scherzo as the middle movement of his concerto; its theme resembles its "model" in its rhythm and course so much that any coincidence must be ruled out. This is followed by a brilliant final rondo (Allegro un poco agitato). The pedal point of the basses and timpani provides a base for the sequential figurations of the solo, this being another technique often found in Saint-Saëns's music.

Traces of the allegro and scherzo themes turn up several times in the course of the movement, thus lending maximum unity to the work. In general, Pierné tends to avoid Classic forms in his concertante works. Rather, he develops his abilities best through structures he has created himself.[56]

I was unable to find any information on Fernand de la Tombelle, whose Piano Concerto in F Minor Op. 26 is deposited at the Bibliothèque Nationale in Paris. The work reveals a pianist who is proficient but not a virtuoso. Traditional in format and more lyrical in its basic mood, as revealed in the long string cantilenas, it is far inferior to Pierné's concerto in inventiveness and refinement.

In the same year, Saint-Saëns responded to the French music world's growing interest in Hispanicisms with his *Havanaise.* Both this work and Op. 94 lose significance if you consider that Brahms produced his double concerto at the same time. And yet—I think it is important to point this out—concertante music outside France cannot diminish Saint-Saëns's merit. Despite his cosmopolitan attitude, he is a true representative of Romantic music culture and, as such, is certainly one of the few to attain international recognition. It would be wrong and pointless to try to pit Saint-Saëns against Brahms or other masters; here stand two great figures who cannot be compared, whose different intentions inevitably led to different results. If anyone is bound and determined to compare the Frenchman with other composers and their concertante works, some possibilities would be Max Bruch, Anton Rubinstein, Peter Tchaikovsky, Antonin Dvorák or Edvard Grieg.

Bordes, a pupil of Franck and close friend of d'Indy, was one of the founders of the Schola Cantorum. He also played an influential role in the renaissance of early music in France.[57] Consequently, liturgical and other sacred music make up the bulk of his compositions. However, he also worked hard to highlight the folk music of his Basque homeland.

In addition to several editions compiled under the title *Archives de la Tradition basque,* his works include a *Trio basque* and a *Suite basque* for flute and strings, both published in 1888, followed by the *Rhapsodie basque* for piano and orchestra in 1890.[58] The format and style of the latter work in particular is unmistakably modeled after Saint-Saëns's *Rhapsodie d'Auvergne*.

The followers of the Schola Cantorum were the first to discover the potential in French folk music. This came at a time when nationalism was spreading everywhere, during the second half of the nineteenth century. D'Indy drew from his extensive folk song collections when he wrote his *Fantaisie* for oboe, Op. 31. The piece was unsuccessful, whether because of an unfortunate choice of solo instrument or because the trite use of already simple melodies did not sit well with audiences. Even the composer later renounced this work, which is a curious combination of folk themes and an "atmosphère ça et là tristanienne" [here and there Tristanlike atmosphere].[59]

The Berceuse Op. 16 for violin by Fauré, an orchestrated version of a chamber music composition written 10 years earlier, is of no great importance.

Imperceptibly, a change had begun to take place in the French music world. The influence of the Italians was long forgotten, the revolutionary newness of Wagner had worn off, and the great names of the nineteenth century, who in their youth had represented the future of French music, were supplanted by their pupils of the new generation. While Lalo was creating his Piano Concerto in F Minor, dedicated to Diémer and no more successful than his other concertante works, while Dubois was enjoying brief success with a monumental *Fantaisie triomphale* for organ, and while Widor was writing his Fantaisie Op. 62,[60] subtitled *Morceau de concert* and overladen with counterpoint and a variation sequence that culminates in a double fugue on the theme—in other words, while French music was indulging in "constructivism,"—Claude Debussy, 1884 winner of the Prix de Rome, was producing his first compositions.

At first Debussy was still under the influence of Wagner, as we sense in the cantata *La Damoiselle élue*. Although he looked back on his training period at the Paris Conservatory with bitterness and hatred, it had infected him with a "Classic" conscience that was not easily overcome.

Debussy's most comprehensive concertante composition tries to deny tradition even in its title, *Fantaisie,* but it turns out to be a concerto [for piano and orchestra] in the traditional sense after all. Vincent d'Indy wanted to premiere the first movement in a Société Nationale concert, but just before the concert, Debussy withdrew the score. He defended his action in a letter to d'Indy:

> It seems to me that playing only the first movement of the Fantaisie would not only be dangerous, but it would give the wrong impression. On reflection, [I feel that] an adequate performance of all three movements would be better than a satisfying performance of only the first.[61]

The argument is threadbare. Deep down, Debussy was afraid of being counted among the "constructivists," from whom he also tried to dissociate himself with his colossal orchestral apparatus.[62]

Just as Saint-Saëns had been forced several decades earlier to choose between the Classic tradition and the lyricism of the Italian school, now Debussy wavered between Saint-Saëns, as representative of tradition, and Wagner. *La Damoiselle élue* continues the ideas of the Bayreuth master, while

> the *Fantaisie* follows the cyclic concerto form favored by Saint-Saëns, Franck, and d'Indy. The themes, which are developed rhythmically, carry over from one movement to the next. When the work was finished, Debussy accused himself of a rash mistake. He realized that his style threatened to betray his belief. He disavowed the *Fantaisie.* Because of its adherence to rules and its contrapuntal framework, it seemed to him to smell of school.[63]

Debussy's terror of walking in the footsteps of tradition ballooned into angry tirades against its authoritative representative, Saint-Saëns. The latter, in turn, saw in Debussy a troublesome innovator who "tends to overestimate musical tone color and must therefore guard against impressionism, one of the most dangerous enemies of true art."[64] Even in the *Fantaisie,* Debussy shows a tendency to dismantle the tonal framework, placing altered chords next to each other (Example 10.12). With

Example 10.12. Debussy, Fantaisie 1, m. 29.

its two movements, the second of which is further divided into two parts, the work does not follow the traditional concertante format. Debussy never uses the piano in solo; it is primarily used for color. Despite his variational treatment of the thematic material, his score in general is geared to tonal considerations.

With Debussy, the heyday of French Romanticism was inevitably headed for its end. The years after the war of 1870–71 had brought new vitality to instrumental music, and the new generation of composers tried to realize at last the French national style that Gounod, Saint-Saëns, and, before them, Berlioz had dreamed of and worked for. The age of the virtuosos was past, and a new aesthetic for instrumental playing was beginning to catch on.

The 30 years between 1870 and the turn of the century saw the deaths of the most important representatives of Romanticism: Auber (1871), de Castillon (1873), Bizet (1875), David (1876), Offenbach (1880), Alkan (1888), Franck (1890), Delibes (1891), Lalo and Guiraud (1892), Gounod (1893), Lekeu and Chabrier (1894), Godard (1895), Thomas (1896), and Chausson (1899). It also saw a new generation born: Schmitt (1870), de Séverac (1873), Roger-Ducasse (1873), Hahn (1874), Ravel (1875), Caplet (1878), Durey (1888), Milhaud, Honegger, and Madame de Tailleferre (1892), Poulenc and Auric (1899). Debussy stands as a link between these fundamentally different worlds. Saint-Saëns remained true to himself, and even if he had wanted to, he could never have become a representative of the new French school.

The Age of Impressionism was dawning in France, and it would change all art forms substantially. The World Exhibition of 1889 had provided new impetus; exoticism, roughly a half-century after David's "Le Désert," was celebrating new triumphs; and success at the Paris Opéra had long since ceased to be a guarantee of fame and recognition. The national schools were striving for a new kind of music, consciously distancing themselves from the Romantic trend that was spreading through all Europe. For the first time, the logic of the tonal structure that Wagner's *Tristan und Isolde* had already set tottering in 1865 was brought under question. All this was happening in France, a country whose music heretofore had been only a peripheral phenomenon on the European cultural scene. Saint-Saëns, once the subject of controversy as a revolutionary himself, was now reputed to be a pedantic follower of outmoded traditions.

11

The French Solo Concerto from 1891 to 1921 (from Op. 89 to Op. 162)

The changed circumstances in the French world of music were also reflected in the concertante productivity of Camille Saint-Saëns. Except for Op. 103 and 119, the concertante works generated in the last 30 years of his life are of minor significance. It is almost as if the boycotting of the concerto form had silenced him completely. Saint-Saëns still defended the solo concerto adamantly as having a promising future,[1] while d'Indy, despite his own concertante works, fought on the opposing side.[2] Yet, Op. 119 essentially marks the end of Saint-Saëns's efforts to reform the concertante concept.

Interestingly, it was not only the concertante concept that died out. Op. 78, written in 1886, was Saint-Saëns's last significant orchestral work. The emphasis was now clearly on the great vocal compositions on the one hand, and on a group of chamber music and piano works on the other hand, which were Classic in every respect: string quartets, duo sonatas, and fugues. Furthermore, we see a disparity of level in Saint-Saëns's works that was never so obvious before: Simple occasional compositions, such as the piece *Sur les bords du Nil,* Op. 125, for military band followed immediately after masterpieces like the Fantasie for Violin and Harp, Op. 124. Such juxtapositions document the composer's helplessness in the face of the new French music, and they show it more clearly, perhaps, than do his writings of that period.

Numerous documents prove that Saint-Saëns had certainly studied the music of Debussy[3] and had acknowledged that he avoided triteness and banality.[4] Presumably Saint-Saëns recognized in Debussy, who was almost 30 years his junior, the chance for some of his own ideas to be perpetuated. At least he felt more of an affinity here than he could ever muster for the "ideas of Mr. Vincent d'Indy."[5] Be that as it may, Debussy, in calling for a distinctly French music reminiscent of the clavecinists, was expressing something that Diémer and Saint-Saëns had advocated many years earlier.

Unlike the graduates of the Schola Cantorum, the new school saw the concerto form as a glorification of the despised constructivism and staunchly opposed the continued existence of the genre as such. Even Fauré, after his unfinished Op. 14, made no further attempt in the area of the solo concerto; Debussy repented of his *Fantaisie* as a sin of youth; and not until the 1930s did Ravel start a new trend with his two piano concertos.

During Saint-Saëns's last creative period, when he distanced himself more and more from the concerto form, most of the concertante works by other composers came from representatives of two trends. On one hand, composers of late-Romantic orientation, who could not subscribe fully to either the Classic or impressionistic ideal, tried to give new meaning to the concerto through unconventional form and content. Foremost among these was Ernest Chausson, with his Concerto in D Major, Op. 21, a sextet that sets concertante piano and violin solos opposite a string quartet.

> Should this unconventional format be seen as an attempt by the musician to revive the old French "concert" of the eighteenth century and the Italian concerto grosso, where two soloists are contrasted, in a kind of new-found ripieno, to a more lavish ensemble with a more orchestral calling?[6]

Though no one knows, it stands to reason that Chausson intended to create a chamber music work along the lines of Franck's piano quintet rather than to revive Baroque forms. At any rate, Chausson has a unique role in French music of the late nineteenth century, apart from any school or trend. His monumental and tremendously sonorous Op. 21 is unmatched by any other work of that period.

On the other side were the efforts to preserve Romantic aesthetics at any price, to continue putting together concertos from lyrical and virtuoso elements that had long since gone out of style.[7] It was primarily composers of this bent who instigated the protest of 1904. Adrien Bérou underscores the outmoded quality of his Op. 46 even in its title. Neither the adjective "romantique" nor the formal designation "concertino" reflect the artistic trends of the 1890s. Also, his emphasis on three-part form must be regarded as a conscious protest against the new school. Bérou, on whom I could find no biographical data, wanted to revive the language of the Ecole Liégoise with his work, but at the same time he wanted to cast aside periodic theme formation—an undertaking that was doomed to failure from the outset.

It also became increasingly common in the ensuing years for composers to ignore the traditional practice of entitling works only with a designation of the form or genre. Even if a work adhered to Classic structures, they would often try, with flowery adjectives—as Dubois did with "religieuse" and "triomphale"—or with newfangled titles, to mislead the audience as to its real nature. Even Saint-Saëns, with his Op. 89, must be regarded as a follower of this new trend.

No doubt Bernard also recognized that a virtuoso piece such as his *Concerto-Fantaisie* was no longer anything to write home about. His one-movement *Concertstück*—the German title originated with the composer himself—Op. 40 is a series of variations followed by a rondo. As for Simon's Piano Concerto, Op. 19, I was able to uncover very little about either the work or its composer. The piece is not inconsequential in that it reveals a preference for rhythmic combinations and syncopations that do not actually come into their own until a later period. Other than that, it is in three movements and conventional in its solo part.

In his *Scènes écossaises,* Op. 138, Godard was just as unsuccessful with the oboe as solo instrument in 1893 as d'Indy had been a few years earlier in his Op. 31. The work is a suitelike composition that recalls the Baroque tradition of hornpipes, here enriched with melodies that are mainly lyrical and whose Scottish origins shall be left an open question.

Jules-Auguste Bordier, known as Bordier d'Angers, was one of the few French composers who made a serious effort to bring culture to the provinces instead of seeking fame and fortune in Paris. Not until the final years of his life did he move from Angers back to the French capital, since the provincial city administration denied him further subsidies for his concert series.[8] Nearly all Bordier's compositions awaken great expectations in the listener, because his original and appealing titles seem to suggest something special. However, as in many of his other works, it turns out that in his *Suite fantaisiste,* Op. 40/1, the subtitle "Airs d'Eglise" is exhausted in a few church-modal expressions; and unfortunately there is also nothing about it suggesting fantasy. Besides, the solo cello part lacks double stops or chords and is rather dull.

As efforts to preserve the solo concerto through these various trends continued in France, music in Germany and Eastern Europe was moving in a new direction. Late Romanticism still influenced the early works of Scriabin, Busoni, and others, but soon a major part of the European music world, including these two composers, turned to expressionism, which would far surpass the efforts of Debussy and his circle in doing away with traditional rules. A work such as Godard's Second Piano Concerto, full of figurative archaisms (Alberti basses, octave chains, and arpeggiated triads) and thematically still in the long outmoded Italian lyrical style, could hardly expect to be successful, even in France. By the end of his life, Godard had to acknowledge with his salon-style instrumental works that he had arrived on the scene about 50 years too late. The same may have been true of Victor Divoir with his *Romance sans paroles* and Alfred Bachelet with his *Poème.* These works are worthy miniature pieces, like those Fauré created in such great numbers. Yet, Divoir and Bachelet were rejected by the new school, which considered the romantic sentimentality exhibited in the two pieces to be an evil second only to constructivism.

Saint-Saëns's symmetrical structures, almost without exception, trace back to Baroque or even older models and are therefore not to be equated with the constructivism condemned by Debussy, which was essentially the preservation of Classic structures as defined in the rules taught at the Paris Conservatory. Debussy, after placing more emphasis on tone and color in the works of his middle period, stands fully under the umbrella of traditional form in his third creative phase. Saint-Saëns's last piano concerto, written in 1896, is quite comparable to Debussy's *Estampes* (1903) in its tendencies.

Saint-Saëns's merit is even more apparent when we compare his

Op. 103 to other French concertante works written in 1896. Louis Lacombe and Edouard Broustet betray the nature of their compositions in their very titles: *Au tombeau d'un hèro* and *Cantilena amorosa.* Both are a mixture of Italian lyricism and new German dramatics, but the accompanying orchestra, through stationary dissonant chords, tries to appear "impressionistic."

Even Paul Lacombe, whose four-movement Suite in A Minor, Op. 52 "seems to trace back to Saint-Saëns in [its] free format," could not shed his image as a composer deeply rooted in Romantic art.[9] His Op. 52 has "a clean polish, appealing character and catchy themes," but still falls far short of Saint-Saëns.[10] Although solo and orchestra are balanced and the thematic material is used skillfully, the harmonic monotony and excessive passage work render the composition meaningless.

Admittedly the Piano Concerto in E-flat Major Op. 16 by Pierre Douillet commands even less interest. The composer remains faithful to the traditional three-movement form and takes up the themes of the first two movements again in the final rondo, but he becomes mired in trite virtuoso phrases that do not even meet Liszt's standards.

After his success with Op. 21, Chausson tried to compose a similar work in 1897, this time for piano, viola, oboe, and string quartet. Unfortunately it was never finished. Dubois, with his Second Piano Concerto in F Minor, comes close to Brahms's style. The four-movement work, with a scherzo as the third movement, appears to be modeled on Brahms Op. 83, especially in the internal structures of the various sections.[11]

The Fantaisie for violoncello by Massenet is one of the deplorable sorties of an operatic composer into the realm of instrumental music. It is as dull as de Joncières's violin concerto. The fact that the work has managed to survive is probably attributable only to the composer's illustrious name and the all-too-meager cellists's repertoire.

In 1898, Bordes and Sauret tried their luck with works inspired by folklore—among them Bordes's *Rhapsodie basque,* which may have been modeled after Saint-Saëns's Op. 73.[12] On the other hand, the disappearance of the Piano Concerto in C Minor by Eugène Anthiome is indeed a pity—a work that would have deserved greater attention for its excellent instrumentation, charming melodies and harmonies, and clear form.

> Chausson came across as extremely ascetic in his orchestral music, scarcely "modernistic," certainly not decadent; he often expanded the basic musical idea, but the thematic intricacies never were mere window dressing. The *Poème* for violin and orchestra—Concerts Colonne, 4 April 1897—seems to me to be the perfect example of what I have just said: It is thoroughly Classic in its tight unity, in the fact that all variations lead back to a savage and darkly expressive central phrase, which gushed forth so movingly from the tumultuous depths of the orchestra under Ysaye's bow.[13]

It is not only this "solide architecture interne [solid internal structure]" that makes Chausson's *Poème,* Op. 25 one of the best concertante works of his day.[14] More importantly, it is one of the few works of that era in which Romantic lyricism is portrayed not as a relic of the past but in a contemporary vein. Even the main theme (Example 11.1) carries enormous tension and is capable of supporting the work's complex five-part structure. The three basic features of Chausson's music, which

Example 11.1. Chausson, *Poème,* Op. 25, m. 31ff.

Debussy defined in 1913 as "freedom of form, harmonious proportions, and dreamy softness," are applied here to perfection.[15] But Chausson, too, had the tragic misfortune of later falling victim to the rabble-rousing campaign of the anti-Wagnerians and being posthumously condemned. Statements such as: "One can scarcely imagine a more complete lack of character, more ridiculous fabrication, more trivial composition and inspiration," said of his opera *Le Roi Arthus,* barred most of Chausson's works from success.[16]

> Louis Aubert, master pupil of Fauré at the Paris Conservatory,[17] belongs to that group of composers who renewed French music from 1895 to 1900 by freeing it from Italian and German influences, thereby leading it back to its unique national character, which ties it, via Saint-Saëns and Berlioz, to Rameau and Couperin.[18]

His Fantaisie in B Minor, Op. 8, is similar in form to his teacher's Ballade Op. 19, but the treatment of the thematic material is novel.

Whereas Delafosse offers little that is new in his "three-movement, somewhat superficial" piano concerto,[19] the Piano Concerto in C Minor/C Major, Op. 16, by André Gédalge is "one of the first to herald the return to the concertante style."[20] The three movements of the work are linked thematically and run together attacca; solo and orchestra are carefully balanced, especially in the middle movement; and the composer skillfully fits contrapuntal passages into the formal framework.

It would, of course, be too great an undertaking to try to discuss every concertante composition of this period in detail. Although the index may give the impression that the turn of the century was the actual heyday of the French solo concerto, one soon realizes that appearances deceive. Most of the works listed are of no interest or consequence; they are only offshoots from the Romantic tradition and could claim very few major successes, even in their day. Since my main concern here is to demonstrate that Saint-Saëns is the actual central figure in the concertante music of France, let me merely touch upon or completely bypass works that are clearly inferior. Among these are Dubois's *Andante cantabile,* Grobet's violin concerto, and Sarasate's Op. 42.

In his Concertino in E Minor, Pugno, "an altogether brilliant pianist," follows the trend of disguising the form.[21] Like Gédalge's concerto, the work has three connected monothematic movements.[22]

Baron Frédéric d'Erlanger, a banker's son from Germany, studied in Paris but settled in England soon afterward, where his Violin Concerto Op. 17 was premiered by Fritz Kreisler on 12 March 1902.[23] The work has a strange coolness, similar to the Violin Concerto of Jean Sibelius. The soloist is active almost continuously and backed by lengthy pedal point passages in the orchestra. At least this concerto is more interesting than the composer's Op. 18, which has a lyrical sentimentality in common with the two cello works by Dubois that were written the same year.

The Morceau de concert for harp by Gabriel Pierné, compared to his piano concerto of 1887, reveals a growing impressionistic influence. This is evident both in the treatment of the solo instrument, and in the themes, which emphasize color elements and leave the clear, periodic structuring of earlier works far behind. The Harp Concerto by Henriette Renié, in contrast, is deeply rooted in Romanticism.

The turn of the century brought increased interest in many solo instruments that had received relatively little attention during the Romantic period because they were ill-suited to the brilliant virtuoso style. The Divertissement for Trumpet by Charles Bordes documents this change, as does d'Indy's Chorale Variations, Op. 55 for saxophone. The latter work, whose tempo marking "Mouvement de Passacaille" was a reference to Bach's famous Organ Passacaglia, reverses the traditional variation structure and does not present the theme until the end of the work.[24] D'Indy had already used the same procedure in 1896 in his symphonic variation work *Istar,* Op. 42. Incidentally, Op. 55 was commissioned by an American, Elisa Hall, who had turned to several French musicians with a request for saxophone literature. Debussy's *Rhapsodie* is another work that owes its origin to Elisa Hall.[25]

Let me also mention the charming Concertino for Flute, Op. 107 by the extremely prolific composer Cécile Chaminade, which, despite its salon-style ease, is impressive in its melodic inventiveness. No less salonlike, but unfortunately less original, is Emile Bernard's *Nocturne,* Op. 51. The piece is a sonata movement in which, in place of the development, a new theme appears; possibly Saint-Saëns's Op. 20 was the inspiration here.

Hans Engel was right when he referred to Jules Massenet's piano concerto as the "nadir of the French solo concerto."[26] The "piquant dance motifs" lose their charm from constant repetition, and the "Airs slovaques" of the finale pander to popular taste without being original.[27] Furthermore, the ethnic origin of the melodies is under dispute. Several biographers speak of Hungarian themes, while the composer himself indicates Slovakian sources.[28] Audiences, too, preferred Massenet's musical theater works. "With a little irreverence, they sent him back to *Manon!* But this concerto was probably no worse than any other."[29]

With his Op. 119, Saint-Saëns bid farewell to the solo concerto form and proved once again, as with Op. 44, that the concerto can also do without Classic models, at least as far as form is concerned. Meanwhile, his concertos were recognized as French music's best contribution to the genre. Composers who cared about perpetuating the genre were orienting themselves more and more to Saint-Saëns's model.

Among them was Léon Moreau, whose Piano Concerto in C-sharp Minor, Op. 35, would have been inconceivable without Saint-Saëns's Op. 44.

> In the two-part first movement [he] develops the main theme in variations . . . In the scherzolike second movement (Intermède) the main theme undergoes further transformation. The slow movement and the rondolike closing movement are fused into one movement.[30]

The work is definitely one of the best French concertos of its time, but even so, the followers of the new school demanded elimination of the genre altogether.

In French and Belgian music of the nineteenth century, the solo concerto (as well as symphonic and chamber music) had existed in the shadow of opera. This state of affairs came to a head early in 1904 when those who championed an aesthetic (influenced by "wagnérisme") that they considered progressive, took the offensive. They would attend every *Concert Colonne* and interrupt, with whistles and catcalls, any performances of concertos and similar works, including those by Beethoven, Saint-Saëns, Paderewski, and Vieuxtemps. A battle raged in the newspapers, lasting several months, and there were several lawsuits. Jacques Bonzon, the leader of the "concerto foes," declared that the future belonged to opera, that the genre of the solo concerto was a "fossil" and that it was high time for it to disappear from concert programs.

Semper aliquid haeret (Something always sticks): though officially the solo concerto was "rehabilitated," the boycott turned out to be fatal for many works. These included the piano concertos of Massenet and Widor, Saint-Saëns's second cello concerto, and the piano concerto by Moreau mentioned above. They were hardly ever performed because concert managers were afraid of more demonstrations.

These events of 1904 continued to affect concert life until the mid 1920s, as is evident from the greatly reduced number of French solo concertos from this period. The scandal of 1904 was also reflected in writings such as Debussy's reviews:

> The mixed reception that greeted this concerto indicates, better than any critique, the path that Mr. Léon Moreau must now take. It has charming orchestral qualities, but their true charm did not come through; the piano part actually seemed to mock them. Without sharing the opinion of a part of the audience who displayed true Parisian wit, I feel that a piano concerto understood in that way clearly calls for the elimination of the piano once and for all.[31]

Oddly enough, Debussy himself turned in the following year to the genre of concertante music that he had so harshly judged. His *Danses* for chromatic harp and strings was written as a commission from the Pleyel firm. The fact that Debussy also met with rejection was admittedly not due to form. "For Mr. Debussy, dissonance has become the rule, consonance the exception. . . . His musical fabric has no structural concept, as it were; it is imprecise, hazy, disquieting, almost sickly."[32] The *Danses* and Saint-Saëns's Op. 122, which was written the same year, are worlds apart. Far removed from both these works is Béla Bartók's Op. 1, whose motor rhythm already points ahead to expressionism.

Just a few decades earlier, the musical world of Europe had been more or less unified, but with the awakening of national awareness and its influence on art, rifts had formed and were becoming increasingly divisive. Whereas Romanticism had been a cosmopolitan trend, composers were now classified according to countless "isms," which created factions even within a country. The diagram in Figure 11.1 may help to clarify this. Only the music of Central Europe shows up as a logical, self-contained development; in both France and Eastern Europe, there was some borrowing during critical phases. Also significant is the fact that French expressionism did not emerge until relatively late.

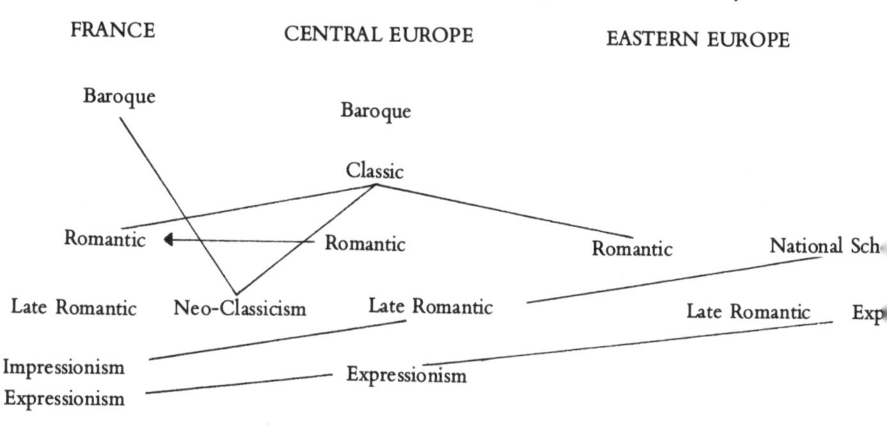

Figure 11.1. Interrelationships in European music.

Widor's Piano Concerto Op. 77 is also in the tradition of Saint-Saëns, whereas the *Villanelle* for horn by Paul Dukas is one of the national character pieces in the style of d'Indy. A very individualistic interpretation of the concertante concept is Ravel's *Introduction et allegro* for harp, accompanied by string quartet, flute, and clarinet. It is a sonata movement with a slow introduction, which, regardless of the septet setting, is a harp concerto in miniature.[33] After Chausson and Ravel, Manuel de Falla also tried using the concerto form in chamber music, with his Concerto for harpsichord, flute, oboe, clarinet, violin, and violoncello (1926). Incidentally, Ravel's work contains a written-out harp cadenza directly before the recapitulation—that is, at a place where room for a cadenza was provided in the violin concertos of Mendelssohn and Tchaikovsky and in Saint-Saëns's Op. 29.

Though the chromatic harp, for which Debussy wrote his *Danses,* never really caught on, André Caplet also devoted a work to this instrument—his multimovement étude based on a short story by Edgar Allan Poe, "The Masque of the Red Death." This work of fascinating tonal quality also has only a string quartet accompanying the solo. Especially impressive is a passage in which harmonies on the bass strings of the harp imitate the striking of a clock, while tremolos played sul ponticello in the strings send shudders down the listener's spine, in keeping with the subject matter.

Like Saint-Saëns's Op. 44, the Variations on an Aeolian Theme in B Minor, Op. 4, by Rhené-Baton has four identifiable sections. All four, which are run together, are variative, and the finale is treated as a fugue.[34] Shorter and relatively insignificant character pieces by Alfred Bachelet, Arthur Coquard, and Georges Brun vacillate between Romantic lyricism and impressionistically veiled sound. At the same time in Dresden, Sergei Rachmaninoff was preparing to depart for America with his Third Piano Concerto. It was a work of such scope and with such an unmistakable profession to virtuosity that it would have been inconceivable in France.

The stylistic differences now become more distinct from year to year. Saint-Saëns continues to stand by Romanticism, as evidenced in his Op. 132; Debussy's Rhapsody for Clarinet is a miniature piece that regards technical intricacies not as virtuoso effects but as an element of the musical development; Arthur van Dooren, with his Concerto Allegro, writes virtuoso music in the traditional sense; Max Reger's Piano Concerto is one of the last central European concertos of the late Romantic period; Glazunov's Piano Concerto appears outmoded next to the young Prokofieff's Op. 10; and Waghalter, Dalcroze, and Dubois try with their works to perpetuate lyricism. In his Op. 14, the Swiss composer Emile Blanchet shows himself to be totally under the influence of his teacher, Busoni.[35]

It would be pointless to devote equal attention to each of the rest of the works listed in Appendix A. Philippe Gaubert's cello concerto is the last French solo concerto for a long time. The new school had actually succeeded in spoiling the genre for composers. With few exceptions, the concertante works of the years between 1910 and 1930 are either harbingers of a completely new trend, expressionism, or they are remnants of that very same Romanticism whose decline composers like Dubois and Dupuis did not want to accept. Nothing was as suspect to expressionism as Romantic music "during which one can close one's eyes," as Jean Cocteau formulated it in *Le Coq et l'Arlequin,* the aesthetic manifesto of the Group de Six.[36]

World War I was another factor. Saint-Saëns became entangled in cultural-political disputes. His music had long ago ceased to be a French export item, and his integrity was questioned from the German as well as from the French side.[37] By the end of the war, if not before, it was clear that Romantic art all over Europe was dead, and it was now a matter of building something new on the ruins. Debussy was dead, and impressionism had died with him. Talk now centered on a group of young artists who wanted music to be understood no longer as an elitist, aesthetic product, but as a part of everyday life.

Igor Stravinsky, with his *Rite of Spring* in 1913, had shaken more than just the French music world. The Romantic aesthetic of ordered euphony had been superseded by motor action, realism, and the cancellation of all previous musical rules. Conservative works such as Saint-Saëns's Op. 154, 156, and 162 were rejected as reactionary and anachronistic. His contributions to French music were forgotten. And yet, after years of opposition, his work would eventually come to be recognized and respected as definitive after all.

12

Summary and Conclusion

"Indeed, Mr. Saint-Saëns's preference for early music is just as notorious as his hostility toward contemporary music."[1]

Saint-Saëns might have been spared such disdain, at least on the part of the French, had he not exposed himself to the cultural-political crossfire at the outbreak of World War I. An artist through and through, he tried to serve his country musically, but his efforts were not appreciated or even recognized.

> I hear that Saint-Saëns told the delighted crowd that during the war he had composed all kinds of theater music, songs, an elegy, and a piece for trombones. If he had made grenade shells instead, music might have been better off.[2]

Despite his anger, Ravel recognized that this same Saint-Saëns, who had discredited himself with his incendiary paper "Germanophilie," was very important to France. Thus, he later wrote to Jean Marnold: "All the idiocies uttered by Wagner, Saint-Saëns and Poueigh are of no importance; it's only their music that matters."[3]

When the war was over, there was too much rebuilding to be done at first for anyone to have given serious thought to musical problems. Furthermore, other young musicians, who made Debussy and Ravel seem like "scrap iron" in comparison, were lifting their voices and shaping the French music world of the future. American jazz had arrived in Paris and, in international thinking, demands for national music no longer had a place. Saint-Saëns still witnessed all this.

But with the passing of the main representatives of the former new school, Saint-Saëns was free of his bitterest opponents. Gradually those who saw him as the greatest French composer of the nineteenth century made their voices heard. Marcel Proust presumably had Saint-Saëns in mind when he had the fictitious composer Vinteuil appear in his massive work *A la recherche du temps perdu.*[4] Ravel placed him next to Mozart as the greatest master of the solo concerto and oriented himself to both while composing his own Concerto in G Major.[5]

Meanwhile, new groups had arisen: the "Société Musicale Indépendante," the "Groupe de Six," and the "Ecole d'Arcueil." Soon "Triton" and "Jeune France" followed as champions of progressive trends.[6] As opposition continued against the operas of Massenet and Gounod, against the salon style of Vieuxtemps, Godard, and all the others, against virtuosity, against the Wagnerians, and against Romantic sentimentality, it became more and more obvious that only a very few French composers were escaping these prejudices: Berlioz, Saint-Saëns, and Fauré.

Berlioz was "rehabilitated" as the most superb representative of symphonic music and musical theater, and Fauré was recognized as the master of chamber music, which had long been held in contempt; but Saint-Saëns was respected as the creator of the best solo concertos French Romanticism had produced. More and more composers emulated him, writing concertos that would have been unthinkable without his example. The fight that Debussy's school had initiated against the genre per se was forgotten, and even the graduates of the Schola Cantorum, most notably Albert Roussel, composed concertos after the style of Camille Saint-Saëns.

To conclude this work, I quote the obituary by Alfred Mortier, published in 1922, which gives an outstanding and far-sighted overview of the nature and work of the composer:

> The passing of Saint-Saëns is symbolic: It is an entire musical age, an entire system of aesthetics that has become part of the past. Saint-Saëns was the epitome of that which we call Tradition. He was the successor and universal heir of Haydn, Bach, Mozart, and Beethoven. His art is the unbreakable link in the chain that connects the eighteenth with the nineteenth century. His work is a mirror that reflects 100 years of music.
>
> Yet for several years Tradition has not fared well; young

musicians behave like those impetuous and ill-bred hooligans who show no respect for old ladies. They have opted to oppose Tradition and embrace the customs of those African villages where, it is said, they drown old people, who are deemed useless encumbrances.

To be sure, every age has had its innovators, and they are essential; without them art would die of paralysis. But the innovators of former times remained respectful toward their masters; they believed one could modify and transform the legacy and still respect the deceased and the wishes of the testator; they did not find it necessary to sully his memory.

We have changed all this. Many young artists want to be safe as they assume their inheritance. Others, thinking they are being more courageous, adamantly refuse the fortune they are offered, claiming they can start over without help from anyone. These are pure illusions, illusions of the ignoramus or scatterbrain. No one can free himself from Tradition. We are permeated with it; we are its beneficiaries from the moment we open our eyes to the light and our ears to sounds, and even before that moment, because we are dependent on our atavism, especially in the musical realm, as demonstrated by the families and dynasties of musicians. It is therefore better to rely openly on Tradition than to attempt a sly and impossible evasion.

So then, what is novelty? A contribution, a small building block. Let us not destroy, let us add on. And originality? It is using heritage in one's own way.

Saint-Saëns is the prototype of the traditionalist. This is also why the New School regarded him with such distrust. Nevertheless, he knew how to combine boldness with wisdom, and he was an innovator in a number of ways. But he had too much good taste to exceed moderation and venture into unknown territory. Musically he bears the stamp of atticism, the search for perfection in form. He was the Anatole France of modern music.

Today, atticism is no longer in vogue. Progressive musicians strive for genius, and everyone knows that genius can forgo moderation and good taste, just as it can forgo elegance and perfection. These are secondary virtues, good for second-rate artists who merely have talent.

Let us console ourselves. Time is a great schoolmaster who has already seen a good many ideas come and go under his rod.

The day will dawn again when people will recognize that taste is no small matter, that a sense of moderation takes great genius, that serenity shows greater mastery than vehemence, and that music that is pleasant to listen to is not necessarily mediocre.[7]

Appendices

A. Thematic List of Saint-Saëns's Concertante Works with Documentation of Sources

The only thematic listing of Camille Saint-Saëns's works is the *Catalogue général et thématique des œuvres de Camille Saint-Saëns* first published in 1897. A second revised printing appeared in 1908 and included all his published works up to and including Op. 124. The more recent listings by Marie Briquet (1963, col. 1276ff.) and James Harding (1965, 230ff.) should be mentioned though they are not thematic. Because of their errors and omissions, these two listings cannot be considered reliable sources.

For several years Sabina Ratner and Yves Gérard have been working on the first complete thematic catalogue of Saint-Saëns's works, including sketches, fragments, and unpublished compositions; they expect to complete their work in 1990. In dating the unnumbered Gavotte and the symphonic fragments to Op. 44/II (Bibliothèque Nationale MS. 909) and positioning several sketches in the chronology, I have gone by their research findings.

Titles, dedications, and movement headings in the following list are given in the original orthography. The list includes all the concertante works by Saint-Saëns of which I am aware. I have omitted the following two sketches, which may possibly also pertain to concertante compositions:

Ms. 823[5] Esquisse pour une oeuvre instrumentale "Allegro n°2" (352×268). The four-page manuscript of a work in F Major, which I could not relate to any piece by Saint-Saëns with which I am familiar; included in the Ratner/Gérard listing as a fragment of unknown date.

Ms. 823[6] Esquisse pour une pièce instrumentale, solo et quatuor (350×270). Another four-page fragment of a presumably concertante work or part of a larger composition for solo (probably for a string or wind instrument) and strings; it could also be a sketch for a chamber-music composition (quintet); included in the Ratner/Gérard listing as a fragment of unknown date.

The source documentation includes only those manuscripts and printed editions that were actually available to me in my work. The numbers in parentheses after autograph sources indicate their format in millimeters.

Op. 6

Tarantelle

pour Flûte et Clarinette avec accompagnement d'Orchestre ou de Piano

à MM. Dorus et Leroy
1re Flûte et 1re Clarinette de l'Académie Impériale (Nationale[1]) de Musique

piccolo, 2 oboes, 2 bassoons, 2 horns, 2 trumpets, 2 trombones, timpani, strings

Date of origin 1857; premiere 1857; published 1857

Presto ma non troppo

496 measures

Sources:

Ms.	2455	(BN)	sketches (350×270)
Ms.	836	(BN)	piano score (350×270)
A:	47178	(BN)	piano score
D & F	3481	(priv.)	piano score
Ac.e[10]	862	(BN)	score (Richault, Paris 1879)

1. D & F 3481: A M.M. DORUS et LEROY de l'Académie Nationale de Musique

Op. 17

Premier Concerto (Ré Majeur)

pour Piano avec accompagnement d'Orchestre

à Madame Alfred Jaëll

2 flutes, 2 oboes, 2 clarinets, 2 bassoons, 4 horns, strings

Date of origin 1858; premiere 1865; published 1875

Andante

386 measures

Andante sostenuto quasi adagio

52 measures

Allegro con fuoco

405 measures

Sources:

Ms.	487	(BN)	piano score (353×270)
D & F	2035	(priv.)	piano score
Ms.	489	(BN)	score (347×263)

Op. 58

Deuxième Concerto (Ut Majeur)

pour Violon avec accompagnement d'Orchestre (ou de Piano[1])

no dedication[2]

2 flutes, 2 oboes, 2 clarinets, 2 bassoons, 2 horns, 2 trumpets, 2 trombones, timpani, harp, strings

Date of origin 1858; premiere 1880; published 1879

Allegro moderato e maestoso

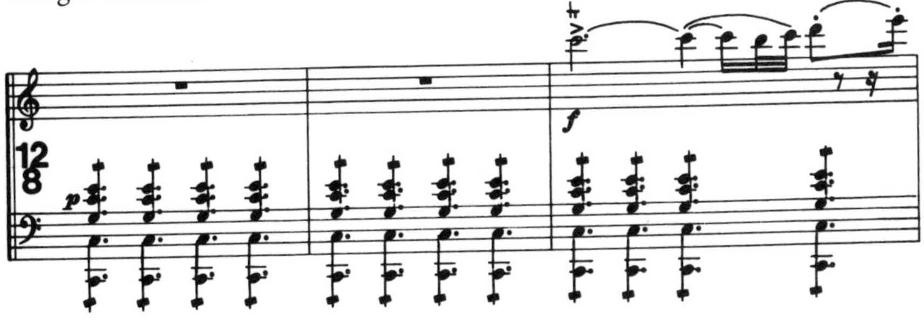

257 measures

Andante espressivo

168 measures

1. On the contemporary edition

2. The dedication "à Achille Dien" listed by Harding is wrong!

Allegro scherzando quasi Allegretto

406 measures

Sources:

Ms.	2493[1]	(BN)	sketches (350×270)
Ms.	484	(BN)	piano score (350×275)
D & F	2628	(priv.)	piano score
Ms.	483	(BN)	score (346×272)

Op. 20

Premier Concerto (Concertstück[1]) (La Majeur)

pour Violon avec accompagnement d'Orchestre

à Monsieur Pablo Sarasate

2 flutes, 2 oboes, 2 clarinets, 2 bassoons, 2 horns, 2 trumpets, timpani, strings

Date of origin 1859; premiere 1867; published 1868

Allegro

314 measures

Sources:

Ms.	2493[2]	(BN)	sketches, Copie Mme. Saint-Saëns (350×270)
Ms.	916[2]	(BN)	sketches (347×271)
Ms.	482	(BN)	score (348×270)
J.M.	757	(priv.)	score (Hamelle & Cie)

1. On the score J. M. 757

Op. 28

Introduction et Rondo Capriccioso

pour Violon avec accompagnement d'Orchestre

à Monsieur Pablo Sarasate

2 flutes, 2 oboes, 2 clarinets, 2 bassoons, 2 horns, 2 trumpets, timpani, strings

Date of origin 1863, premiere undated, published 1870

Andante malinconico

342 measures

Sources:

Ms.	2454bis	(BN)	Copie de Mme Saint-Saëns, préparée pour la gravure (350×270)
Ms.	2455	(BN)	sketches (350×270)
Ms.	916[2]	(BN)	sketches (347×271)
Ms.	2454	(BN)	piano score (350×270)
D & F	2041	(priv.)	piano score
D & F	7125	(priv.)	score

Op. 22

Deuxième Concerto (Sol Mineur)

pour Piano avec accompagnement d'Orchestre

à Madame (la Marquise[1]) A. de Villers née de Haber

2 flutes, 2 oboes, 2 clarinets, 2 bassoons, 2 horns, 2 trumpets, timpani, strings

Date of origin 1868; premiere 1868; published 1868

Andante sostenuto

116 measures

Allegro scherzando

346 measures

Presto

343 measures

Sources:

Ms.	488	(BN)	score (350×272)
F.S.	39[73]	(BN)	copy of a sketch for the first movement

1. Does not appear on score D & F 7137

			("voici un bout de phrase de mon concerto de piano, avec mille compliments C.S.")
D & F	2037	(priv.)	piano score
D & F	7137	(priv.)	score
Ms.	875[a]	(BN)	Esquisses et Brouillons
Ms.	928	(BN)	"Love's prayer" (mélodie arrangée sur l'adagio [sic] du deuxième Concerto pour piano et orchestre par une admiratrice de l'auteur et copiée par celle-ci; paroles d'"Emilie." Notice explicative de Ch. Mahlherbe.[2]) (350×244)

2. This suggestive treatment may possibly have come from Marie Reiset, later Vicomtesse de Grandval, who, as Saint-Saëns's pupil, had a brief affair with the composer.

Op. 27

Romance

pour Piano, Orgue et Violon[1]

à Monsieur Gustave Doré

2 flutes, 2 oboes, 2 clarinets, 2 bassoons, harp, strings

Date of origin 1868; premiere undated; unpublished

Andantino

115 measures

Sources:

Ms.	667	(BN)	score of the orchestrated version (350×270)
D & F	2040	(priv.)	original version

1. D & F 2040: pour Violon, Piano ou Harpe et Orgue

Op. 29

Troisième Concerto (Mi^{b})

pour Piano avec accompagnement d'Orchestre

à Monsieur E. M. Delaborde

2 flutes, 2 oboes, 2 clarinets, 2 bassoons, 2 horns, 2 trumpets, 3 trombones, timpani, strings

Date of origin 1869; premiere 1869; published 1875

Moderato assai

327 measures

Andante

109 measures

Allegro non troppo

437 measures

Sources:

D & F	2134	(priv.)	piano score
D & F	2176	(priv.)	score
D & F	8827	(priv.)	Allegro pour le piano d'après le Troisième Concerto Op. 29 (Ed. 1913)

Op. 37

Romance (Ré^b)

pour Flûte (ou Violon) avec accompagnement d'Orchestre ou de Piano

à Monsieur A. de Vroye

2 oboes, 2 clarinets, 2 bassoons, 4 horns, 2 trumpets, timpani, strings

Date of origin 1871; premiere undated; published 1874

Moderato assai

115 measures

Sources:

Ms.Cons.D.	8398	(BN)	piano score (240×304) (mais pas autographe, d'après Mme Yvonne Rokseth, Bibliothéquaire à la BN)
D & F	1953	(priv.)	piano score
K.	947	(BN)	score (D & F, Paris 1874)

Op. 33

Premier Concerto (La Mineur)

pour Violoncelle avec accompagnement d'Orchestre

à Monsieur A. Tolbecque

2 flutes, 2 oboes, 2 clarinets, 2 bassoons, 2 horns, 2 trumpets, timpani, strings

Date of origin 1872; premiere 1873; published 1873

Allegro non troppo

657 measures

Sources:

Ms.	824	(BN)	sketches (352×268)
Ms.	485	(BN)	piano score (348×270)
D & F	1746	(priv.)	score

Op. 36

Romance (Fa Majeur)

pour Cor (ou Violoncelle) avec accompagnement d'Orchestre ou de Piano

à Monsieur H. Garigue

2 flutes, oboe, 2 clarinets, bassoon, strings

Date of origin 1874; premiere undated; published 1874

Moderato

93 measures

Sources:

Ms.	837	(BN)	score (350×270)
D & F	1952	(priv.)	piano score

Op. 48

Romance (Ut Majeur)

pour Violon et Piano ou Orchestre

à Monsieur Alfred Turban

flute, oboe, clarinet, bassoon, 2 horns, strings

Date of origin 1874[1]; premiere undated; published 1876

Allegretto

190 measures

Sources:

Ms.	659	(BN)	score (352×270)
D & F	2289	(priv.)	piano score

1. Note on the handwritten score: "1er Août"

Op. 43

Allegro Appassionato

pour Violoncelle avec accompagnement de Piano ou d'Orchestre

à Monsieur Jules Lasserre

2 flutes, 2 oboes, 2 clarinets, 2 bassoons, 2 horns, strings

Date of origin 1875; premiere undated; published 1875; orchestrated 1876

Allegro appassionato

215 measures

Sources:

Ms.	852	(BN)	score (350×270), "signé et daté 1876 à la fin, Ms. ayant servi à la gravure."
Ms.	558	(BN)	piano score
Augener Ed.	10020	(priv.)	piano score
Ms.	852	(BN)	score

Unnumbered opus

Gavotte (Sol) N° 3

(pour Violoncelle avec accompagnement d'Orchestre ou de Piano[1])

no dedication

flute, English horn, 2 clarinets, strings

Date of origin 1875[2]; premiere undated; unpublished

Allegro non troppo

103 measures

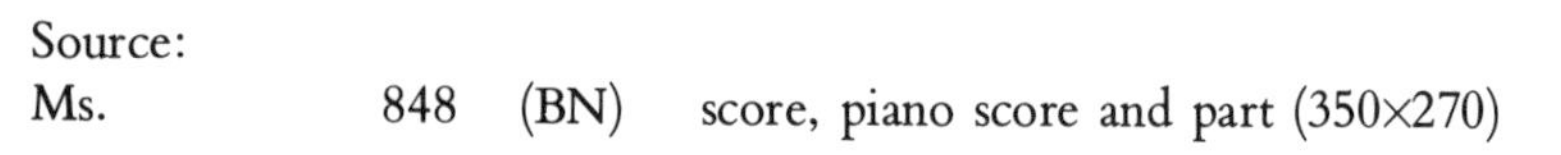

Source:
Ms. 848 (BN) score, piano score and part (350×270)

---

1. Not noted on the manuscript

2. Cf. discussion in Chapter 1.

Op. 44

Quatrième Concerto (Ut Mineur)

pour Piano avec accompagnement d'Orchestre

à Monsieur Antoine Door (Professeur de Piano au Conservatoire de Vienne[1])

2 flutes, 2 oboes, 2 clarinets, 2 bassoons, 2 horns, 2 trumpets, 3 trombones, timpani, strings

Date of origin 1875; premiere 1875; published 1877

Allegro moderato

116 measures

Andante

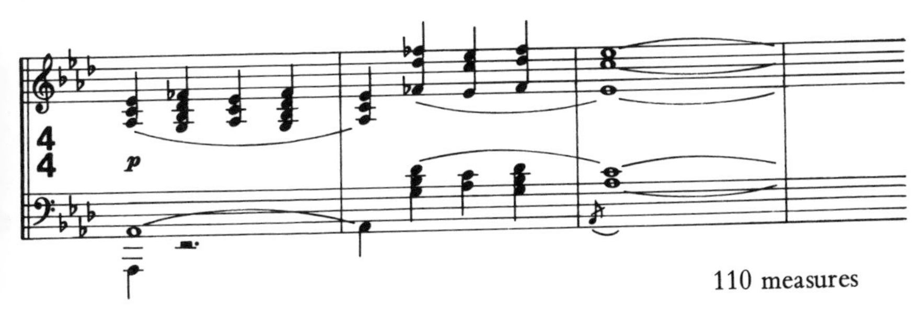

110 measures

Allegro Vivace

258 measures

Andante

37 measures

Allegro

368 measures

Sources:

Ms.	909	(BN)	Sketches of a symphonic movement[2] (350×270)
D & F	2280	(priv.)	piano score
D & F	7138	(priv.)	score

---

1. On the score D & F 7138

2. Cf. Chapter 2, note 22 (see next page)

Unnumbered opus (Op. 44)

no title[1]

no dedication

2 flutes, 2 oboes, 2 clarinets, 2 bassoons, 2 horns, 2 trumpets, strings, timpani

Date of origin 1854[2]; no premiere; unpublished

Lento assai

112 measures

Source:

Ms.	909	(BN)	score[3] (350×270)

---

1. Note on the manuscript: "N° 1"

2. Cf. Chapter 2, note 22

3. There are 112 continuous measures completed and fully orchestrated; then the manuscript breaks off, and subsequent pages clearly pertain to another work.

Op. 61

Troisième Concerto (Si Mineur)

pour Violon avec accompagnement d'Orchestre

à Monsieur Pablo Sarasate

2 flutes, 2 oboes, 2 clarinets, 2 bassoons, 2 horns, 2 trumpets, 3 trombones, timpani, strings

Date of origin 1880[1]; premiere 1880; published 1881

Allegro non troppo

294 measures

Andantino quasi allegretto

152 measures

Molto moderato e maestoso

468 measures

1. Note on the handwritten score: "mars"

Sources:

Ms.	916[9]	(BN)	sketches for the first movement (Par St. Saëns d'après l'écriture—au haut de la page[1]: "juillet 1874") The legibility of the date is extremely poor and could be "1894." I was unable to obtain any further information at the BN; I agree with Yves Gérard that 1874 is the more probable date. (350×270)
Ms.	720	(BN)	Allegro de Concert pour Violon et piano d'après le Troisième Concerto Op. 61 (350×270)
Ms.	731	(BN)	piano score (La partie du violon ne semble pas de la main du compositeur) (350×270)
Ms.	486	(BN)	score (353×272)
Ms.	899	(BN)	arrangement pour violon et piano d'Adam Laussel (350×270)
D & F	7139	(priv.)	score

Op. 62

Morceau de Concert

pour Violon avec accompagnement d'Orchestre (ou de Piano[1])

à Monsieur Ovide Musin

2 flutes, 2 oboes, 2 clarinets, 2 bassoons, 2 horns, 2 trumpets, timpani, strings

Date of origin 1880[2]; premiere undated; published 1880

Largamente

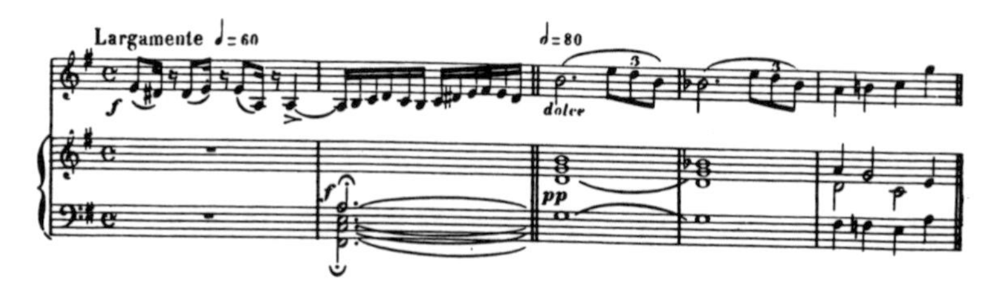

311 measures

Sources:

Ms.	900	(BN)	sketches (350×270)
Ms.	701	(BN)	score (350×270)
Ms.	733	(BN)	piano score (On-y-a joint le Point d'orgue composé pour ce morceau, signé et daté d'Ismaïlia) (350×270)
D & F	2803	(priv.)	piano score

---

1. On D & F 2803

2. Note on the handwritten piano score: "juillet 1880"

Op. 70

Allegro appassionato

pour Piano seul (ou[1]) avec accompagnement d'Orchestre

no dedication

2 flutes, 2 oboes, 2 clarinets, 2 bassoons, 2 horns, 2 trumpets, strings

Date of origin 1884; premiere undated; published 1884

Allegro

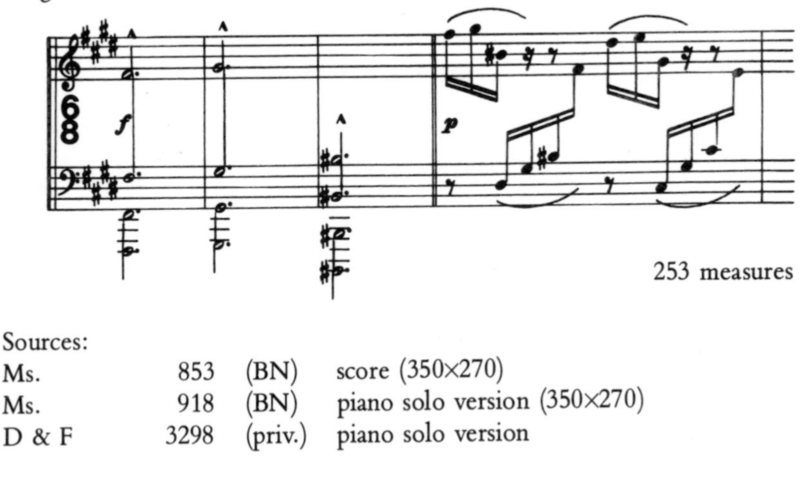

253 measures

Sources:

Ms.	853	(BN)	score (350×270)
Ms.	918	(BN)	piano solo version (350×270)
D & F	3298	(priv.)	piano solo version

1. Not listed in *Catalogue général et thématique des œuvres de Camille Saint-Saëns*.

Op. 73

Rapsodie[1] d'Auvergne

pour Piano et Orchestre[2]

à Monsieur Louis Diémer

3 flutes, 2 oboes, 2 clarinets, 2 bassoons, 4 horns, 2 trumpets, 3 trombones, timpani, percussion, strings

Date of origin 1884[3]; premiere undated; published 1884

Lento ad libitum

351 measures

Sources:

Ms.	546	(BN)	score (350×270)
D & F	3406	(priv.)	piano solo version

---

1. D & F 3406: Rhapsodie . . .

2. D & F 3406: . . . pour Piano

3. Note on the handwritten score: "Décembre"

Op. 83

Havanaise

pour Violon avec accompagnement d'Orchestre ou de Piano[1]

à Monsieur Diaz Albertini

2 flutes, 2 oboes, 2 clarinets, 2 bassoons, 2 horns, 2 trumpets, timpani, strings

Date of origin 1887[2]; premiere undated; published 1888

Allegretto lusinghiero[3]

326 measures

Sources:

Ms.	846	(BN)	score (350×270)
Ms.	735	(BN)	piano score (350×270)
D & F	3914	(priv.)	score

---

1. *Catalogue général et thématique*: pour Violon et Orchestre

2. Note on the handwritten score: "septembre"

3. *Catalogue général et thématique*: Allegretto

Op. 94

Morceau de Concert

pour Cor avec accompagnement de Piano ou d'Orchestre[1]

à Monsieur Henri Chaussier

2 flutes, 2 oboes, 2 clarinets, 2 bassoons, 3 trombones, timpani, strings

Date of origin 1887[2]; premiere undated; published 1893

Allegro moderato

253 measures

Sources:

Ms.	663	(BN)	piano score and full score (350×270)
D & F	4605	(priv.)	piano score
D & F	6527	(priv.)	score

1. *Catalogue général et thématique*: Morceau de Concert pour Cor

2. Note on the handwritten piano score: "octobre"; note on the handwritten full score: "2 novembre"

Op. 89

Africa

Fantaisie pour Piano et Orchestre[1]

à Madame Roger-Miclos

2 flutes, 2 oboes, 2 clarinets, 2 bassoons, 2 horns, 2 cornets, 3 trombones, timpani, percussion, strings

Date of origin 1891[2]; premiere 1891; published 1891

Molto allegro

589 measures

Sources:

Ms.	916[10]	(BN)	sketches ("Danse des Almées," pas signé, par St. Saëns d'après l'écriture) (351×270)
Ms.	2445	(BN)	score (440×310)
D & F	4476	(priv.)	score

1. D & F 4476: . . . avec accompagnement d'Orchestre

2. Ms. 916[10] originated in 1890; the handwritten score bears the note "1er Avril" (1891).

Op. 103

Cinquième Concerto (Fa Majeur)

pour Piano et Orchestre

à Monsieur Louis Diémer

2 flutes, 2 oboes, 2 clarinets, 2 bassoons, 4 horns, 2 trumpets, 3 trombones, timpani, percussion, strings

Date of origin 1896[1]; premiere 1896; published 1896

Allegro animato

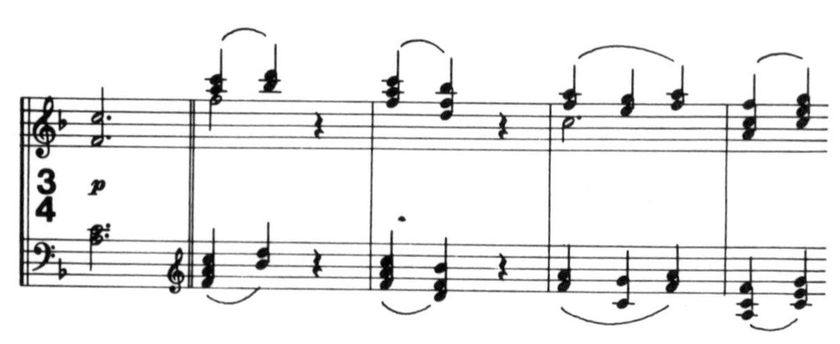

542 measures

Andante

270 measures

Molto allegro

435 measures

---

1. Ms. 916[6] originated in 1894

Sources:

Ms.	916^6	(BN)	sketches for the first movement (Première esquisse du concerto faite aux Canaries deux ans avant/esquisse du Ier morceau) (315×212)
Ms.	916^5	(BN)	sketches (Esquisse donée les . . . 96/esquisse du finale) (350×270)
D & F	5135	(priv.)	piano score
D & F	7593	(priv.)	score
D & F	55876	(priv.)	Toccata d'après le Final du Cinquième Concerto Op. 111/VI, à Monsieur Raoul Pugno (Date of origin 1899—published 1899)

Op. 119

Deuxième Concerto (Ré Mineur)

pour Violoncelle et Orchestre

à Monsieur Joseph Hollman

2 flutes, 2 oboes, 2 clarinets, 2 bassoons, 4 horns, 2 trumpets, timpani, strings

Date of origin 1902[1]; premiere 1902; published 1902

Allegro moderato e maestoso

108 measures

Andante sostenuto (Le double plus lent)

94 measures

Allegro non troppo

148 measures

1. Note on the handwritten score: "novembre"

Mouvement du premier morceau

65 measures

Sources:

Ms.	707	(BN)	score (350×270)
Ms.	708	(BN)	piano score (350×270)
D & F	6188	(priv.)	piano score

Op. 122

Caprice Andalous

pour Violon avec accompagnement d'Orchestre

à Monsieur Johannes Wolff

2 flutes, 2 oboes, 2 clarinets, 2 bassoons, 2 horns, 2 trumpets, 3 trombones, timpani, harp[1], strings

Date of origin 1904; premiere 1904; published 1904

Allegretto moderato

428 measures

Sources:

Ms.	706	(BN)	score (355×272)
Ms.	879	(BN)	piano score (esquisse datée postérieurement, par erreur sans doute, de 1894) (350×270)
D & F	6417	(priv.)	piano score

1. ad libitum

Unnumbered opus

Fantaisie

pour Orgue-Eolian[1]

no dedication

Date of origin 1906[2]; no premiere; unpublished

Lento[3]

(38 pages[4])

Source:
Ms. from the private archives of Hans Schneider (Tutzing)[5]

---

1. According to the title page. The manuscript, or rather copies of the first three pages and the last one which Mr. Schneider kindly made available, contains the complete piano score of the work. Whether Saint-Saëns ever orchestrated it is still uncertain.

2. Signed and dated on the last page.

3. According to the movement heading on page 1; presumably the tempo changes several times in the course of the work, which may even be in several movements. This seems all the more likely, considering the Fantaisie begins in A-flat major (without key signature) but ends in B-flat major (with the appropriate key signature).

4. Unfortunately the number of measures could not be determined; the performance time is noted at the top of the first page in Saint-Saëns's own hand: "-4′/8″-".

5. I am grateful to Yves Gérard for sharing the following letter from Saint-Saëns to Charles Lecocq (Ms. Dieppe, Musée du Chateau, fonds Saint-Saëns), which reveals the occasion for and nature of the work:
London, 21 July 1906:

> You will understand my silence when you learn that I visited this familiar city to see if I couldn't compose a piece for one of the Eolian company's semi-mechanical organs, and that I had to study the instrument and write a

great Fantaisie within a few days—I had a deadline. If I were to tell you that this Fantaisie is a masterpiece, you would not believe me and you would be right, but there are still a few little sections that are not totally dull; there is even a canon in fifths, supported by pedal ornamentation. . . . What was fun was the possibility of writing things that human fingers and feet can't play. Man intervenes in the execution through his choice of stops and tempos. The result is very strange but demands good finger technique, and if amateurs should buy this instrument, which costs something like 4,000 pounds(!), and have it installed in their palace—there are such people—I imagine they might be somewhat at a loss as to how to use it. In any case, this is a way of making music quite different from what we are used to.

Op. 132[1]

La Muse et le Poète

Duo pour Violon et Violoncelle avec accompagnement d'Orchestre ou de Piano

à la mémoire de Madame J.-Henry Carruette[2]

2 flutes, 2 oboes, 2 clarinets, 2 bassoons, 2 horns, 2 trumpets, 3 trombones, timpani, harp, strings

Date of origin 1910; premiere 1910; published 1910; withdrawn by the publisher 1921

Andantino

522 measures

Sources:

Ms.	916[3]	(BN)	esquisse primitive (353×270)
Ms.	825	(BN)	esquisse: duo pour violon et piano (350×270)
Ms.	2451	(BN)	trio version and score ("Duo pour violon et violoncelle avec accmt. d'orchestre" rayée) (445×320)
D & F	7870	(priv.)	score

1. Not in Catalogue *général et thématique,* which ends with Op. 124.

2. Harding erroneously lists "à Madame Henry Carruette" for the trio version.

Op. 154

Morceau de Concert

pour Harpe avec accompagnement d'Orchestre

à Mademoiselle Nicole Anckier

2 flutes, 2 oboes, 2 clarinets, 2 bassoons, 2 horns, 2 trumpets, timpani, strings

Date of origin 1918; premiere undated; published 1919

Allegro non troppo

587 measures

Sources:

Ms.	2471	(BN)	piano score (350×270)
D & F	9625	(priv.)	piano score
Ac.e[10]	464	(BN)	score (Durand, Paris 1919)

1. D & F 9625 erroneously has 4/4

Op. 156

Cyprès et Lauriers

Fantaisie pour Orgue et Orchestre

à Monsieur Raymond Poincaré

3 flutes, 2 oboes, 2 clarinets, 3 bassoons, 4 horns, 3 trumpets, 3 trombones, tuba, timpani, percussion, 2 harps, strings

Date of origin 1919; premiere 1919; published 1919

Sources:

Ms.	835	(BN)	Cyprès (350×270)
Ms.	646	(BN)	1. esquisse pour les "Lauriers" 2. parties d'orgue pour les deux morceaux 3. arrangement pour deux pianos 4. partition d'orchestre de "Lauriers" (350×270)
D & F	9800	(priv.)	score

Op. 162

Odelette

pour Flûte avec accompagnement d'Orchestre

à Monsieur François Gaillard

2 oboes, 2 bassoons, strings

Date of origin 1920; premiere 1920; published 1920

Andantino

169 measures

Sources:

Ms.	661	(BN)	score and piano score (352×276)
D & F	9870	(priv.)	piano score
D & F	9868	(priv.)	score

Unnumbered opus

Fantaisie

pour Clarinette avec accompagnement d'orchestre[1] (en mi bémol majeur)

no dedication

2 flutes, 2 oboes, 2 bassoons, 2 horns, 2 trumpets, 3 trombones, timpani, strings

Date of origin unknown (presumably late 1850s or early 1860s); no premiere; unpublished

No tempo marking

14 measures

Source:

Ms.	(priv.)	In the Yves Gérard collection

1. The score (in horizontal format) bears, presumably by another's hand, the heading "Fantaisie pr Clarinette Manuscrit préparé par Camille Saint-Saëns." The fragment, in which only the parts of the first violin (m. 1–12), the second violin (m. 13–14), and the solo entrance (m. 14) are recorded, breaks off after m. 14. So far, I have been unable to find references to this work in the relevant literature. The manuscript suggests a date of origin between 1858 and 1865.

Joël-Marie Fauquet (1986, 155) mentions a "Fantaisie pour clarinette" by Saint-Saëns, performed on 9 April 1860 by Adolphe Leroy in a concert of the *Société Armingaud* in the Salle Erard. His source of information is *Revue et Gazette Musicale de Paris* 16 (15 April 1860): 142. It was not possible to ascertain to what extent the present manuscript is related to this Fantaisie, about which nothing further is known and which must be considered lost.

B. List of French Solo Concertos and Concertante Works from 1850 to 1920

The following table is a chronological summary of the works discussed in Chapters 9–11. Also listed below are Saint-Saëns's concertos and concertante compositions. The third column lists the most important solo concertos of this period originating outside France.

The basis for this table was the cataloged holdings of the Bibliothèque Nationale (BN), Paris. Without any claim to comprehensiveness, it should certainly offer a representative overview of the concertante music of France between 1850 and 1920. By and large, I considered only those published works for which a score was also available; the exceptions, for reasons mentioned in Chapters 9 and 10, are the violin concertos of Jules Garcin and Victorin de Joncières and the Concertino for Violin by the Vicomtesse de Grandval.

The dates given in the Bibliothèque Nationale's union catalog generally refer to the year of publication. Since it was a common publishing practice at that time for a work to be printed directly after completion of the composition, or after the premiere at the latest, I could assume that the dating of the source document usually coincided with the beginning of its effective history (through publication or performance). Insofar as possible, I have checked the dating I chose against lists of works or reviews of premiere performances.

I decided to forgo the inclusion of catalog number (BN), format, movement sequence, length, and instrumentation. The titles of the works are given in the original orthography.

A few of the works included in the table were neither written in France nor published there. However, Francois Lesure told me that the Bibliothèque Nationale's collection of nineteenth- and early twentieth-century editions is made up almost exclusively of works acquired from private collections or archives of smaller libraries or conservatories in Paris. Therefore, it is safe to assume that these works, though not composed or published in France, were nevertheless performed in Paris and thus could have influenced the French solo concerto. In a few cases, such as the compositions of Peter Benoist, this theory has been confirmed by contemporary reviews in Paris music journals.

Unfortunately the holdings of the Bibliothèque Municipale at Dieppe have not yet been cataloged. Naturally it would have been helpful to check Camille Saint-Saëns's estate, most of which is kept there, to find out which of the compositions mentioned here were in his possession. Then correspondence might have been studied to determine which of the works he was familiar with or had even played himself. The latter could be determined with certainty only in the case of de Castillon's piano concerto.

	C. Saint-Saëns	France	Europe
1850		*Gastinel,* Léon Concerto pour deux violons	*Schumann,* Robert Konzert a-moll für Violoncello, Op. 129
		Vieuxtemps, Henri IV. Concert pour violon en ré mineur, Op. 31	
1851		*Dancla,* Charles III. Fantaisie pour violon, Op. 47	
		Litolff, Henri IV. Concerto symphonique pour piano en ré mineur, Op. 102	

	C. Saint-Saëns	France	Europe
		Offenbach, Jacques Concertino pour violoncelle	
1852		*Léonard,* Hubert II. Concert pour violon en ré mineur, Op. 14	
1853		*Wieniawski,* Henri I. Concert pour violon en fa dièse mineur, Op. 14	*Schumann,* Robert Konzert d-moll für Violine, Op. posth.
1856		*Alard,* Delphin II. Symphonie concertante pour deux violons, Op. 31	
		Dupont, Auguste Symphonie-Concerto pour piano	
1857	Tarantelle (la mineur) pour flûte et clarinette, Op. 6	*Alkan,* Charles Valentin Concerto pour piano solo, Op. 39	
		Alard, Delphin III. Symphonie concertante pour deux violons, Op. 34bis	
		Dupont, Auguste I. Concerto pour piano	
1858	I. Concerto pour piano en ré majeur, Op. 17	*Herz,* Henri IV. Concerto pour piano, orchestre et choeurs, Op. 192	*Brahms,* Johannes I. Konzert d-moll für Klavier, Op. 15
	II. Concerto pour violon en ut majeur, Op. 58		
1859	I. Concerto pour violon en la majeur, Op. 20	*Pfeiffer,* Georges I. Concert pour piano, Op. 11	

	C. Saint-Saëns	France	Europe
		Singelée, Jean Baptiste Concert pour la saxophone soprano ou ténor en si bémol, Op. 57	
1860		*Dancla,* Charles IV. Symphonie concertante pour deux violons, Op. 98	
		Vieuxtemps, Henri V. Concerto pour violon en la mineur, Op. 37 ("Grétry")	
1862		*Dancla,* Charles Symphonie concertante pour deux violons et violoncelle, Op. 105	
		Servais, A. François Concerto militaire pour violoncelle, Op. 18	
		Wieniawski, Henri II. Concerto, pour violon en ré mineur, Op. 22	
1863	Introduction et Rondo capriccioso pour violon, Op. 28	*Servais,* A. François Souvenir de Bade—grande fantaisie pour violoncelle, Op. 20	
1864		*Benoit,* Peter Symphonisch Gedicht voor Klavier, Op. 43	
		Pfeiffer, Georges II. Concert pour piano en mi bémol majeur, Op. 21	

	C. Saint-Saëns	France	Europe
1865		*Fétis,* François Joseph Fantaisie pour orchestre et orgue	
1866		*Benoit,* Peter Symphonisch Gedicht voor Fluit	
		Bergson, Michael Concerto symphonique pour piano, Op. 62	
		Dupont, Auguste III. Concerto pour piano en fa mineur	
		Joncières, Victorin de (II.)Concerto pour violon en ré mineur	
		Léonard, Hubert IV. Concert pour violon, Op. 26	
1868	II. Concerto pour piano en sol mineur, Op. 22	*Wrobleski,* Emile Grand concerto symphonique pour piano	*Bruch,* Max I. Konzert g-moll für Violine, Op. 26
	Romance pour violon, Op. 27		*Grieg,* Edvard Konzert a-moll für Klavier, Op. 16
1869	III. Concerto pour piano en mi bémol, Op. 29	*Fétis,* François Joseph Concerto pour flûte	
1871	Romance pour flûte ou violon en ré bémol majeur, Op. 37	*Castillon,* Alexis de Concerto pour piano en ré majeur, Op. 12	
		Léonard, Hubert V. Concert pour violon, Op. 28	

	C. Saint-Saëns	France	Europe
		Swert, Jules de Fantaisie pour violoncelle, Op. 25	
		Widor, Charles Marie Concert pour violoncelle en mi mineur, Op. 42	
1872	I. Concerto pour violoncelle en la mineur, Op. 33	*Garcin,* Jules Concerto pour violon en ré mineur, Op. 14	
1873		*Dancla,* Charles Hymne à Ste Cécile pour violon, Op. 114	
		Lalo, Edouard Symphonie espagnole pour violon en ré mineur, Op. 21	
1874	Romance pour cor ou violoncelle en fa majeur, Op. 36	*Grandval,* Marie Vicomtesse de (Marie *Reiset*) Concertino pour violon en ré majeur	
	Romance pour violon en ut majeur, Op. 48	*Lalo,* Edouard Concerto pour violon en fa majeur, Op. 20	
		Swert, Jules de Concerto pour violoncelle en ré mineur, Op. 32	
1875	Allegro appassionato pour violoncelle (si mineur), Op. 43		*Tchaikovsky,* Peter I. Konzert b-moll für Klavier, Op. 23
	IV. Concerto pour piano en ut mineur, Op. 44		

	C. Saint-Saëns	France	Europe
	Gavotte (sol mineur) pour violoncelle, unnumbered opus		
1876		*Dubois,* Théodore Concert-Capriccio pour piano en ut mineur	*Dvorák,* Antonin Konzert g-moll für Klavier, Op. 33
		Lalo, Edouard Concerto pour violoncelle en ré mineur	*Tchaikovsky,* Peter Variations on a Rococo Theme for Cello and Orchestra, Op. 33
1877		*Godard,* Benjamin Concerto romantique pour violon en la mineur	
		Swert, Jules de II. Concerto pour violoncelle en ut mineur, Op. 38.	
		Vieuxtemps, Henri Concert pour violoncelle en la mineur, Op. 46	
1878		*Fauré,* Gabriel Concerto pour violon en la majeur, Op. 14 (unfinished)	*Brahms,* Johannes Konzert D-Dur für Violine, Op. 77
		Sarasate, Pablo de Zigeunerweisen für Violine, Op. 20	*Tchaikovsky,* Peter Konzert D-Dur für Violine, Op. 35
1879		*Dancla,* Charles "La Clochette"—Air de danse brillant pour violon, Op. 148	

	C. Saint-Saëns	France	Europe
		Dancla, Charles[1] Nocturne-Meditation pour violon, Op. 148	
		Franco-Mendès, Jacques III. Grand Concerto en ré pour violoncelle, Op. 46	
		Godard, Benjamin Concerto pour piano en la mineur, Op. 31	
1880	III. Concerto pour violon en si mineur, Op. 61	*Dupont,* Auguste Morceau de concert pour piano, Op. 42	*Dvorák,* Antonin Konzert a-moll für Violine, Op. 53
	Morceau de concert pour violon, Op. 62	*Lalo,* Edouard Fantaisie Norvégienne pour violon	*Tchaikovsky,* Peter II. Konzert G-Dur für Klavier, Op. 44
1881		*Bériot,* Charles Wilfrid de I., II., III. et IV. Concert pour piano (ed.)	*Brahms,* Johannes II. Konzert, B-Dur für Klavier, Op. 83
		Dupont, Auguste IV. Concert pour piano en fa mineur, Op. 49	
		Fauré, Gabriel Ballade pour piano en fa dièse majeur, Op. 19	
		Godard, Benjamin Introduction et allegro pour piano	

[1]The composer inadvertently used the opus no. 148 twice.

	C. Saint-Saëns	France	Europe
1882		*Bruneau,* Alfred Romance pour cor, Op. 6	*Strauss,* Richard Konzert d-moll für violine, Op. 8
1883		*Diémer,* Louis Morceau de concert pour piano, Op. 31	*Strauss,* Richard Konzert Es-Dur für Waldhorn, Op. 11
		Diémer, Louis I. Concert pour piano en ut mineur, Op. 32	
		Diémer, Louis Morceau de concert pour violon, Op. 33	
		Lalo, Edouard Concerto russe pour violon, Op. 29	
		Pfeiffer, Georges III. Concert pour piano en si majeur, Op. 86	
1884	Allegro appassionato, Op. 70	*Brassin,* Louis III. Concerto pastorale pour piano	*d'Albert,* Eugene Konzert h-moll für Klavier, Op. 2
	Rapsodie d'Auvergne pour piano, Op. 73	*Franck,* César "Les Djinns" pour piano	*Tchaikovsky,* Peter Konzertfantasie G-Dur für Klavier, Op. 56
		Guiraud, Ernest Caprice pour violon	
		d'Indy, Vincent Lied pour violoncelle, Op. 19	
		Sauret, Emile Concerto pour violon en ré mineur, Op. 26	

C. Saint-Saëns	France	Europe
	Vieuxtemps, Henri II. Concerto pour violoncelle en si mineur, Op. 50	
1885	*Bernard,* Emile Romance pour flûte, Op. 33	*Strauss,* Richard Burleske d-moll für Klavier
	Florence, H. Balthasar Concert pour violon en la mineur (en un seul mouvement)	
	Franck, César Variations symphoniques pour piano	
	Lalo, Edouard Fantaisie-Ballet pour violon	
	Sauret, Emile Rapsodie russe pour violon en sol majeur, Op. 32	
1886	*Bernard,* Emile Concerto-Fantaisie pour piano	
	Gounod, Charles Fantaisie sur l'Hymne nationale russe pour piano	
	Hollman, Joseph II. Concert pour violoncelle en la mineur	
	Pierné, Gabriel Fantaisie-Ballet pour piano, Op. 6	

	C. Saint-Saëns	France	Europe
1887	Havanaise pour violon, Op. 83	*Hérold,* Louis IV. concerto pour piano	*Brahms,* Johannes Doppelkonzert a-moll für Violine und Violoncello, Op. 102
	Morceau de concert pour cor, Op. 94	*Pierné,* Gabriel Concerto pour piano en ut mineur, Op. 12	
		Tombelle, Fernand de la Concert pour piano en fa mineur, Op. 26	
1888		*Bernard,* Emile Romance pour violon, Op. 27	
		Bordes, Charles Suite basque pour flûte et cordes	
		Fauré, Gabriel Berceuse pour violon, Op. 16	
		Gounod, Charles Suite concertante pour piano	
		d'Indy, Vincent Fantaisie en sol majeur pour hautbois principal sur des thèmes populaires français, Op. 31	
1889		*Debussy,* Claude Fantaisie pour piano	
		Dubois, Théodore Fantaisie triomphale pour orgue	
		Lalo, Edouard Concerto pour piano en fa mineur	

	C. Saint-Saëns	France	Europe
		Widor, Charles Marie Fantaisie (Morceau de concert) pour piano, Op. 62	
1890		*Bordes,* Charles Rhapsodie basque pour piano	
		Pierné, Gabriel Scherzo-Caprice pour piano, Op. 25	
1891	Africa pour piano, Op. 89	*Bérou,* Adrien Concertino romantique en trois suites pour violon, Op. 46	*Rachmaninoff,* Sergej I. Konzert fis-moll für Klavier, Op. 1
		Chausson, Ernest Concert pour piano, violon et cordes en ré majeur, Op. 21	
		Dubois, Théodore Mélodie religieuse pour violon	
1892		*Bernard,* Emile Concertstück pour piano, Op. 40	
		Dubois, Théodore II. Fantaisie triomphale pour orgue	
		Simon, A. Concerto pour piano, Op. 19	
1893		*Bordier,* J. d'Angers Suite fantaisiste n° I (Airs d'Eglise) pour violoncelle, Op. 40, No. 1	*d'Albert,* Eugen Konzert E-Dur für Klavier, Op. 12
		Godard, Benjamin Scènes eccossaises pour hautbois, Op. 138	*Tchaikovsky,* Peter III. Konzert Es-Dur für Klavier, Op. 75

	C. Saint-Saëns	France	Europe
1894		*Divoir,* Victor Romance sans paroles pour violon ou violoncelle	*Scriabin,* Alexander Konzert fis-moll für Klavier, Op. 20
		Godard, Benjamin II. Concert pour piano, Op. 148	
1895		*Accolay,* J. B. Concerto pour violon en ré majeur	*Dvorák,* Antonin Konzert h-moll für Violoncello, Op. 104
		Bachelet, Alfred Poème pour violoncelle	
		d'Indy, Vincent Symphonie sur un chant montagnard français (Symphonie cévenole) pour piano, Op. 25	
1896	V. Concerto pour piano en fa majeur, Op. 103 ("Egyptien")	*Broustet,* Edouard Cantilena amorosa—Romance sans paroles pour violon	
		Douillet, Pierre Concerto pour piano en mi bémol majeur, Op. 16	
		Guilmant, Alexandre Marche funèbre pour orgue et cordes en ut mineur, Op. 41	
		Lacombe, Louis "Au tombeau d'un héro", Elégie pour violon	
		Lacombe, Paul Suite pour piano en la mineur, Op. 52	

	C. Saint-Saëns	France	Europe
1897		*Chausson,* Ernest Concert pour piano, alto, hautbois et cordes (sketch)	*Busoni,* Ferruccio Konzert D-Dur für Violine, Op. 35 a.
		Dubois, Théodore II. concerto pour piano en fa mineur	
		Massenet, Jules Fantaisie pour violoncelle	
1898		*Anthiome,* Eugène Concert pour piano en ut mineur	
		Chausson, Ernest Poème en mi bémol majeur pour violon, Op. 25	
		Dubois, Théodore Concerto pour violon en ré mineur	
		Sauret, Emile Rapsodie suèdoise pour violon en mi mineur, Op. 59	
1899	Six Etudes pour piano, Op. 111 (No. 6: Toccata d'après le final du Concerto, Op. 103)	*Accolay,* J. B. Concerto pour violon en mi mineur	
		Aubert, Louis Fantaisie pour piano en si mineur, Op. 8	
		Delafosse, Léon Concerto pour piano en la majeur	
		Dubois, Théodore Andante cantabile pour violoncelle	

C. Saint-Saëns	France	Europe
	Gédalge, André I. Concert pour piano en ut majeur/mineur, Op. 16	
	Grobet, Louis Concerto pour violon en ré mineur	
	Sarasate, Pablo de Introduction et Tarantella pour violon, Op. 43	
1900	*Jongen,* Joseph Concerto pour violon en si mineur, Op. 17	*d'Albert,* Eugen Konzert C-Dur für Violoncello, Op. 20
	Pugno, Raoul Concertstück pour piano en mi mineur	
1901	*Dubois,* Théodore Entr'acte et Rigaudon de Xavière pour violoncelle	*Rachmaninoff,* Sergej II. Konzert c-moll für Klavier, Op. 18
	d'Erlanger, Baron Frédéric Concerto pour violon, Op. 17	
	d'Erlanger, Baron Frédéric Andante symphonique pour violoncelle, Op. 18	
	Pierné, Gabriel Poème symphonique pour piano et orchestre, Op. 37	
	Pierné, Gabriel Morceau de concert (Konzertstück) pour harpe, Op. 39	

	C. Saint-Saëns	France	Europe
		Renié, Henriette Concerto pour harpe en ut mineur	
1902	II. concerto pour violoncelle en ré mineur, Op. 119	*Bernard,* Emile Nocturne pour piano, Op. 51	
		Bordes, Charles Divertissement pour trompette	
		Chaminade, Cécile Concertino pour flûte, Op. 107	
		Dalcroze, Jacques I. Concert pour violon en ut mineur, Op. 50	
1903		*Dubois,* Théodore Fantaisie pour harpe	*Sibelius,* Jean Konzert d-moll für Violine
		d'Indy, Vincent Choral varié pour saxophone, Op. 55	
		Massenet, Jules Concert en mi bémol majeur pour piano	
		Moreau, Léon I. Concert pour piano en ut dièse mineur, Op. 35	
		Pennequin, J. G. Concerto pour violon en la mineur, Op. 7	
		Pierné, Gabriel Poème symphonique pour piano	

	C. Saint-Saëns	France	Europe
1904	Caprice andalous pour violon, Op. 122	*Debussy,* Claude Deux danses pour harpe chromatique et cordes	*Bartók,* Béla Rhapsodie für Klavier, Op. 1
			Glasunow, Alexander Konzert a-moll für Violine, Op. 84
1905		*Widor,* Charles Marie Concerto pour piano, Op. 77	
1906	Fantaisie pour Orgue-Eolian	*Dubois,* Théodore Nocturne pour violoncelle	*Busoni,* Ferruccio Konzert für Klavier (with choral finale), Op. 39
		Dukas, Paul Villanelle pour cor	
		Godard, Benjamin Fantaisie persane pour piano, Op. 152	
		Ravel, Maurice Introduction et allegro pour harpe	
1907		*Bachelet,* Alfred Dans la montagne, Ballade pour cor ou violoncelle	
		Coquard, Arthur Légende pour violoncelle	
		Coquard, Arthur Sérénade pour violoncelle	
1908		*Caplet,* André La Masque de la Mort Rouge, Etude symphonique pour harpe chromatique	

	C. Saint-Saëns	France	Europe
		Rhené-Baton Variations sur un mode éolien pour piano en si mineur, Op. 4	
1909		*Brun,* Georges Calme du soir, pour violoncelle	*Rachmaninoff,* Sergej III. Konzert d-moll für Klavier, Op. 30
		Giraud, Frédéric Concert pour violon en la mineur, Op. 12	
1910	"La Muse et le Poète", pour violon et violoncelle, Op. 132	*Debussy,* Claude I. Rapsodie pour clarinette (orch. Roger-Ducasse)	*Elgar,* Edward Konzert h-moll für Violine, Op. 61
		van Dooren, A. Allegro de Concert pour piano	*Glasunow,* Alexander I. Konzert f-moll für Klavier, Op. 92
		Waghalter, Henri Concert pour violoncelle, Op. 15	*Reger,* Max Konzert f-moll für Klavier, Op. 114
1911		*Dalcroze,* Jacques II. concert (Poème) pour violon	*Prokofieff,* Sergej I. Konzert Des-Dur für Klavier, Op. 10
		Dubois, Théodore Cavatine pour cor	
		Blanchet, Emile Morceau de concert pour piano	
1912		*Dubois,* Théodore Fantaisie-Stück pour violoncelle	
		Gaubert, Philippe Concerto pour violoncelle ("Lamento")	

	C. Saint-Saëns	France	Europe
1913		*Dupuis,* Sylvain Concertino pour hautbois	*Prokofieff,* Sergej II. Konzert g-moll für Klavier, Op. 16
1915			*de Falla,* Manuel "Noches en los jardines de España", Impressions symphoniques pour piano
1916			*Glasunow,* Alexander II. Konzert H-Dur für Klavier
1917			*Prokofieff,* Sergej I. Konzert D-Dur für Violine, Op. 19
1918	Morceau de concert pour harpe, Op. 154	*Jongen,* Joseph Concertino pour violoncelle en ré majeur, Op. 18	
1919	Cyprès et Lauriers pour orgue, Op. 156	*Dupré,* Marcel Fantaisie en trois parties pour piano *Fauré,* Gabriel Fantaisie pour piano, Op. 111 *Roger-Ducasse,* Jean Romance pour violoncelle *Tailleferre,* Germaine Ballade pour piano	
1920	Odelette pour flûte, Op. 162	*Milhaud,* Darius Cinq Etudes pour piano	

	C. Saint-Saëns	France	Europe
		Samuel-Rousseau, Marcel Rhythmes de Danse sur le même thème pour piano	
1921	Romance pour violon, Op. 27 (orch.)	*d'Erlanger,* Baron Frédéric Concerto symphonique pour piano	
		Witkowski, Georges Martin "Mon Lac", pour piano.	

List of Abbreviations

BM	Bibliothèque Municipale, Dieppe
BN	Bibliothèque Nationale, Paris
col.	column
Cons.	Conservatoire
CSS.	Camille Saint-Saëns—articles and essays in the bibliography (numbered alphabetically)
D & F	Editions Durand et Fils
i.a.	inter alia / among others
K.	Köchel listing
m.	measure
N.p.; n.p.	no publisher given, and/or no place of publication
Op.; op.	opus
priv.	in the author's private possession

Notes

Introduction

1. Neitzel 1899.
2. Harding 1965.
3. Cf. i.a. *Neue Musik-Zeitung* 27, no. 19 (1906): 424.
4. Cf. i.a. Stegemann 1976, 267ff.
5. Qtd. in Goldron 1966, 110.

1. A Biographical Sketch

1. The family name is a French distortion of *Sanctus Sidonius.* In 675, an Irish monk by this name became the abbot of a monastery in Normandy (Seine-Inférieure) founded by Thierry III. In the town that grew up around the monastery and still bears the name Saint-Saëns today, we find mention of the composer's earliest verifiable ancestor, Jean Baptiste Nicolas Saint-Saëns, in 1775. Cf. Dumaine 1936.
2. Saint-Saëns tells of his childhood while under the care of both women; cf. CSS-32.
3. Cf. Hervey 1970, 4; also Harding 1965, 26f.
4. Qtd. in Harding 1965, 27.
5. Cf. Hervey 1970, 5. The date 1853 given by Bonnerot (1922e, 28) and Harding (1965, 49) is incorrect.
6. *La France Musicale* 24, no. 12 (18 March 1860), qtd. in Fallon 1973,

79 [Fallon's Eng. trans.].

7. Cf. Bonnerot 1922e, 28f.
8. The composer himself relates the odd circumstances surrounding the premiere performance; cf. CSS-51, 204f.
9. Baumann 1923, 218f.
10. Cf. also Chapter 2, note 10.
11. Dandelot 1930, 46f.
12. Qtd. in Servières 1930, 136.
13. Qtd. in Dandelot 1930, 47.
14. Cf. Stegemann 1976, 267ff; this article includes additional documents and references to the Wagner/Saint-Saëns relationship. Cf. also Ecorcheville 1899.
15. Cf. Bruneau 1903, 79; also Hervey 1970, 7.
16. CSS-4, 884.
17. Saint-Saëns to his cousin Léon (priv.).
18. Qtd. in *Neue Musik-Zeitung* 36, no. 10 (1915): 110.
19. CSS-4, 884.
20. CSS-52, 113 (trans. F. Rothwell).
21. Dandelot 1930, 41.
22. Baumann 1923, 219.
23. Bonnerot 1922e, 40.
24. In 1974, Philips issued a recording of the complete concertante cello works of Saint-Saëns with Christine Walewska and the Orchestre National de l'Opéra de Monte Carlo under Eliahu Inbal (6500.459). The recording included the Suite Op. 16, with the Gavotte added as a third movement. There was no reference to the orchestrated version of Op. 16, which could hardly have been written by the composer himself, since nothing is known of a manuscript. The Gavotte was not recorded in the original orchestration, but in a revised instrumentation that is not authentic. My inquiry to Philips about this has brought no response. In any case, the combination of the Gavotte with Op. 16 is very dubious, as a close examination of the original (MS. 848 of the Bibliothèque Nationale, Paris) reveals. The title page of the piano part does indeed bear the notation "No. 3," which points to a cyclic work, and the title and form suggest a suite. Yet a comparative analysis of handwriting, paper, and style indicates that it probably was not written until the mid 1870s. Thus, a belated completion of Op. 16

is conceivable but highly unlikely.

25. Cf. Prod'homme 1929, 131 [Fr. orig.]; 1922, 471 [Eng. trans.].
26. Cf. *Neue Musik-Zeitung* 27, no. 19 (1906): 24.
27. Cf. Baumann 1923, 190f., and Hervey 1970, 199. It should also be noted that the time of origin in the English translation of Prod'homme's text (see note 25 above, p. 472) is given incorrectly as 1860, while it appears correctly in the French original as 1863.

    César Franck's Op. 1 is proof of how hard it was in those days to succeed with chamber music in Paris. The young composer entitled this collection of three piano trios (1838–1841) *Trois Trios concertans,* which was equivalent to the usual designation at that time of *Trio de Salon.* In doing this, he denied the seriousness of these works in order to gain public favor. Cf. i.a. Mohr 1969, 77.
28. Cf. Bonnerot 1922e, 42.
29. Ibid., 43.
30. Alberte L'Hôte in *La France Musicale* 31, no. 15 (4 April 1867).
31. *Revue et Gazette Musicale de Paris* 34, no. 14 (4 April 1867).
32. See note 30.
33. See note 31.
34. Cf. i.a. Bonnerot 1922e, 47ff.
35. Ibid., 54.
36. Albert L'Hôte in *La France Musicale* 32, no. 19 (6 May 1868).
37. Isidore Philipp, qtd. in Prod'homme 1929, 132 [Fr. orig.], and 472 [Eng. trans.]. The date of origin is given incorrectly in both the French original (1854) and in the English translation (1864).
38. Liszt to Saint-Saëns, in letter collection of La Mara (Marie Lipsius), no. 91:146, qtd. in Dandelot 1930, 55. Possibly Liszt's endorsement of Saint-Saëns here, and in connection with the opera *Samson et Dalila,* was partially responsible for the Frenchman's occasionally being classed with the disciples of the so-called new German school.
39. *Allgemeine Musik-Zeitung* 4, no. 50 (15 December 1869): 398f.
40. Adolphe Jullien in *Le Ménestrel* 37, no. 15 (17 March 1870).
41. H. M. in *Le Ménestrel* 43/9, no. 2427 (21 January 1877).
42. This sincere declaration of loyalty to his fatherland was soon forgotten; in the political turmoil of the First World War, the French press accused Saint-Saëns of lacking national commitment.
43. Romain Bussine, president; Camille Saint-Saëns, vice president;

Alexis de Castillon, first secretary; Jules Garcin, second secretary; Charles-Ferdinand Lenepveu, treasurer. (The bylaws of the Société Nationale were drafted by Alexis de Castillon). Qtd. in Bonnerot 1922e, 61.

44. Actually Saint-Saëns's *Rouet d'Omphale* marked the founding of a musical genre that was of great significance in France on into the twentieth century. I mention these as the most important works:
    1873—*Phaëton* (C. Saint-Saëns, Op. 39)
    1873—*Les Eolides* (C. Franck)
    1874—*Danse macabre* (C. Saint-Saëns, Op. 40)
    1877—*La Jeunesse d'Hercule* (C. Saint-Saëns, Op. 50)
    1878—*La Forêt enchantée* (V. d'Indy, Op. 8)
    1881—*Wallenstein* (V. d'Indy, Op. 12)
    1881—*Poème de montagne* (V. d'Indy, Op. 15, pianoforte)
    1882—*Viviane* (E. Chausson, Op. 5)
    1882—*Le Chasseur maudit* (C. Franck)
    1884—*Les Djinns* (C. Franck)
    1886—*Solitude dans les bois* (E. Chausson, Op. 10)
    1897—*Soir de fête* (E. Chausson, Op. 32)
    1897—*L'Apprenti sorcier* (P. Dukas)
    1903—*Résurrection* (A. Roussel, Op. 4)
    1905—*Jour d'été à la montagne* (V. d'Indy, Op. 61)
    1920—*Pour une fête de printemps* (A. Roussel, Op. 22)
45. The performance turned into a fiasco, but amid the pandemonium of shouting and whistling, Saint-Saëns and Pasdeloup continued playing with stoic calm. De Castillon's concerto did not receive a second performance until Raoul Pugno played it 27 years later.
46. Saint-Saëns wrote of Op. 22: "Elle était le résultat d'une improvisation sur l'orgue de Saint-Augustin [It was the result of an improvisation on the St. Augustine organ]."
47. Sketches of both works are found on a single sketch sheet (MS. 834, Bibliothèque Nationale, Paris), notated with the same pen.
48. Bonnerot 1922e, 69.
49. *Revue et Gazette Musicale de Paris* 40, no. 4 (19 January 1873): 30.
50. Cf. i.a. Mies 1972, 82.
51. Qtd. in Bonnerot 1922e, 73.
52. Cf. Appendix A.
53. Cohen 1875.

54. *Neue Musik-Zeitung* 13, no. 11 (November 1892): 261.
55. *Le Journal de Musique* 1, no. 5 (1 August 1876): 3.
56. Armand Gouzien in *Le Journal de Musique* 1, no. 12 (19 August 1876): 5.
57. A German translation of the article appears in *Die Musik* 1902, 2: 879ff; cf. CSS-4.
58. The sixth of these Etudes, *en forme de valse,* was later orchestrated, with Saint-Saëns's approval, by the Belgian violinist Eugène Ysaye.
59. Richard Pohl had also translated Berlioz's *Béatrice et Bénédict* into German for performance in Weimar on 8 April 1863.
60. *Le Journal de Musique* 2, no. 31 (15 December 1877): 1.
61. Ibid. 1, no. 47 (21 April 1877): 4.
62. Bonnerot's claim that the mother was no longer able to nourish the child after the shock of André's death has been disproved on the basis of several letters (priv.).
63. Marie Laure Emilie Saint-Saëns died in Cauderan near Bordeaux on 30 January 1950, at the age of 95.
64. Saint-Saëns to a friend, 18 July 1878 (priv.).
65. H. B. in *Le Ménestrel* 46/12, no. 2547 (15 February 1880).
66. Qtd. in Bondeville 1971, 15.
67. Qtd. in Servières 1930, 202.
68. Qtd. in Bondeville 1971, 8.
69. Qtd. in Servières 1930, 203.
70. Qtd. in Bonnerot 1922e, 111.
71. Ibid., 113. Cf. also Saint-Saëns's account of the genesis of the work (CSS-45).
72. Harding erroneously gives 1886 as the date of origin. Bonnerot and the *Catalogue général et thématique des œuvres de Camille Saint-Saëns* indicate that the piece was written in 1885 but not published until 1886.
73. Qtd. in Bonnerot 1922e, 119f.
74. Ibid., 121.
75. *Neue Musik-Zeitung* 7, no. 3 (February 1886): 37.
76. Ibid., no. 5 (February 1886,): 50.
77. Qtd. in Bonnerot 1922e, 127.
78. Ibid., 139.
79. Ch. G. in *L'Art Musical* 30, no. 20 (25 October 1891).
80. H. M. in *Le Ménestrel* 57/44, no. 3162.

81. Qtd. in Bonnerot 1922e, 158.
82. Qtd. in Dandelot 1930, 147.
83. Victor Debay in *Ouest Artiste* (1899); qtd. in Dandelot 1930, 148.
84. Qtd. in Dandelot 1930, 148.
85. Qtd. in Bonnerot 1922e, 165.
86. Stojowsky 1901, 320.
87. J. T. in *Revue Musicale de Paris* 3, no. 3 (8 March 1903).
88. René Doire in *Le Courrier Musical, Artistique et Littéraire du Littoral* (1911); qtd. in Dandelot 1930, 203f.
89. J. Jemain in *Le Ménestrel* 70/47, no. 3843 (13 November 1904).
90. A. L. in *Revue Musicale de Paris* 4, no. 23 (13 November 1904).
91. Jean Huré in *Le Courrier Musical, Artistique et Littéraire du Littoral,* (13 November 1904); qtd. in Dandelot 1930, 201.
92. Qtd. in Bonnerot 1922e, 189.
93. Cf. i.a. letter from Saint-Saëns to his cousin Léon, 20 December (priv.).
94. S. in *Revue Musicale de Paris* 10, no. 21 (20 October 1910).
95. Qtd. in Bonnerot 1922e, 190.
96. Cf. i.a. Stegemann 1976, 267ff.; and Linden 1915, 82.
97. Qtd. in Bonnerot 1922e, 206.
98. A. Noty in *Le Courrier Musical, Artistique et Littéraire du Littoral* 22, no. 17 (24 October 1920).
99. Cf. Chantavoine 1921a, 239.
100. From Charles Widor's address at the Paris funeral service; qtd. in Aguétant n.d. (after 1921), 174.

2. *The Form of the Concertos and Concertinos [Morceaux de Concert]*

1. Raymond Tobin (1952, 12) is somewhat vague in his characterization when he calls "the first movement more energetic than fast, the middle movement more lyrical than slow, and the finale light and frivolous."
2. Cf. Mies 1972, 88.
3. Cf. i.a. Foss 1952, 143ff.
4. Triple Concerto in C Major, Op. 56; Fourth Piano Concerto in G Major, Op. 58; Violin Concerto in D Major, Op. 61; Fifth Piano Concerto in E-flat Major, Op. 73.

5. E.g., Robert Schumann's Violoncello Concerto in A Minor, Op. 129.
6. Cf. Mies 1972, 85.
7. Cf. i.a. Engel 1958, col. 1574.
8. Qtd. in Dandelot 1930, 198ff. Cf. also Lalo 1903.
9. In the remainder of the text, the concertante works by Saint-Saëns, as a rule, are referred to only by opus number; the thematic list of these works and their sources in Appendix A serves for orientation.
10. In emulation of Viotti and Paganini, Charles Auguste de Bèriot strove for a lyric-cantabile violin style, as found in the bel canto of the Italian operas of Donizetti, Bellini, and Rossini, which were very successful in Paris, and in the no less successful works of their imitators, Meyerbeer and Massenet. The Ecole Liégoise was founded around 1850 by Henri Vieuxtemps, a pupil of de Bériot, together with Hubert Léonard, Lambert-Joseph Massart and Jehin Prume; it was later continued by Eugène Ysaye. Vieuxtemps deserves primary credit for bringing virtuosity back into a healthy relationship with the orchestra. Since the other two violinist personalities of the Romantic period in France, Henri Wieniawski and Pablo de Sarasate, did not become prominent until later, Saint-Saëns was forced to seek his inspiration from the Ecole Liégoise.
11. Cf. i.a. Fallon 1973, 33, 78, and 120.
12. Cf. i.a. Cooper 1969a, 211; and Harding 1965, 105f.
13. César Franck uses a similar procedure in his Symphony in D Minor. After a slow introduction and fast main subject, instead of the expected exposition, he repeats the introduction and main subject, this time in a different key.
14. Cooper 1969a, 217. Cooper separates the work, which he erroneously lists as the Second Cello Concerto, into three movements run together attacca and calls the middle movement an intermezzo. A similar interpretation of the form is found in contemporary critiques; cf. i.a. Chapter 1, note 49.
15. Cf. i.a. Lyle 1923, 101.
16. Cf. Cooper 1969a, 211; Lyle 1923, 92.
17. Cf. Hervey 1970, 103 and 99.
18. Cf. Neitzel 1899, 72.
19. Cf. Baumann 1923, 227.
20. Cf. Harding 1965, 140.

21. Mies 1972, 85.
22. MS. 909 (1), Bibliothèque Nationale, Paris. Unlike Op. 44, this score is marked *lento assai.* Cf. Appendix A, Unnumbered opus (Op. 44).
23. Qtd. in Cooper 1969a, 215.
24. Cf. Mies 1972, 66.
25. Cf. Lyle 1923, 103.
26. E.g., Andante and Rondo Ungarese for Bassoon in C Minor, Op. 35 (C. M. Weber, 1813); Serenade and Allegro gioioso for Piano, Op. 43 (F. Mendelssohn-Bartholdy, 1838); Introduction and Allegro Appassionato for Piano in G Major, Op. 92 (R. Schumann, 1849); Concerto Allegro with Introduction for Piano in D Minor, Op. 134 (R. Schumann, 1853); Introduction et Allegro pour piano, Op. 49 (B. Godard, 1881); Konzertstück (Introduction and Allegro) for Piano (F. Busoni, 1890); Introduction et Tarantelle pour violon, Op. 43 (P. de Sarasate, 1899); Entr'acte et Rigaudon de Xavière pour violoncelle (Th. Dubois, 1901); Introduction et Allegro pour Harpe etc. (M. Ravel, 1905–06).
27. In this sense, the finale of Op. 61 approximates a two-part concertante form.
28. Johann Sigismund Scholze, *Sperontes Singende Muse an der Pleisse in 2.mahl 50 Oden, der neuesten und besten mus. Stücke mit den dazu gehörigen Melodien zu beliebter Clavier-Übung und Gemüths-Ergötzung* [Sperontes' singing muse in twice 50 odes, the newest and best musical pieces with their respective melodies, for popular keyboard practice and delight of the soul]. Cf. Karl 1963, col. 853.
29. Cf. Marcel Marnat, jacket notes, Philips 6504.055; and James Harding, jacket notes, Electrola Music Inc. 1 C 157-02.917/19.
30. Cf. Marcel Marnat, jacket notes, Philips 6504.055.
31. The list of works in the biography by James Harding (1965, 230ff.) makes no reference to Op. 94. When I asked the author about this, he replied that he had simply forgotten the work (priv. corresp.); this is not the only gap in the list, incidentally. This blatant contradiction to the express claim that this was a list of the "Complete Musical Works of Camille Saint-Saëns" seems to me to be symptomatic of the flaws of the publication and the inadequacy of the author's research.
32. As a rule, however, the variation form was expressed right in the

title, as in Chopin's Op. 2 or Tchaikowsky's Op. 33.

33. Harding 1965, 179.
34. Cf. author's correspondence with Harding and Gérard (priv.); and Saint-Saën's correspondence (Bibliothèque Municipale in Dieppe, Bibliothèque Nationale in Paris, and priv.).
35. Cf. Tobin 1952, 13.
36. Cf. Mies 1972, 54f.
37. Ibid., 79.
38. Ibid., 67ff.
39. Berlioz 1947 [Eng. trans. of *Memoires*], 442. Unsuccessful attempts were made by Balakireff, Mikuli, Minhejmer, and Tausig to revise the orchestra part for the Piano Concerto in E Minor, Op. 11; and by Burmester and Klindworth, for Op. 21 in F Minor. Cf. Rehberg and Rehberg 1948, 407f.
40. Cf. Mies 1972, 72. In checking through the issues between 1850 and 1880 of the following periodicals in the Bibliothèque Nationale, Paris—*L'Art Musical; Le Courrier Musical, Artistique et Littéraire du Littoral; La France Musicale; Le Guide Musical; Le Journal de Musique; Le Ménestrel; Le Monde Musical;* and *Revue Musicale de Paris*—I frequently encountered reviews that describe extremes in solo concerto performance. For example, it seems to have been common practice for the soloist not to step onto the stage until some point during the orchestral prelude and to be greeted with a storm of applause even though the concerto had already begun. A few virtuosos adopted especially "effective" mannerisms aimed at steering the audience's attention to themselves; one soloist—regrettably, he could not be identified, since the reviewer refers to him simply as "le soliste" and mentions no specific concert whose soloists could have been checked—is said to have established the habit of entering wearing white kid gloves and making a big show of stripping them off during the prelude. During lengthy orchestral passages, he carried on loud conversations with the guests of honor. Cf. i.a. *Le Journal de Musique* 3/141 (8 February 1879): 2.
41. Cf. i.a. Rehberg and Rehberg 1947, 60.
42. Cf. i.a. Myers 1968, 77; and Stuckenschmidt 1960, 290.
43. Cf. Mies 1972, 71.
44. Cf. Schering 1927, 198.
45. Cf. Cooper 1969a, 210.

46. Cf. Hervey 1970, 103.
47. Cf. i.a. Wolfurt 1926, 162.
48. Cf. i.a. Engel 1974, 262.
49. Engel 1974, 109; cf. Lyle 1923, 93.
50. Cf. Cooper 1969a, 21.
51. Cf. Schröter 1971, 33f.
52. The only reference to the monothematic character of Op. 62 is found in jacket notes by Marcel Marnat, Philips 6504.055.
53. Cf. Heldt 1973, 134.
54. Cf. i.a. Mies 1972, 31 and 41.
55. Tobin 1952, 11. More recent studies of the concerto form of the Venetian Baroque period cast doubt on this theory.
56. Ansermet 1965, 319.
57. Mellers 1964, 17.
58. Robertson and Stevens 1968, 57.
59. Cf. Robertson and Stevens 1968, 59.
60. Cf. Tobin 1952, 12.
61. Cf. Mies 1972, 31.
62. Ibid., 31 and 41.
63. Cooper 1969a, 210.
64. Hugo Leichtentritt, *Musikalische Formenlehre,* qtd. in Müller-Blattau 1955, col. 555f.
65. Cf. von Fischer 1966, col. 1298.
66. One of Franck's early works, the *Variations brillantes* for piano and orchestra, Op. 8 (ca. 1834), continues the tradition of Chopin's Op. 2 and in no way resembles the arrangement of Franck's later variations.
67. Cf. i.a. Mohr 1969, 136ff.
68. Emmanuel 1922, 28.
69. Parker 1919, 567.
70. Prod'homme 1922, 476.

3. The Relationship of Solo and Orchestra

1. Berlioz 1955, 406.
2. *Monatshefte für Musikwissenschaft* 37 (1905): 31.
3. Cf. Engel 1974.
4. MS. 13.893, Bibliothèque Nationale, Paris; cf. Chapter 9.

5. Cf. Schottky 1909.
6. Chevillard 1922, 5.
7. Jehin 1922, 5.
8. Hue 1922, 5.
9. Carse 1964, 300.
10. In the early 1920s, pianist Harold Bauer (1873–1951) made a piano roll recording of Op. 22 in a version for solo piano, which is as interesting as it is unsatisfying.
11. In his *Memoirs* Berlioz repeatedly refers to the lack of discipline of the Paris orchestras, their unartistic insistence on providing only the minimal services required, and their slovenly execution of the music, whereby notes were changed and simplified arbitrarily. However, one could surmise that Berlioz often generalized on the basis of individual boycotts directed against him.
12. These settings were taken from a table by Heinz Becker in *Die Musik in Geschichte und Gegenwart,* ed. Friedrich Blume, vol. 10 (1962): col. 192ff.
13. Cf. i.a. Harding 1965, 106.
14. Baumann 1923, 221.
15. Lyle 1923, 99.
16. Cooper 1969a, 215.
17. Baumann 1923, 213 and 217.
18. Ibid., 216.
19. Qtd. in Baumann 1923, 223.
20. Qtd. in *Le Monde Musical* 20 (31 January 1901): 307.
21. Qtd. in Aguétant n.d. (after 1921), 39; also qtd. in Mason n.d., 196ff.
22. Boschot 1926, 206.
23. CSS-37, 222f.
24. Baumann 1923, 214.
25. Cf. i.a. Parker 1919, 564, and Delage 1978.
26. Knosp 1905.
27. Henri Blanchard, qtd. in Eckart-Bäcker 1965, 173.
28. Adolphe Blotte, qtd. in Eckart-Bäcker 1965, 173.
29. Saint-Saëns was one of the first musicians to become interested in the Welte-Mignon system. His recordings on the player piano, which was invented in 1904, include Chopin's Impromptu in F-sharp Major, Op. 36, as well as the following compositions of his

own: Dance of the priestesses and aria of Dalila from the finale of the first act of *Samson et Dalila; Rapsodie d'Auvergne,* Op. 73; the Mazurkas Ops. 21 and 66; Valse mignonne, Op. 104; Valse nonchalante, Op. 110; Gavotte from the suite Op. 90; and "Reverie a Blidah" and "Marche militaire française" from the *Suite algérienne,* Op. 60. There is also an acoustic recording of a few parts of Op. 89 in existence, recorded in 1904 on Gramophone and Typewriter Company Matrix 3464p. However, a recording of the first movement of Op. 22 seems unfortunately to be lost without a trace. All recordings reveal Saint-Saëns as an extremely cultivated pianist, with no trace of the romantic exaggeration typical of recordings by the young Alfred Cortot.

30. Philippe 1922, 40.
31. Busoni 1957, 172.
32. Cf. i.a. Schonberg 1963, 267.
33. A. K. 1905, 23.
34. Qtd. in Georges Servières 1930, 136.
35. CSS-34, xi.
36. CSS-33, 122.
37. CSS-15, 127 [Ger. trans.].

4. *The Cadenza*

1. Qtd. in E. Thiel 1962, 229.
2. Cf. E. Thiel 1962, 229.
3. For more on this and the following cf. Mies 1972, 31.
4. This pedal-pointlike fermata also gave rise to the French term "point d'orgue" for the concerto cadenza.
5. Ernst Hess, qtd. in Mies 1972, 32.
6. Cf. Mies 1972, 32.
7. In 1976 I had the opportunity to hear a performance of the work with Alkan's cadenza. K. 466 in general seems to be especially susceptible to arbitrary cadenzas, as demonstrated more recently by Arthur Schnabel's cadenza, which ventures into atonal realms.
8. Saint-Saëns wrote cadenzas to Beethoven's Op. 58 (1878) and Op. 61, for violin (1900), as well as to the Mozart concertos K. 365 (for two pianos), K. 482, and K. 491, which are not dated.
9. Cf. Mies 1972, 41f.

10. At this point I would like to express special thanks to Ulf Hoelscher, who gave me some very interesting insights into the violin cadenzas of the nineteenth century. Among other things, he pointed out that certain technical combinations are possible only when separated by a fermata and that they were therefore used mainly outside the actual movement (in the cadenza).
11. Mies 1972, 43f.
12. See Chapter 3, note 19.
13. Cf. i.a. Stengel 1931, 96.
14. Baumann 1923, 214.
15. Similarly independent cadenzas are found in the Concerto in A Minor for Violin, Op. 54 (1904), by Glazunov; in the *Tzigane* for violin (1924), by Ravel; and in the First Concerto for Violin, Op. 99 (1948), by Shostakovich.

5. *Horizontal and Vertical Structures*

1. See quote in Chapter 3 connected to note 36.
2. Qtd. in E. Thiel 1962, 308.
3. Cf. i.a. contemporary reviews in French music journals.
4. Baumann 1923, 142ff.
5. Cf. Baumann 1923, 231.
6. I am indebted to Yves Gérard for the suggestion that the composer may have taken this theme from Breton folk music, even though in altered rhythmic form. However, our cooperative research has so far failed to confirm this theory.
7. Marty 1907, 91.
8. Bernard 1935, 241.
9. Cf. Debussy 1974 [Ger. trans.], 53.
10. Ceillier 1922, 30.
11. Qtd. in Ceillier 1922, 29.
12. Cf. i.a. Schonberg 1973 [Ger. trans.], 103.
13. See note 1 above.
14. CSS-34, i ff.
15. For these and the other examples, cf. Chapters 9–11.
16. Cf. i.a. Leichtentritt 1951, 88.
17. Qtd. in Hervey 1970, 39.
18. Qtd. in Baumann 1923, 121.

19. Jules Combarieu, *Théorie du rythme,* qtd. in Baumann 1923, 121; cf. also Chapter 7.
20. Chantavoine 1947, 80.
21. Cf. Chapter 1, note 39.
22. Baumann 1923, 127.
23. Ibid., 128.
24. Cf. i.a. Stegemann 1976, 267ff.; and Jullien 1887.
25. Baumann 1923, 128f.
26. Ibid., 131.
27. Cf. Baumann 1923, 131f.
28. Baumann 1923, 132.
29. CSS-21, 8.
30. Saint-Saëns to Fauré, 27 December 1915, qtd. in Nectoux 1973, 108.

6. *Folk and Oriental Elements*

1. Cf. i.a. Cooper 1969a, 44.
2. As a follower of Saint-Simonism, David, with a few friends, had fled the country in March 1833 to escape political persecution. His wanderings led him through almost every country in the Middle East. He made notes on many of the melodies and rhythms that he heard, which he developed after returning to his homeland in the summer of 1835. Saint-Saëns appreciated the unabashed naiveté of David's composition. Cf. i.a. Brancour 1911; and Lebeau 1954, col. 47ff.
3. Cf. i.a. Quittard 1906, 107ff.
4. Dubcek 1978, 86ff.
5. Cf. i.a. Dubcek 1978, 86.
6. Cf. i.a. Myers 1968, 159f.
7. Cf. Saint-Saëns correspondence in the Bibliothèque Municipale, Dieppe.
8. According to a letter from Saint-Saëns to Jacques Durand, which Yves Gérard told me about, but which I was unfortunately not able to examine personally.
9. Cf. i.a. Niemöller 1973, 402ff. This source includes further references to the papers of Georg Capellen on the subject.
10. See note 8 above.

11. Cf. Chapter 1, note 84.
12. Tiersot 1889.
13. Ibid., 88.
14. Qtd. in *Grand Larousse encyclopédique.*
15. Cf. MS. 916^{10}, 1890, Bibliothèque Nationale, Paris; also Bonnerot 1922e, 148.
16. Cf. Chapter 2, note 22.
17. MS. 916^{5} and MS. 916^{6}, Bibliothèque Nationale, Paris: "Première esquisse du Concerto faite aux Canaries deux ans avant esquisse du 1er morceau [First sketch of the Concerto made in the Canaries two years before the sketch of the first piece]."
18. Baumann 1923, 223.
19. Cf. i.a. Chottin 1951, col. 590.
20. Cf. Wirth 1951, col. 679.
21. CSS-16, 125.
22. Cf. i.a. Schneider 1965, col. 1010.
23. Cf. Bonnerot 1922e, 104.
24. Cf. i.a. Fuchs 1956, col. 186.
25. Tiersot 1889, 92.
26. Cf. i.a. "Saint-Saëns" in *The New Grove Dictionary of Music and Musicians.*
27. Ibid.
28. Cf. i.a. Vallas 1946, 1950.

7. *Camille Saint-Saëns's Personality, Aesthetics, and Approach to Composition*

1. Cf. Chapter 3, note 33.
2. Thorel 1907b, 92.
3. Bonnerot, Préface to *La Vie.*
4. Cf. Chapter 2, notes 68–70.
5. Qtd. in Rutz 1954, 227f.
6. CSS-42, 9ff.
7. Cf. i.a. Harding 1965, 105f.
8. Ibid., 91ff.
9. Cf. i.a. Cortot 1948, 75f.
10. Cf. i.a. Bonnerot 1922e, 54.

8. *Historical Background*

1. The source below gives the opus number incorrectly as 10.
2. Cf. i.a. Engel 1958, col. 1572.
3. Qtd. in Engel 1958, col. 1574.
4. Johannes Brahms to Clara Schumann, June 1878, qtd. in Rehberg and Rehberg 1947, 183.
5. Qtd. in Doukan 1951, col. 1089.
6. Cf. i.a. Quittin 1960, col. 633.
7. Cf. i.a. Lavignac and Laurencie 1925, 3:1838.
8. Cf. i.a. Heldt 1973, 20.
9. Hans Engel, qt. in Heldt 1973, 20.
10. Cf. i.a. Parker 1918, 46.
11. Cf. i.a. Klingenbeck 1962, col. 1356.
12. Stengel 1931, 9.
13. Cf. i.a. Stengel 1931, 31ff.
14. Cf. Engel 1958, col. 1580. Engel's rather vague reference is mainly to the genre names then current in France: "concerto brillant," "concerto romantique," and "concerto de salon."
15. Qtd. in Ferchault 1962, col. 773.
16. Cf. i.a. Goldron 1966, 91.
17. Pierre Lalo, qtd. in Goldron 1966, 91. Saint-Saëns later defended Meyerbeer (cf. CSS-35), whose "grand opéra" he himself emulated in works such as *Henry VIII* or *Les Barbares.*
18. Platzbecker 1905, 12; cf. also Favre 1947.
19. Cf. i.a. Mohr 1969, 77; and Chapter 1, note 27.
20. Qtd.in Engel 1958, col. 1580.

9. *The French Solo Concerto from 1850 to 1873 (from Op. 6 to Op. 33)*

1. Neitzel 1899, 69.
2. For this and all subsequent references to French solo concertos, cf. Appendix B.
3. *Die Musik in Geschichte und Gegenwart* errs on two points: Hans Engel's article (1958b, col. 1580) refers to the Second Concerto symphonique as "based on Dutch themes," while Fritz Stein's article (1960, col. 1004) gives the opus number incorrectly as 54.

4. Schonberg 1963, 192.
5. Cf. Chapter 1, note 8.
6. Cf. Baumann 1923, 219.
7. Cf. Appendix A, Op. 58, note 2.
8. Schering 1927, 160; and Hanslick 1876.
9. Cf. i.a. Schonberg 1963, 179.
10. Heldt 1973, 22.
11. Schumann 1974, 236.
12. Cf. Baumann 1923, 210 ff.; Carraud (1907) also sees this connection.
13. Cf. i.a. Barzun 1969, 2:251.
14. Stengel (1931, 94) gives the date of origin incorrectly as 1862.
15. Cf. i.a. Mies 1972, 68.
16. Ibid., 82.
17. Cf. i.a. Lavignac and Laurencie 1925, 1792.
18. Servais's first name, according to Alexander Vander Linden (1965, col. 579), is Adrien-François. Lavignac and Laurencie (1925, 1838) give his first name as François-André.
19. Qtd. in Vander Linden 1965, col. 579.
20. Cf. i.a. Göthel 1963a, col. 1400f.
21. Shaw 1961, 359.
22. Ibid., 132.
23. Cf. i.a. Parker 1918, 46; and Wells-Harrison 1915, 77ff.
24. Cf. i.a. Göthel 1963a, col. 1401.
25. Van der Borren 1951, col. 1965.
26. Lavignac and Laurencie 1925, 1838. It is interesting that Lavignac speaks here of "Concerto pour piano" and "Concerto pour flûte."
27. Cf. i.a. Stengel 1931, 106.
28. Berlioz 1979 [Ger. trans.], 193.
29. Wangermée 1955, col. 132. [The German word is *Verkalkt,* literally referring to "hardening of the arteries." Ed.]
30. Ibid., col. 132f.
31. Cf. i.a. Ferchault 1958, col. 158.
32. Qtd. in Lavignac and Laurencie 1925, 1798.
33. MS. 13.893, Bibliothèque Nationale, Paris, with the note "Paris 1 juin 1866."
34. See note 32.
35. Cf. i.a. Savari 1890.

36. Cf. i.a. Dandelot 1923.
37. Stengel 1931, 95.
38. Imbert 1897; and Séré 1922, 69ff.
39. Cf. i.a. d'Indy 1965, 46.
40. Qtd. in Séré 1922, 73.
41. Cf. i.a. Gauthier 1952, col. 903f.
42. Ibid., col. 902.
43. Cf. i.a. Harding 1965, 110.
44. Fourcaud 1896.
45. Cf. i.a. Raicich 1965, col. 1785.
46. Qtd. in Lavignac and Laurencie 1925, 1776.
47. Qtd. in Bondeville 1971, 11.
48. Widor 1922.
49. K. 3513, (Vm^{24}:108), Bibliothèque Nationale, Paris, has the note: "Jules Garcin, violon solo de l'opéra, membre de la chapelle impériale et de la société des Concerts du Conservatoire. Dédié à Monsieur Ambroise Thomas de l'Institut." Garcin's concerto was published by Editions Richault in 1872.
50. Cf. Mies 1972, 51ff.
51. Cf. i.a. Cooper 1969a, 31f.; also Servières n.d.
52. Séré 1922, 257.
53. H. C. Colles, qtd. by Foss 1952, 151.
54. Lavignac and Laurencie (1925, 1788) refer to the work as "2e Concerto, Op. 21 appelé *Symphonie espagnole*."
55. Pitrou 1957, 44.
56. Cf. i.a. Ferchault 1960, col. 108.
57. Boschot 1954, 102f.
58. CSS-16, 125.
59. Cf. i.a. Guichard 1955.
60. CSS-22, 220.
61. Cf. i.a. Stegemann 1976, 267ff.
62. Cf. CSS-4 and *Le Journal de Musique* 1, no. 14 (2 novembre 1876): 3.
63. Cf. i.a. Servières 1923b.
64. Cf. i.a. Stegemann 1976, 267ff; also Weingartner 1915, 82.
65. Cf. Vallas 1946 and 1950, 287, Figure 16.
66. d'Indy 1930.

10. *The French Solo Concerto from 1874 to 1890 (from Op. 36 to Op. 94)*

1. CSS-6, 37f.
2. Cf. i.a. Kahl 1963, col. 853.
3. Ibid., col. 855.
4. CSS-55, 202f.
5. Cf. i.a. Harding 1965, 72.
6. Lavignac and Laurencie 1925, 1970.
7. Cf. i.a. Buffenoir 1894.
8. The piano arrangement I used (K. 37.420, Bibliothèque Nationale, Paris) was published in Paris (Editions Hartmann) in 1874. Since I was unable to find more exact information, I decided to go by this date and list the work under 1874 in Appendix B.
9. E. Thiel 1962, 93.
10. Pitrou 1957, 43f.
11. Raugel 1954, col. 840.
12. Cf. i.a. Tiersot 1918, 72ff.
13. Cf. i.a. Cooper 1969b, 128f.
14. Other sources list "Concerto capriccioso."
15. Stengel 1931, 97.
16. Lavignac and Laurencie 1925, 1803.
17. Haraszti 1956, col. 391.
18. Stengel 1931, 97. The year of origin is given erroneously as 1882.
19. Cf. i.a. Cooper 1969b, 90; also Schmitz 1966, 40.
20. Cf. Mies 1972, 66f.
21. Lavignac and Laurencie 1925, 1788.
22. Pitrou 1957, 44.
23. Ibid., 44f.
24. See note 21.
25. Cf. i.a. Quittin 1973, col. 1882.
26. Stengel 1931, 31.
27. Ibid., 31. A similar encapsulation is found in Tchaikovsky's First Piano Concerto in B-flat Minor, Op. 23, where the slow movement contains a scherzo section.
28. Mey 1904, 167.
29. Stengel 1931, 23.
30. Qtd. in Nectoux 1972b, 39f.

31. Cf. i.a. Cooper 1969b, 83.
32. Qtd. in Nectoux 1972b, 40.
33. Ibid.
34. Mark Hambourg, qtd. in Schonberg 1963, 269.
35. Cf. i.a. Boschot 1922–26 1:240.
36. Cf. *Monatshefte für Musikgeschichte* 37 (1905).
37. Qtd. in Cotte and Haultier 1954, col. 435.
38. Although the work premiered in 1881, the composer speaks of 1883 as the date of origin in his correspondence (Bibliothèque Nationale, Paris).
39. Pitrou 1957, 45.
40. Stengel 1931, 97.
41. Ibid., 50f.
42. Göthel 1963b, col. 1436f.
43. d'Indy 1965, 163.
44. Cf. Cooper 1969b, 46.
45. Cf. i.a. Horton 1952, 431.
46. Cf. Rehberg 1961, 472.
47. Qtd. in Lavignac and Laurencie 1925, 1788.
48. Lavignac and Laurencie 1925, 1838.
49. Cf. Lavignac and Laurencie 1925, 1812.
50. Stengel 1931, 97. He gives both the wrong title (*Fantasie*) and the wrong date (1888).
51. The Fantasia is based on the so-called Czar hymn ("God keep the Czar"), written in 1833 by Alexey Fyodorovitch Lvov, which was also among the themes Tchaikovsky worked into his *1812 Overture* and his *Slavic March,* Op. 31.
52. Qtd. in Séré 1922, 235.
53. As nearly as I could determine, the title, which was common for this period, goes back to a concertante work for violin by de Bériot called *Scènes de Ballet.*
54. Stengel (1931, 98) erroneously gives 1895 as the date of origin.
55. Stengel 1931, 98.
56. Cf. i.a. Cooper 1969b, 203.
57. Cf. i.a. Raugel 1952, col. 139f.
58. Cf. i.a. Cooper 1969b, 60.
59. Ibid.
60. Stengel (1931) erroneously lists the opus number as 69.

61. Qtd. in Vallas 1961 [Ger. trans.], 80f.
62. Cf. related discussion in Section 3.1; also Rutz 1954, 47f.
63. Maurice Emmanuel, "Les Ambitions de Claude Achille," *Revue Musicale de Paris* 5 (1926), qtd. in Rutz 1954, 48.
64. Strobel 1940, 48.

11. *The French Solo Concerto from 1891 to 1921 (from Op. 89 to Op. 162)*

1. Cf. p. 57.
2. D'Indy 1904.
3. Cf. i.a. p. 184.
4. Cf. Strobel 1940, 48.
5. CSS-21; also Vallas 1947, 79ff.
6. Gallois 1967, 157.
7. Boschot 1922–26, 3:101ff.
8. Cf. i.a. Verchaly 1973, col. 949.
9. Stengel 1931, 54.
10. Ferchault 1960, col. 40.
11. Cf. i.a. Stengel 1931, 97.
12. Ibid., 96.
13. Camille Mauclair, *Souvenir sur Ernest Chausson,* qtd. in Séré 1922, 114.
14. Gallois 1967, 146.
15. Qtd. in Pitrou 1957, 155.
16. Marnold 1920, 123.
17. Cf. i.a. Cooper 1969b, 204.
18. Machabey 1949–51, col. 777.
19. Stengel 1931, 32.
20. Ibid., 33.
21. Schonberg 1963, 270.
22. Cf. i.a. Stengel 1931, 32f.
23. Cf. i.a. Cotte 1954, col. 1504.
24. Cf. Vallas 1950, 224.
25. Cf. i.a. Vallas 1950, 243f.
26. Engel 1974, vol. 2.
27. Schering 1927, 199.

28. I.a. Lavignac and Laurencie 1925, 1725.
29. Debussy 1971, 173.
30. See note 19.
31. Debussy 1971, 77.
32. Vallas 1958, 292.
33. Cf. i.a. Myers 1968, 181.
34. Cf. i.a. Stengel, 1931, 58.
35. Ibid., 40; also Dent 1974, 224.
36. Cocteau 1979, 50.
37. Cf. i.a. Stegemann 1976, 267ff.; also Marnold 1920, 29ff.

12. *Summary and Conclusion*

1. Marnold 1920, 29.
2. Ravel to Jean Marnold, Chalons-sur-Marne, 7 October 1916, qtd. in Gal 1966, 514.
3. Qtd. in Myers 1968, 52.
4. Cf. i.a. Myers 1971, 131f.
5. Cf. i.a. Myers 1968, 84 and 106.
6. Cf. i.a. Myers 1971, 56f.
7. Mortier 1922, 4.

Bibliography

All the sources quoted in this study appear in alphabetical order in the following bibliography. I have also included books and magazine articles not quoted in the text that provided valuable information on the life and work of Camille Saint-Saëns and thus helped me gain a feeling for the musical world of French Romanticism and the cultural history behind the artistic trends. Especially informative in this regard were the composer's own writings.

Wherever possible I have listed a book's publisher. There are several magazine articles listed for which page numbers could not be given, since I had access only to photocopies on which the pagination was illegible or cut off.

Not included in the bibliography, but given in the body of the text, are record jacket texts, which are not scholarly sources but offer comments on special aspects of Saint-Saëns's concertante works found nowhere else.

It would exceed the scope of this study and hence, this bibliography, to undertake a detailed evaluation of Saint-Saëns's works within French Romanticism with appropriate literary documentation. The classification of the composer as a representative of "salon music," initiated by d'Indy and Debussy and still widely accepted today, merits greater attention, but refutation of this classification must be reserved for another time. In this context I would cite just one source, which to my knowledge contains the most comprehensive bibliography on the intellectual history of France during the Romantic period and the early twentieth century:

Klein, Jean-René. 1975. *Introduction à l'étude du langage boulevardier,* p. XXff. Paris Ed. Nouvelarts.

A thorough study of the writings in this bibliography, which to a large extent also deal with salon music, should dispel the notion once and for all that Saint-Saëns was merely an affable composer of superficial salon pieces.

I have refrained from evaluating the sources compiled on the following pages. Let me only say in conclusion that the biographies by Emile Baumann (*Les grandes formes de la musique: L'œuvre de M. Camille Saint-Saëns*) and Jean Bonnerot (*La vie et l'œuvre de Camille Saint-Saëns*) provided the greatest help and, in my opinion, can still be regarded today as standard works.

[In the bibliography, "Blume" refers to *Die Musik in Geschichte und Gegenwart.* Ed.]

A., K. 1905. *Saint-Saëns als Kind.* In: *Neue Musik-Zeitung* 27:23f

Aguétant, Pierre. n.d. (after 1921). *Saint-Saëns par lui-même.* Paris: Alsatia.

Allgemeine Musik-Zeitung. Ed. Selmar Bagge et al. Leipzig, 1874–.

Ansermet, Ernest. 1965. *Die Grundlagen der Musik im menschlichen Bewuβtsein.* Munich: Piper. (Fr. orig. pub. in 1961.)

L'Art Musical. Ed. Léon Escudier. Paris.

Aubry, G. Jean. 1922. "Camille Saint-Saëns." *Chesterian* 20:97ff.

Augé de Lassus, Lucien. 1914. *Saint-Saëns.* Paris: Delagrave.

Babin, Gustave. 1908. "L'assassinat du Duc de Guise." *L'Illustration* (October 31).

Barrès, Maurice. 1885. "Musiques—A propos du livre de M. Saint-Saëns: *Harmonie et Melodie.*" *La Revue Illustrée* (December 15).

Barzun, Jacques. 1969. *Berlioz and the Romantic Century.* 2 vols. New York: Columbia University Press.

Baumann, Emile. 1900. *Camille Saint-Saëns et* Déjanire. Paris: n.p.

———. [1905] 1923. *Les grandes formes de la musique: L'œuvre de M. Camille Saint-Saëns.* 2d ed. Paris: Ollendorff.

———. 1927. "Histoire de mon amitié pour Camille Saint-Saëns." In *Intermèdes,* 170ff. Paris.

Becker, G. 1919. "La idee di V. d'Indy quelle di Camille Saint-Saëns." *Rivista Musicale Italiana* 19:381ff.

Bellaigue, Camille. 1888–1893. *L'année musicale.* 6 vols. Paris: n.p.

______. 1889. *Monsieur Camille Saint-Saëns.* Paris: Durand.
______. 1898. *Etudes musicales et nouvelles silhouettes de musiciens.* Paris: n.p.
______. 1926. "Lettres de Saint-Saëns et Camille Bellaigue." *Revue des Deux Mondes* 4.
Berlioz, Hector. [1843] 1948. *Grand traité d'instrumentation et d'orchestration modernes.* Trans. by Th. Front. New York: n.p. (1st Eng. ed. 1858, rev. several times.)
______. [1948] 1955. *Instrumentationslehre.* Repr. Rev. and updated by Richard Strauss. Leipzig: n.p.
______. 1969. *Mémoires.* 2 vols. Repr. Paris: Flammarion. (Eng. trans. by Rachel Holmes and Eleanor Holmes, under the title *Memoirs.* 1947. Rev. and updated by Ernest Newman. New York: A. A. Knopf. Ger. trans. *Memoiren.* 1979. Munich: n.p.)
Bernard, Robert. 1935. "Camille Saint-Saëns." *La Revue Musicale* 16, no. 160 (November): 241ff.
Bernier, Conrad. 1937. "Emile Baumann et l'œuvre de Camille Saint-Saëns." *Georgetown University French Review* 1:3ff.
Besnard, Charles. 1922. *Notice sur la vie et les œuvres de Monsieur Camille Saint-Saëns.* Paris: Firmin-Didot.
Bierné, Maria. "Camille Saint-Saëns et son œuvre." *Le Guide Musical* 57, no. 50:763ff.
Blanchard, Henri. 1852. "Le premier concert de la Société Sainte-Cécile." *Revue et Gazette Musicale de Paris* 19, no. 4.
Blondel, C. n.d. (probably 1896). *Le cinquantenaire artistique de C. Saint-Saëns.* Paris: Durand.
Blume, Friedrich, ed. 1949/51–1979. *Die Musik in Geschichte und Gegenwart.* 15 vols. Kassel: Bärenreiter.
Bondeville, Emmanuel. 1971. *Un grand musicien mal connu—Camille Saint-Saëns.* Paris: Firmin-Didot.
Bonnerot, Jean. 1911a. "A propos de *Proserpine*." *Echo de Paris* (November 6).
______. 1911b. "*Déjanire* de Saint-Saëns." *Echo de Paris* (November 18).
______. 1912. "La vingtième année de *Samson et Dalila*." *Echo de Paris* (November 22).
______. 1913a. "La création de *Proserpine*." *Massilia* (December).
______. 1913b. "Les souvenirs de Saint-Saëns." *L'Action* (February 23).

———. 1919. "Une œuvre inédite de Saint-Saëns—*Le carnaval des animaux*." *Mercure de France* (June 1).

———. 1921. "*Ascanio* de Camille Saint-Saëns." *Echo de Paris* (November 3).

———. 1922a. "Camille Saint-Saëns: Souvenirs." *Comoedia* (December 18).

———. 1922b. "*Le carnaval des animaux* de Saint-Saëns." *Le Guide de Concert (et des Théâtres Lyriques)* (February 24).

———. 1922c. "Les dernières années de Saint-Saëns." *Le Guide de Concert (et des Théâtres Lyriques)* 3, numéro spécial Saint-Saëns.

———. 1922d. "Mort de Camille Saint-Saëns." *Mercure de France* (January 1).

———. [1914] 1922e. *La vie et l'œuvre de Camille Saint-Saëns.* 2d rev. ed. 1922. Paris: Durand.

———. 1925. "Les domiciles Parisiens de Saint-Saëns." *Mercure de France* (March 1).

———. 1927. "Saint-Saëns à Saint-Germain." *Gazette Artistique et Littéraire de Seine-et-Oise* (October 1).

———. 1933. "Saint-Saëns bibliophile." *Archives de la Société des Collectionneurs d'Ex-Libris* (October–December).

———, ed. 1957. "Saint-Saëns et Romain Rolland—Lettres inédites publiées par Jean Bonnerot." *Revue de Musicologie* 39, no. 40:196ff.

Boschot, Adolphe. 1922–1926. *Chez les musiciens.* 3 vols. Paris: Plon-Nourrit.

———. 1954. *Saint-Saëns et sa correspondance générale—Mélanges d'histoire littéraire et de bibliographie offerts à Jean Bonnerot.* Paris: n.p.

Botte, Adolphe. 1860. "Camille Saint-Saëns." *Revue et Gazette Musicale de Paris* 27, no. 16.

Bragard, R. n.d. *Concertos célèbres.* Brussels: n.p.

Brancour, René. 1911. *Félicien David.* Paris: Laurens.

Briquet, Marie. 1963. "Charles-Camille Saint-Saëns (Werke)." Blume, vol. 11.

Bruneau, Alfred. 1900. *Musiques d'hier et de demain.* Paris: Fasquelle.

———. 1901. *La musique française.* Paris: Fasquelle.

———. 1903. *Musiques de Russie et musiciens de France.* Paris: Fasquelle.

Brussel, Robert. 1901. "*Les Barbares.*" *L'Art Dramatique et Musical* (October).

———. 1906. "Le soixantième anniversaire musical de M. Saint-

Saëns." *Le Courrier Musical, Artistique et Littéraire du Littoral* (June 1).
Buffenoir, Hippolyte. 1894. *Nos contemporaines—La Vicomtesse de Grandval.* Paris: Librairie du Mirabeau.
Bülow, Hans von. 1908. *Briefe.* Vol. 7. Leipzig: n.p.
Busoni, Ferruccio. 1957. "Reminiscences of Saint-Saëns." In *The Essence of Music.* New York: Dover Press.
Calvocoressi, Michail Dimitrij. 1922. "Camille Saint-Saëns." *Monthly Musical Record* (London) 614:25f.
Carraud, G. 1907. "Mendelssohn et Monsieur Saint-Saëns amateurs." *Le Courrier Musical, Artistique et Littèraire du Littoral* 2.
Carse, Adam. [1925] 1964. *The History of Orchestration.* Repr. New York: Dover Press.
Castera, R. de. 1903. "Les variations de Monsieur Saint-Saëns." *L'Occident* 3.
Catalogue de l'exposition commémorative à l'occasion du cent cinquantième anniversaire de la naissance de Camille Saint-Saëns. 1985. Château-Musée de Dieppe.
Catalogue du Musée de Dieppe: Archéologie, histoire locale, beaux-arts, Musée Saint-Saëns, histoire naturelle. 1904. Dieppe.
Catalogue général et thématique des œuvres de Camille Saint-Saëns. [1897] 1908. 2d rev. ed. Paris: Durand.
Ceillier, Laurent. 1922. "Personnalité et évolution de Saint-Saëns." *Le Guide de Concert (et des Théâtres Lyriques)* 3, numéro spécial Saint-Saëns: 29f.
Chantavoine, Jean. 1921a. "Camille Saint-Saëns." *Neue Musik-Zeitung* 37:239ff.
———. 1921b. *L'œuvre dramatique de Camille Saint-Saëns.* Paris.
———. 1922. "Sur Saint-Saëns." *Le Ménestrel* 88, no. 2 (January 13): 9ff.
———. 1947. *Camille Saint-Saëns.* Paris: Richard-Masse.
Chase, Gilbert. 1975. "Charles Camille Saint-Saëns." In *The International Cyclopedia of Music and Musicians.* New York: n.p.
Chevillard, Camille. 1922. "Hommage à Saint-Saëns." *Le Courrier Musical, Artistique et Littèraire du Littoral* 24, no. 1.
Chottin, Alexis. 1951. "Arabische Musik." Blume, vol. 1, col. 577ff.
Clozanet, Albert [Jean d'Udine]. 1904. *Paraphrases musicales sur les grands concerts du dimanche 1900–1903.* Paris: A. Joanin.
———. 1908. "Saint-Saëns." *Le Courrier Musical, Artistique et Littèraire* 6.

Cocteau, Jean. [1918] 1979. *Le coq et l'arlequin.* New ed. Paris: n.p.
Coeuroy, A. 1922. *La musique française moderne.* Paris.
Cohen, Henry. 1875. [Review.] *L'Art Musical* (Paris) 14, no. 44 (October 31).
Combarieu, Jules. 1901. "Saint-Saëns et l'opinion musicale." *Revue d'Histoire et de Critique* 1:355ff. and 390ff.
______. 1903. "Saint-Saëns, l'homme et le musicien." *La Revue Musicale* 3:590f.
______. 1919. *Histoire de la musique.* 3 vols. Paris: A. Collin.
Cooper, Martin. [1951] 1969a. "Camille Saint-Saëns." In *The Concerto.* Ralph Hill, ed. Rev. ed. London: Penguin.
______. [1951] 1969b. *French Music From the Death of Berlioz to the Death of Fauré.* Rev. ed. 1969. London: Oxford University Press.
Cortot, Alfred. [1932] 1948. *La musique française de piano.* 2d ed. 3 vols. Paris: Presses Universitaires de France. (Pub. orig. in Paris by Rieder.)
Cotte, Roger. 1954. "D'Erlanger." Blume, vol. 3.
Cotte, Roger and Bernard Haultier. 1954. "Diémer." Blume, vol. 3.
Le Courrier Musical, Artistique et Littéraire du Littoral. Ed. A. Diot, René Doire, et al. Paris, 1899–.
Croze, J. L. 1890. "M. Saint-Saëns—Fantaisies et pages intimes." *La Revue Illustrée* (March 15).
______. 1900. "*Javotte* à l'Opéra-Comique." *Le Théâtre* 28 (February).
"C. Saint-Saëns et le mouvement musical contemporain." 1898. *Le Guide Musical* (January 9).
"C. Saint-Saëns et l'opinion musicale à l'étranger." 1901. *La Revue Musicale* (October–November 1901).
Curzon, H. de. 1912. "Le premier contact de M. Camille Saint-Saëns avec le public." *Le Guide Musical* (August 4 and 11).
Dandelot, Arthur. 1923. *La Société des Concerts du Conservatoire (1828–1923) avec une étude historique sur les grands concerts symphoniques avant et depuis 1828.* Paris.
______. 1930. *La vie et l'œuvre de Saint-Saëns.* Paris.
Debay, Victor. 1899, 1903. "Saint-Saëns." *Le Courrier Musical, Artistique et Littéraire du Littoral* 1, nos. 3 and 4 (1899); 6, no. 11 (1903).
Debussy, Claude. 1922. *Monsieur Croche Antidilettante.* Paris: Dorbon. (Eng. trans. 1928, 1948; rev. Ger. trans. 1974, Stuttgart.)
______. 1971. *Monsieur Croche et autres écrits.* Paris: Gallimard.

Delage, Roger. 1978. "Saint-Saëns humaniste." *L'Avant-Scène Opéra* (Paris) 15.

Dent, Edward J. 1974. *Ferruccio Busoni.* Repr. London: Eulenburg.

Destranges, Etienne. 1893. *Etude sur* Samson et Dalila. Paris: n.p.

______. 1895. *Une partition méconnue*—Proserpine *de Camille Saint-Saëns.* Paris: n.p.

______. 1906. *Consonances et dissonances.* Paris: Fischbacher.

Dommange, René and Lola Dommange. 1969. *Livre du centenaire des Editions Durand & Cie.* Mulhause: n.p.

Doukan, Pierre-Bernard. 1951. "Baillot." Blume, vol. 1.

Dubcek, Marina. 1978. "L'orientalisme dans *Samson.*" *L'Avant-Scène Opéra* (Paris) 15.

Dukas, Paul. 1896. "Concert-Festival donné par M. Saint-Saens." *Chronique des Arts* (June 13).

______. 1948. *Ecrits sur la musique.* Paris: n.p.

______. 1980. *Chroniques musicales sur deux siècles 1832–1932.* Repr. Paris: Stock.

Dumaine, R. 1936. *Les origines normandes de Camille Saint-Saëns.* Laine: n.p.

Dumesnil, Roger. 1930. *La musique contemporaine en France.* 2 vols. Paris: n.p.

______. 1946. *La musique en France entre les deux guerres 1919–1939.* Geneva: n.p.

Durand, Jacques. 1910, 1925. *Quelques souvenirs d'un editeur de musique (I. 1865–1909; II. 1910–1924).* Paris: Durand.

Eckart-Bäcker, Ursula. 1965. *Frankreichs Musik zwischen Romantik und Moderne—Die Zeit im Spiegel der Kritik.* Regensburg: Bosse.

Ecorcheville, Jean. 1899. "Monsieur Saint-Saëns et le wagnérisme." *Revue de Paris* 8 (August 1).

Emmanuel, Maurice. 1922. "L'esthétique de Saint-Saëns." *Le Guide de Concert (et des Théâtres Lyriques)* 3, numéro spécial Saint-Saëns: 27f.

Engel, Hans. 1958. "Instrumentalkonzert." Blume, vol. 7, col. 1569ff.

______. 1974. *Das Instrumentalkonzert.* 2 vols. Wiesbaden: Breitkopf & Härtel.

Epordand, E. 1923. "Saint-Saëns." *Musik* (Copenhagen) (January 1).

Fallon, Daniel Martin. 1973. *The Symphonies and Symphonic Poems of Camille Saint-Saëns.* Diss., Yale.

______. 1978. "Saint-Saens and the Concours de Composition

Musicale in Bordeaux." *Journal of the American Musicological Society* (Boston): 309ff.

Fauchois, René. 1938. *La vie prodigieuse de Camille Saint-Saëns.* Paris: n.p.

Fauquet, Joël-Marie. 1986. *Les sociétés de musique de chambre à Paris de la restauration à 1870.* Paris: n.p.

Fauré-Frémiet, Philippe. 1957. *Gabriel Fauré.* 2d ed. Paris: n.p.

Fauré, Gabriel. 1922. "Camille Saint-Saëns." *La Revue Musicale* 2.

———. 1930. *Opinions musicales.* Paris: n.p.

Favre, Max. 1947. *Gabriel Faurés Kammermusik.* Diss. Zurich: Max Niehaus.

Ferchault, Guy. 1958. "Joncières." Blume, vol. 7.

———. 1960. "Lalo." Blume, vol. 8.

———. 1962. "Paris (19.Jahrhundert)." Blume, vol. 10.

———. 1960. "Lacombe." Blume, vol. 8.

Fétis, François-Joseph. 1833–1844. *Biographie universelle des musiciens et bibliographie générale de la musique.* 8 vols. Brussels: n.p. (2d ed. pub. in Paris 1860–1865. 2 supplemental vols. by A. Pougin, 1870–1875, Paris: Firmin-Didot.)

Foss, Hubert. 1952. "The virtuoso violin concerto." In *The Concerto.* Ralph Hill, ed. London: Penguin.

Foureaud, Louis de. 1896. "La carrière d'un maître—Saint-Saëns." *Le Gaulois* (June 8).

La France Musicale. J. Maurel, M. Escudier et al, G. Laurens. Paris.

Fuchs, Arno. 1956. "Habanera." Blume, vol. 5.

Funérailles de Saint-Saëns. 1922. Discours prononcés le 24 octobre (sic) 1921 au cimetière du Montparnasse. Paris: Durand.

Gal, Hans, ed. 1966. *In Dur und Moll—Briefe großer Komponisten.* Frankfurt: G. B. Fischer. (Pub. in Eng. as *Great Composers in Their Letters.*)

Gallet, Louis. 1895. "Saint-Saëns et *Brunhilda* (*Frédégonde*)." *Le Ménestrel* (February 24 and March 17).

———. 1898. "Camille Saint-Saëns." *Revue de l'Art Ancien et Moderne* 11.

Gallois, Jean. 1967. *Chausson.* Paris: Seghers.

Gauthier, André. 1952. "Castillon." Blume, vol. 2.

Gauthier-Villars, Henry [Willy]. 1898. "Camille Saint-Saëns et le mouvement musical contemporain." *Le Guide Musical* 1.

———. 1907. "Monsieur Saint-Saëns et la clarté." *Comoedia* (October 12).

Gérard, Yves. n.d. *Saint-Saëns and the Problems of Nineteenth-Century French Music, Seen Through the Saint-Saëns Archives.* Unpub. MS.

Goldron, Romain. 1966. *Die nationalen Schulen—Neuer Frühling in Frankreich.* Lausanne: Rencontre. [German transl.]

Göthel, Folker. 1963a. "Sarasate." Blume, vol. 11.

______. 1963b. "Sauret." Blume, vol. 11.

Gounod, Charles. 1887. "*Proserpine* de Camille Saint-Saëns." *La France* (March 18).

______. 1890. Ascanio *de Camille Saint-Saëns.* Paris: n.p.

______. 1895. *Mémoires d'un artiste.* Paris: Calman-Lévy. (Eng. trans. 1896. New York: n.p.)

Gourmont, R. de. 1904. *Promenades littéraires.* Paris: n.p.

Grand Larousse encyclopédique. 1960. Vol. 1. Paris: Larousse.

Guichard, Léon. 1955. *La musique et les lettres au temps du romantisme.* Paris: Presses Universitaires de France.

Le Guide du Concert (et des Théâtres Lyriques). G. Bender, G. Jannel et al., eds. Paris, 1910–.

Le Guide Musical. F. Delhasse, M. Kufferath et al., eds. Brussels, 1855–.

Guy-Ropartz, Jean. 1891. *Notations artistiques.* Paris: Lemerre.

Handschin, Jacques. 1930. *Camille Saint-Saëns.* Hundertundachtzehntes Neujahrsblatt der Allgemeinen Musikgesellschaft in Zürich auf das Jahr 1930.

Hanslick, Eduard. 1876. "Camille Saint-Saëns." *Neue Freie Presse* (Vienna) (April).

______. 1896. *Fünf Jahre Musik.* Berlin: Allgemeiner Verein für deutsche Literatur.

Haraszti, Emile. 1956. "Godard." Blume, vol. 5.

Harding, James. 1965. *Saint-Saëns and His Circle.* London: Chapman & Hall.

Heldt, Gerhard. 1973. *Das deutsche nachromantische Violinkonzert von Brahms bis Pfitzner.* Diss. Regensburg: Bosse.

Henderson, A. M. n.d. "Personal memories of Saint-Saëns." *Musical Opinion* (London) 6, no. 55:531ff.

Hervey, Arthur. 1894. *Masters of French Music.* London: n.p.

______. 1903. *French Music in the Nineteenth Century.* London: G. Richards: n.p.

______. [1922] 1970. *Saint-Saëns.* New York. Repr., Westport.

Hill, Ralph, ed. 1952. *The Concerto.* London: Penguin. (8th ed. 1968; rev. ed. 1969).

Hippeau, Edmond. 1883. Henry VIII *et l'opéra français.* Paris: n.p.
Horton, John. 1952. "Variation forms." In *The Concerto.* Ralph Hill, ed. London: Penguin.
Hue, Georges. 1922. "Hommage à Saint-Saëns." *Le Courrier Musical, Artistique et Littéraire du Littoral* 24, no. 1.
Humbert, Georges. 1913. *Fêtes musicales en l'honneur de Saint-Saëns.* Vevey: n.p.
Imbert, Hugues. 1888. *Profils des musiciens.* Paris: Fischbacher.
———. 1892. *Nouveaux profils de musiciens.* Paris: Fischbacher.
———. 1894. *Portraits et études.* Paris: n.p.
———. 1897. *Profils d'artistes contemporains.* Paris: Fischbacher.
———. 1902. *Médaillons contemporains.* Paris: Fischbacher.
d'Indy, Vincent. 1904. *Le sifflet au concert—Lettre dans la plaidoirie de Jacques Bonzon devant le Tribunal de simple police de Paris.* Vannes: n.p.
———. 1915. "Musique française et musique allemande." *La Renaissance* (June 12).
———. 1916. "Se libérer soi-même de la domination musicale allemande." *Musical Courrier* (April 27).
———. 1928. "Où en est la musique française?" *Comoedia* (February 21).
———. 1930. *Richard Wagner et son influence sur l'art musical français.* Paris: Delagrave.
———. [1910] 1965. *César Franck.* London: Dover. Repr., New York.
Jehin, Léon. 1922. "Hommage à Saint-Saëns." *Le Courrier Musical, Artistique et Littéraire du Littoral* 24, no. 1.
Jenn, Pierre. 1984. "*L'assassinat du Duc de Guise.*" *L'Avant-Scène Cinema* (Paris) no. 334.
Le Journal de Musique. A. Bourdilliat and Armand Gouzien. eds. Paris.
Jullien, Adolphe. 1887. "Le Wagner français et l'autre." *L'Indépendance Musicale et Dramatique* (April 15).
———. 1892–1894. *Musiciens d'aujourd'hui.* 2 vols. Paris: Librairie de l'Art.
———. 1896. *Musique.* Paris: Fischbacher.
———. 1910. *Musiciens d'hier et d'aujourd'hui.* Paris: Fischbacher.
Karl, Willi. 1963. "Die instrumentale Romanze." Blume, vol. 11.
Kit, Charles and Paul Loanda. 1889. *Musique savante—Sur la musique de M. Saint-Saëns.* Lille: Imprimerie de L. Danel.
Klein, Jean-René. 1975. *Introduction à l'étude du langage boulevardier.* Paris: n.p.

Klingenbeck, Josef. 1962. "Pleyel." Blume, vol. 10.

Knosp, Gaston. 1905. "Camille Saint-Saëns—Zu seinem 70.Geburtstage." *Neue Musik-Zeitung* 27.

Koechlin, Charles. 1927. *Gabriel Fauré.* Paris: n.p.

______. 1939. "L'orientalisme dans la musique française." *Plaquettes de la Schola* (April–May).

______. 1938. "Situation actuelle de la musique en France." *La Revue Internationale de Musique* (Brussels).

______. 1948. "A propos de Camille Saint-Saëns." *La Pensée* 10:27ff.

Lacroux, Jean. 1985. "Camille Saint-Saëns, amateur d'astronomie." *Cahiers Ivan Tourguéniev—Pauline Viardot—Maria Malibran* 9:126ff.

La Grange, Henri-Louis De. 1952. "Tableau chronologique des principales œuvres musicales de 1900 à 1950." *La Revue Musicale* no. 216.

Lalo, Pierre. 1900. "M. Saint-Saëns et le quatuor à cordes." *Le Temps* (January 18).

______. 1903. "Une opinion de M. Saint-Saëns—A propos de l'interpretation des œuvres de Bach et de Haendel." *Le Temps* (February 24).

______. 1904. "La reforme de la musique sacrée. Les idées et les contradictions de M. Saint-Saëns." *Le Temps* (July 12 and 19).

______. 1906. "A propos d'un anniversaire de M. Saint-Saëns." *Le Temps* (May 29).

______. 1907. "La journée de M. Saint-Saëns—M. Saint-Saëns compositeur, pianiste et chef d'orchestre." *Le Temps* (October 29).

______. 1947. *De Rameau à Ravel.* Paris.

Laloy, Louis. 1905. "C. Saint-Saëns et les Italiens." *Le Ménestrel* 7:180f.

______. 1928. *La musique retrouvée 1902–1927.* Paris: n.p.

Landormy, Paul. 1932. "Vincent d'Indy." *The Musical Quarterly* 18, no. 4:507ff.

______. 1943. *La musique française de Franck à Debussy.* Paris: Gallimard.

Lara, René. 1896. "Le cinquantenaire du premier concert de M. Saint-Saëns." *Le Figaro* (June 2).

Laurencie, Lionel de la and Albert Lavignac. See Albert Lavignac and Lionel de la Laurencie.

Lavignac, Albert. 1896. *La musique et les musiciens.* Paris: Delagrave.

Lavignac, Albert and Lionel de la Laurencie. 1913–1939. *Encyclopédie de la musique et dictionnaire du conservatoire.* 11 vols. Paris: Delagrave.

Lavoix, Henri. 1891. *La musique française.* Paris: n.p.

Lay, Jacques. 1985. "La maison de Camille Saint-Saëns à Louveciennes." *Cahiers Ivan Tourguéniev—Pauline Viardot—Maria Malibran* 9:125f.

Lebas, Georges. 1924. "Lettres inédites de Lecoq à Saint-Saëns." *La Revue Musicale* 5:119ff.

Lebeau, Elisabeth. 1954. "Félicien David." Blume, vol. 3.

Lefevre, Maurice. 1907. "Camille Saint-Saëns jugé par ses pairs." *Musica* 6, no. 57 (June): 82.

Legrand, Albert. 1937. *Camille Saint-Saëns.* Dieppe: Imprimerie Dieppoise.

Leichtentritt, Hugo. 1951. *Musical Form.* Cambridge.

Lenoir, P. 1956. "Résumé de la conférence sur Saint-Saëns." *La Montagne Ste Geneviève* 5.

Liess, Andreas. 1950. *Deutsche und französische Musik in der Geistesgeschichte des 19.Jahrhunderts.* Vienna: n.p.

Linden, Ilse. 1915. "Saint-Saëns in Nöten." *Neue Musik-Zeitung* 36:82.

Lindenlaub. n.d. (probably 1896). *Le jubilé de Saint-Saëns.* Paris: Quantin.

Liszt, Franz. 1966. *Briefe aus ungarischen Sammlungen 1835–1886.* Kassel: Bärenreiter.

———. [1880–1883] 1978. *Gesammelte Schriften.* 6 vols. Repr., Hildesheim/New York: n.p. (Orig. pub. in Leipzig.)

Loanda, Paul and Charles Kit. See Charles Kit and Paul Loanda.

Locard, Paul. 1900. *Les maîtres contemporains de l'orgue.* Paris: n.p.

Lockspeiser, Edward. 1952. "Maurice Ravel." In *The Concerto.* Ralph Hill, ed. London: Penguin.

Longyear, Rey M. [1969] 1988. *Nineteenth-Century Romanticism in Music.* 3rd ed. Englewood Cliffs, NJ.

Lyle, Watson. 1923. *Camille Saint-Saëns—His Life, His Art.* New York: n.p.

Machabey, Armand. 1949–1951. "Aubert." Blume, vol. 1.

Malherbe, Charles. 1890. *Notice sur* Ascanio, *opéra de Camille Saint-Saëns.* Paris: n.p.

———. 1898. "Saint-Saëns jugé par un Anglais." *Revue Internationale de Musique* (May 1).

———. 1910. "Camille Saint-Saëns." *Mercure Musical et Bulletin Français de la Société Internationale de Musique* 8.

Marmontel, Antoine-François. 1882. *Virtuoses contemporains.* Paris: n.p.

_______ . 1888. *Pianistes célèbres.* 2d ed. Paris: n.p.

Marnold, Jean. 1907. "L'œuvre de M. Saint-Saëns." *Mercure de France* (November 16).

_______ . n.d. (1912). *Musique d'autrefois et d'aujourd'hui.* Paris: n.p.

_______ . 1917. *La musique pendant la guerre.* Paris: n.p.

_______ . 1920. *Le cas Wagner.* Paris: Georges Crès.

Martin, Jules. 1897. *Nos auteurs et compositeurs dramatiques.* Paris: n.p.

Marty, Georges. 1907. "L'œuvre symphonique de Saint-Saëns." *Musica* 6, no. 57 (June): 91.

Mason, Daniel Gregory. n.d. "Camille Saint-Saëns—A modern classicist." *New Music Review* (New York) 14, no. 162: 196ff.

Massenet, Jules. 1912. *Mes souvenirs.* Paris: Pierre Lafitte. (Eng. trans. 1919. Boston.)

McCarty, Clifford. 1957. "Film music for silents." *Films in Review* 8, no. 3 (March).

Mellers, Wilfrid. 1946. *Music and Society.* London: n.p.

Melos/Neue Zeitschrift für Musik. Carl Dahlhaus et al., eds. Mainz.

Le Ménestrel. Paris: Heugel & Co., 1833–1940.

Ménétrier, Jean-Alexandre. 1978. "Saint-Saëns: Un musicien de la Troisième République." *L'Avant-Scène Opéra* (Paris) 15.

Mey, Kurt. 1904. "Neuere französische Musikästhetik." *Neue Musik-Zeitung* 25:167ff.

Mies, Paul. 1972. *Das Konzert im 19.Jahrhundert—Studien zu Formen und Kadenzen.* Bonn: Bouvier.

Mohr, Wilhelm. 1969. *Caesar Franck.* Tutzing: Hans Schneider.

Le Monde Musical. R. Dick and E. Mangeot, eds. Paris, 1889–1940.

Monatshefte für Musikgeschichte. 1905. No. 37.

Montargis, Jean. 1919. *Camille Saint-Saëns—L'œuvre, l'artiste.* Paris: La Renaissance du Livre.

Mortier, Alfred. 1922. "D'un siècle à l'autre." *Le Courrier Musical, Artistique et Littéraire du Littoral* 24, no. 1 (January 1).

Müller-Blattau, Josef. 1955. "Form." Blume, vol. 4.

Musica. Xavier Leroux and Jarrice, eds. Paris, 1902–1914.

The Musical Quarterly. O. Sonneck, C. Engel et al., eds. New York, 1915–.

Myers, Rollo H. [1960] 1968. *Ravel—Life and Works.* New York: n.p.

_______ . 1971. *Modern French music—Its Evolution and Cultural Background From 1900 to the Present Day.* Oxford: Basil Blackwell.

Nectoux, Jean-Michel. 1972a. "Correspondance Saint-Saëns—Faure." *Revue de Musicologie* 58:65ff.

———. 1972b. *Fauré.* Paris: du Seuil.

———, ed. 1973. *Camille Saint-Saëns et Gabriel Fauré—Correspondance (soixante ans d'amitié).* Paris: Heugel.

———. 1984. *Gabriel Fauré: His Life Through Letters.* London: n.p.

Neitzel, Otto. 1899. *Camille Saint-Saëns.* Berlin: Harmonie.

Néronde, Chassaigne de. 1922. "Un grand musicien français: Camille Saint-Saëns." *Athéna* 1:423ff.

Neue Musik-Zeitung. Leipzig/Cologne/Stuttgart, 1881–1928.

Niemöller, Klaus Wolfgang. 1973. "Zur Musiktheorie im frühen 20.Jahrhundert." *Musicae Scientiae Collectanea (Festschrift Karl Gustav Fellerer).*

Nussy Saint-Saëns, Marcel. 1936. *Camille Saint-Saëns et La Musique française.* Bayonne: Imprimerie du Courrier de Bayonne.

Olivier-Bernard, Elisabeth. 1971. "Jules Pasdeloup et les concerts populaires." *Revue de Musicologie* 57.

Parker, D.C. 1917. "A modern Proteus—Saint-Saëns and the repertory." *Musical Standard* (London) 10, no. 256:346ff.

———. 1918. "Saint-Saëns and the violin." *The Strad* (London) 24, no. 338:44ff.

———. 1919. "Camille Saint-Saëns—A critical estimate." *The Musical Quarterly* 5:560ff.

Philippe, Isidore. 1922. "Saint-Saëns pianiste et compositeur pour le piano." *Le Guide de Concert (et des Théâtres Lyriques)* 3, numéro spécial Saint-Saëns: 40f. First pub. in 1907 in *Musica* 6, no. 57 (June): 90.

Pioch, Georges. 1907. "Saint-Saëns écrivain et poète." *Musica* 6, no. 57 (June): 95.

Pitrou, Robert. 1957. *De Gounod à Debussy—Une "belle époque" de la musique française.* Paris: Albin Michel.

Platzbecker, Heinrich. 1905. "Camille Saint-Saëns—Zu seinem 70.Geburtstage." *Neue Musik-Zeitung* 27:12ff.

Poueigh, J. See Octave Séré.

Pougin, Arthur. 1900. "Monsieur Camille Saint-Saëns comme écrivain." *Zeitschrift der Internationalen Musikgesellschaft* 1:259ff.

Prod'homme, J. G. 1917. "Music and musicians in Paris during the first two seasons of the war." *The Musical Quarterly* 3:135ff.

———. 1929. "Camille Saint-Saëns" (Fr. orig.). *Rivista Musicale*

Italiana 29:129ff. (Eng. trans. in 1922 in *The Musical Quarterly* 8:468ff.).

Quittard, Henri. 1906. "L'orientalisme musical—Saint-Saëns orientaliste." *La Revue Musicale* 6 (March 1): 107ff.

Quitin, José. 1960. "Léonard." Blume, vol. 8.

______. 1973. "Dupont." Blume, vol. 15.

Raicich, Jan. 1965. "De Swert." Blume, vol. 12.

Ratner, Sabina. 1973. *The Piano Music of Camille Saint-Saëns.* Diss. Michigan: University Microfilms.

______. 1985. "La genèse et la fortune de *Samson et Dalila.*" *Cahiers Ivan Tourguéniev—Pauline Viardot—Maria Malibran* 9:109ff.

Raugel, Félix. 1952. "Bordes." Blume, vol. 2.

______. 1954. "Dubois." Blume, vol. 3.

Récy, René de. 1889. "Camille Saint-Saëns." *Revue Bleue* (February 2 and 16).

Rehberg, Paula. 1961. *Franz Liszt.* Zurich: n.p.

Rehberg, Walter and Paula Rehberg. 1947. *Johannes Brahms.* Zurich: Artemis.

______. 1948. *Frédéric Chopin.* Zurich: Artemis.

Revue d'Histoire Musicale. 1901. *Numéro spécial Saint-Saëns* (October).

Revue et Gazette Musicale de Paris. Charles Dezauche, ed., 1834–1880.

Revue Musicale de Paris.

Reyer, Ernest. 1909. *Quarante ans de musique.* Paris: Calman-Lévy.

Richard, Albert, ed. "Camille Saint-Saëns 1835–1921—Correspondance inédite." *La Revue Musicale* 358/360.

Rivista Musicale Italiana. Turin, 1894–.

Robert, Frédéric. 1963. *La musique française au XIXeme siècle.* Paris: Presses Universitaires de France.

Robert, Gustave. 1896. *La musique a Paris 1895–1896.* Paris: Fischbacher.

Robertson, Alec and Denis Stevens. 1960–1968. *The Pelican History of Music.* Harmondsworth: n.p.

Rohozinski, L., ed. 1925. *Cinquante ans de musique française 1874–1925.* 2 vols. Paris: n.p.

Rolland, Romain. 1904. *Paris als Musikstadt.* Berlin: Bard, Marquart & Co.

______. 1908. *Musiciens d'aujourd'hui.* Paris: Librairie Hachette. (Eng. trans. 1915. Repr. 1969.)

Romain, Louis de. 1890. *Essais de critique musicale.* Paris: Lemerre.
Rutz, Hans. 1954. *Debussy.* Munich: C. H. Beck.
Sachs, Leo. 1922. "Souvenirs de Saint-Saens." *La Revue Musicale* 2.
Sadie, Stanley, ed. 1980. *The New Grove Dictionary of Music and Musicians.* London: Macmillan.
Saint-Saens, Charles-Camille. 1900. *Portraits et souvenirs.* Paris: Société d'Edition Artistique. [abbrev. *PS.*]
———. 1922a. *Divagations sérieuses.* Paris: Flammarion. [abbrev. *DS.*]
———. 1922b. *Outspoken Essays on Music.* Authorized Eng. trans. by Fred Rothwell. New York: n.p. [abbrev. *OE.*]
———. 1969. *Musical Memories.* Eng. trans. New York: Da Capo Press. [abbrev. *MM.*]
[Articles by Saint-Saëns.]
CSS-1 "Anarchy in music." *MM.*
CSS-2 "Antoine Rubinstein." *PS.*
CSS-3 "Art for art's sake." *MM.*
CSS-4 "Bayreuth und der Ring des Nibelungen." 1902. *Die Musik* 2:879ff.
CSS-5 "Berlioz's *Requiem.*" *MM.*
CSS-6 "Charles Gounod." *PS, OE.*
CSS-7 "Charles Gounod on Mozart's *Don Juan.*" *OE.*
CSS-8 "Chopin." *OE.*
CSS-9 "A Chopin M.S.: The F major ballade in the making." *OE.*
CSS-10 "La Défense de l'Opéra-Comique." *PS.*
CSS-11 "Delsarte." 1969. *MM.*
CSS-12 "Docteur a Cambridge." *PS.*
CSS-13 "*Don Giovanni.*" *PS.*
CSS-14 "The false masterpieces of music." *OE.*
CSS-15 "Franz Liszt." *PS.* [Ger. trans. by Marie Bessmertny, under the title "Saint-Saëns über Liszt." 1913. *Neue Musik-Zeitung* 34:428ff.]
CSS-16 "Georges Bizet." *PS.*
CSS-17 "Hector Berlioz." *PS.*
CSS-18 "Hélène." *OE.*
CSS-19 "History and mythology in opera." *MM.*
CSS-20 "The history of an opéra-comique." *MM.*
CSS-21 "The ideas of Monsieur Vincent d'Indy." *OE.*

CSS-22 "L'illusion wagnérienne." *PS.*
CSS-23 "Impressions of America." *OE.*
CSS-24 "Jacques Offenbach." *MM.*
CSS-25 "Joseph Haydn and the seven words." *MM.*
CSS-26 "Jules Massenet." *MM.*
CSS-27 "Lettre de Las Palmas." *PS.* [Ger. trans. by Marie Bessmertny, under the title "Ein Brief aus Las Palmas von Camille Saint-Saens." 1903. Trans. of "L'art et les artistes," *Neue Musik-Zeitung* 34 (1913) :125ff.]
CSS-28 "The Liszt centenary at Heidelberg (1912)." *MM.*
CSS-29 "Liszt, the pianist." *OE.*
CSS-30 "Louis Gallet." *PS, MM.*
CSS-31 "The manuscript libretto of *Faust*." *OE.*
CSS-32 "Memories of my childhood." *MM.*
CSS-33 "The metronome." *OE.*
CSS-34 "Le métronome et l'espace céleste." *DS.*
CSS-35 "Meyerbeer." *MM.*
CSS-36 "Modern music." *OE.*
CSS-37 "Le mouvement musical." *PS.*
CSS-38 "Music in the church." 1916. *The Musical Quarterly* 2:1ff.
CSS-39 "Musical digressions." *OE.*
CSS-40 "Musical painters." *MM.*
CSS-41 "A note on Rameau." *OE.*
CSS-42 *Notes sur les décors de théâtre dans l'antiquité romaine.* 1866. Paris: Baschet.
CSS-43 "The old conservatoire." *MM.*
CSS-44 "The organ." *MM.*
CSS-45 "The origin of *Samson and Delilah*." *OE.*
CSS-46 "Orphée." *PS, MM.*
CSS-47 "Pauline Viardot." *MM.*
CSS-48 "Popular science and art." *MM.*
CSS-49 "Preface to *Pièces de clavecin de Jean-Philippe Rameau*." 1905. Paris: Durand.
CSS-50 "Problèmes et mystères." *DS.*
CSS-51 "Rossini." *MM.*
CSS-52 "Sarasate." *OE.*
CSS-53 "Seghers." *MM.*
CSS-54 "Spiritualisme et matérialisme." *DS.*

CSS-55 "Le théâtre au concert." *PS.*
CSS-56 "Their majesties." *MM.*
CSS-57 "Transformisme." *DS.*
CSS-58 "Un engagement d'artiste." *PS.*
CSS-59 "Une lettre à l'astronome Hirn." *PS.*
CSS-60 "Une traversée en Bretagne." *PS.*
CSS-61 "Victor Hugo." *MM.*
CSS-62 "Victor Massé." *PS.*

Sallés, Antoine. 1917. "Lalo, Saint-Saëns, Bruneau, Charpentier." In *Pour la musique française.* Paris: Georges Crès.

———. 1922. *Saint-Saëns à Lyon.* Paris: Fromart.

Samazeuilh, Gustave. 1947. *Musiciens de mon temps.* Paris: n.p.

Savari, Pauline. 1890. "Le Musée Saint-Saëns à Dieppe." *Le Guide Musical* 36 (November 9).

Schering, Arnold. 1927. *Geschichte des Instrumentalkonzerts.* 2d ed. Leipzig: n.p.

Schmitz, Robert E. 1966. *The Piano Works of Claude Debussy.* Repr. New York: n.p.

Schneider, Marius. 1965. "Die Volksmusik Spaniens und der 'arabische' Einfluβ." Blume, vol. 12, col. 1010ff.

Schonberg, Harold C. 1963. *The Great Pianists.* New York: Simon and Schuster.

———. 1967. *The Great Conductors.* New York. (Ger. trans. 1973. *Die Groβen Dirigenten.* Munich.)

Schottky, J. M. [1830] 1909. *Paganinis Leben und Treiben als Künstler und Mensch.* Repr. Prague.

Schröter, Werner. 1971. *Das Klavierkonzert.* Wolfenbüttel: Möseler.

Schumann, Robert. 1974. *Gesammelte Schriften.* New ed. Leipzig: n.p.

Séré, Octave [J. Poueigh]. [1911] 1922. *Musiciens français d'aujourd'hui.* 2d rev. ed. Paris: Société du Mercure de France.

Servières, Georges. 1896. *La musique française moderne.* Paris: Havard.

———. 1922. "L'amitié de Liszt et de Saint-Saëns." *Le Ménestrel* 7.

———. 1923a. *Saint-Saëns.* Paris: Librairie Felix Alcan.

———. 1923b. "Le 'wagnérisme' de Saint-Saëns." *Rivista Musicale Italiana* 23.

———. 1930. *Les maîtres de la musique—Saint-Saëns.* Paris: n.p.

———. n.d. *Edouard Lalo.* Paris: Laurens.

Shaw, George Bernard. 1961. *London Music in 1888–89 as Heard by Corno di Bassetto (Later Known as Bernard Shaw) With Some Further Autobiographical Particulars.* New York: Dodd, Mead & Company. (1937 by GBS.)

Sordet, Dominique. 1924. *Douze chefs d'orchestre.* Paris: n.p.

Stegemann, Michael. 1976. "Camille Saint-Saëns und Deutschland." *Melos/Neue Zeitschrift für Musik* 4: 267ff.

______. 1985. "Der Mord als schöne Kunst betrachtet—Camille Saint-Saëns und die Anfänge der Filmmusik." *Melos/Neue Zeitschrift für Musik* 10:8ff.

______. 1987. "Attizismus und Modernität—Camille Saint-Saëns und die Wiederbelebung der Alten Musik." In *Kongreßbericht des Internationalen Musikwissenschaftlichen Kongresses Stuttgart 1985.* Kassel.

Stein, Fritz. 1960. "Litolff." Blume, vol 8.

Stengel, Theophil. 1931. *Die Entwicklung des Klavierkonzerts von Liszt bis zur Gegenwart.* Diss. Berlin: Paul Funk.

Stevens, Denis and Alec Robertson. See Alec Robertson and Denis Stevens.

Stojowsky, Sigismund. 1901. "Die 'Barbaren' von Camille Saint-Saëns an der Pariser großen Oper." *Die Musik* 1:316ff.

Stoullig, Edmond, ed. 1897. *Les annales du théatre et de la musique.* Publication annuelle à Paris depuis 1897. Paris: Ollendorff.

Strobel, Heinrich. 1940. *Claude Debussy.* Zurich: Atlantis.

Stuckenschmidt, H. H. 1960. *Ravel.* Frankfurt: n.p.

Tenroc, C. 1911. "*Déjanire* sera sa dernière *œuvre.*" *Comoedia* (July 21).

Thiel, Eberhard. 1962. *Sachwörterbuch der Musik.* Stuttgart: Kröner.

Thiel, Wolfgang. 1978. "Pariser Filmmusik-Premiere anno 1908." *Musik und Gesellschaft* 28, no. 12 (December): 712f.

Thorel, René. 1906. "Le Musée Saint-Saëns à Dieppe." *Musica* 5 (March).

______. 1907a. "Les Deux Saint-Saëns à Dieppe." *Comoedia* (October 28).

______. 1907b. "Saint-Saëns intime." *Musica* 6, no. 57 (June): 92ff.

Tiersot, Julien. 1889. *Musiques pittoresques (promenades musicales)—L'exposition de 1889.* Paris: Fischbacher.

______. 1902. "La symphonie en France." *Bulletin Mensuel de la Société Internationale de Musique* (July).

______. 1918. *Un demi siècle de musique française—Entre les deux guerres, 1870–1917.* Paris: Félix Alcan.

Tobin, J. Raymond. 1952. "The concerto and its development." In *The concerto.* Ralph Hill, ed. London: Penguin.

d'Udine, Jean. See Albert Clozanet.

Vallas, Léon. 1944. *Achille Claude Debussy.* Paris: Presses Universitaires de France.

———. 1946, 1950. *Vincent d'Indy.* 2 vols. Paris: Albin Michel.

———. 1947. "Une discussion entre Saint-Saëns et d'Indy." *La Revue Musicale* (Paris) 2:79ff.

———. 1958. *Claude Debussy et son temps.* Paris: Albin Michel. (Ger. trans. pub. in 1961 as *Debussy und seine Zeit.* Munich: n.p.)

van der Borren, Charles. 1951. "Benoit." Blume, vol. 1.

Vander Linden, Alexander. 1965. "Servais." Blume, vol. 12.

Verchaly, André. 1973. "Bordier." Blume, vol. 15.

Viardot, Pauline. 1907. "La jeunesse de Saint-Saëns." *Musica* 6, no. 57 (June): 83f.

von Fischer, Kurt. 1966. "Variation." Blume, vol. 13.

Wangermée, Robert. 1955. "Fétis." Blume, vol. 4.

Weingartner, Felix. 1915. "Ein offener Brief an Saint-Saëns." *Neue Musik-Zeitung* 36:82.

Wells-Harrison, W. 1915. "Saint-Saëns' violin concerto." *The Strad* (London) 26, no. 303:77ff.

Widor, Charles-Marie. 1922. *Notice sur la vie et les œuvres de Monsieur Camille Saint-Saëns.* Paris: Firmin-Didot.

Willy. See Henry Gauthier-Villars.

Wirth, Helmut. 1951. "Enrique Granados." Blume, vol. 5.

Wolfurt, Kurt von. 1926. "Das Problem Mussorgskij." *Die Musik* 19:162ff.

Zimmermann, Reiner, ed. 1978. *Charles-Camille Saint-Saëns—Musikalische Reminiszenzen.* Leipzig: Reclam.

Zviguilsky, Alexandre. 1985. "L'exécution du second acte de *Samson et Dalila* à Croissy." *Cahiers Ivan Tourguéniev—Pauline Viardot—Maria Malibran* 9:123ff.

Indices

A. Index of Saint-Saëns's Works

1. Works with Opus numbers

2. Works without Opus numbers

B. *Index of Names*